MW01488191

Convergence in Career Development Theories

Convergence in Career Development Theories

Implications for Science and Practice

Mark L. Savikas
Robert W. Lent, Editors

CPP BOOKS
Palo Alto, California
A Division of Consulting Psychologists Press, Inc.

98 97 96 95 94   10 9 8 7 6 5 4 3 2 1

Credits appear on pages 279 and 280, which constitute a continuation of the copyright page.

Library of Congress Cataloging-in-Publication Data

Convergence in career development theories: implications for science
   and practice / Mark Savickas, Robert Lent, editors. -- 1st ed.
      p.   cm.
   Includes bibliographical references and index.
   ISBN 0-89106-066-9
   1. Career development I. Savickas, Mark. II. Lent, Robert W. (Robert William).
   HF5381.C6873 1994
   158.7--dc20   93-42895
                                                    CIP

Printed in the United States of America
First edition
   First printing 1994

Contents

ORDER
ON
VIDEO
① BORDIN
④ DAWIS
③ HOLLAND
⑤ KRUMBOLTZ
② SUPER

Mark L. Savickas
Northeastern Ohio Universities College of Medicine
Robert W. Lent
Michigan State University

John D. Krumboltz
Stanford University

René V. Dawis
University of Minnesota

John L. Holland
Professor Emeritus, Johns Hopkins University

Acknowledgment

WE GRATEFULLY ACKNOWLEDGE the assistance of the following groups and organizations whose generous support made possible the convergence project and conference: The American Psychological Association's Vocational Behavior and Career Intervention Special Interest Group, Counseling Psychology Division; Consulting Psychologists Press; Loyola University Chicago's Department of Counseling and Educational Psychology; Michigan State University's Counseling Center and Department of Counseling, Educational Psychology and Special Education; the National Career Development Association; Northeastern Ohio Universities College of Medicine's Division of Basic Medical Sciences; Western Michigan University's Department of Counselor Education and Counseling Psychology; and the University of North Texas' Department of Psychology.

CHAPTER ONE

Introduction

A Convergence Project for Career Psychology

Mark L. Savickas
Northeastern Ohio Universities College of Medicine

Robert W. Lent
Michigan State University

THEORISTS AND RESEARCHERS in diverse psychological special-ties have increasingly been lending their voices to the call for unified science. Noting the array of competing theories of psychotherapy, Goldfried and Padawer (1982) asserted that theoretical diversity may be taken as a sign of the field's healthy development, but concluded that "there nonetheless comes a time when one needs to question where fruitful diversity ends and where chaos begins" (p. 3). Staats (1991) raised strong concern about the fragmentation of modern psychology, arguing that psychological science is facing a crisis of disunity, reflected by "many unrelated methods, findings, problems, theoretical languages, schismatic issues, and philosophical positions" (p. 899). Efforts to address questions about fragmen-tation within the psychological sciences have produced a robust movement called *unification psychology*. This movement has been particularly animated in the field of psychotherapy, where its aim has been to integrate or bridge the many competing theoretical approaches to comprehending and conducting psychotherapeutic interventions.

The domain of career psychology, like psychotherapy, is characterized by a plethora of theories, philosophical positions, and research camps (although not nearly as profuse or diverse as those found in psychotherapy). However, calls for unification of career theories and research have been relatively faint. Career psychologists have never endured the sort of disharmony that currently besets certain other psychological disciplines. We have been able to coexist more or less peacefully, possibly because of our roots in the study of individual differences or because our theories deal with different but overlapping problems. Nevertheless, like their peers in other psychological domains, career psychologists are becoming increasingly sensitized to the value of scientific rapprochement. Krumboltz and Nichols (1990), for example, recently compared three theories of career decision making to Krumboltz's social learning theory, then integrated the different theories using Ford's (1987) overarching conceptual model, the living systems framework.

Sensitivity to convergence in career theories seems to have been heightened by a series of invited articles celebrating the 20th anniversary of the *Journal of Vocational Behavior*. These articles prompted scholarly reflection concerning the course that career psychology had traversed since the journal's founding in 1970. The first contribution was written by Samuel Osipow (1990). Osipow's article directed our attention to the topic of convergence in theories of career choice and development, tracing how such theories have shaped vocational research and counseling practice for more than 40 years. He identified a group of four theories that spanned this era and remain influential today: trait and factor (Holland, 1985), social learning (Mitchell, Jones, & Krumboltz, 1979), developmental (Super, Starishevsky, Matlin, & Jordaan, 1963), and work adjustment (Dawis & Lofquist, 1984). Osipow asserted that these four theories have come to resemble each other in important ways. By identifying significant convergence in these theories, Osipow roused his colleagues' interest in theory integration (e.g., see the invited contribution by Borgen, 1991).

Joining Osipow in this concern with convergence, Donald Super proposed that a conference be convened to explore in greater depth the prospects for further theory convergence. Super (1992) had recently written how the question of "which theory is better" is specious because no theory in itself is sufficient. The theories need each other to comprehensively address the complexity of career development. Furthermore, the results of research studies acquire deeper meaning when they are viewed from the perspectives of two or more theories.

Super's idea for a convergence project received an enthusiastic welcome, perhaps because of growing concerns about disunity fueled by other invited articles in the *Journal of Vocational Behavior,* such as a review article by Hackett, Lent, and Greenhaus (1991). In reflecting upon 20 years of theoretical and empirical activity in career psychology, Hackett and her colleagues suggested that the time is ripe for integrative efforts that will

> (a) bring together conceptually related constructs (e.g., self-concept, self-efficacy); (b) more fully explain outcomes that are common to a number of career theories (e.g., satisfaction, stability); (c) account for the relations among seemingly diverse constructs (e.g., interests, needs, ability, self-efficacy); and (d) identify the major variables crucial to an overarching theory of career development. (p. 28)

A number of recent reviews note the proliferation of vocational constructs that are incompletely incorporated into existing theory and research. Careful examination of the operational definitions of many of the new constructs reveals great similarity to the operational definitions of existing constructs. Because many new constructs are not explicitly linked to career theories (although they may have connections to theory in developmental, organizational, social, or personality psychology), their relation to existing career constructs is often elusive. Although novel constructs can expand the scope of career inquiry, a comprehensive understanding of vocational behavior will require concerted efforts to (a) identify core constructs that cut across major theories, (b) agree upon operational definitions for these constructs, and (c) develop and disseminate a research agenda for theory integration.

THE CAREER CONVERGENCE PROJECT

We developed a convergence project to address these issues. The project sought to facilitate theory convergence, stimulate theory unification research, and prompt more explicit use of theory in guiding vocational research. To accomplish these goals, we enlisted the help of a group of preeminent scholars who were eager to discuss the topic of theoretical convergence. This group of distinguished colleagues agreed to participate in a conference that would consider prospects for convergence among theories of career choice and development. They also agreed to expand their presentations into chapters discussing their view on a convergence agenda for career theory. These chapters compose this book.

The book has four parts. Part 1 consists of five chapters in which major career theorists each consider how their approach converges with, or could be made to bridge, one or more other career theories. The career theorists included in part 1 represent the five theories that currently serve as the foundation for the field of career development and counseling: John D. Krumboltz, René V. Dawis, John L. Holland, Edward S. Bordin, and Donald E. Super. The theorists have made important, long-lasting contributions to career psychology, and all have received major awards from professional organizations recognizing their contributions.

In preparing their chapters, we asked the theorists to address the following question: "How does your theory converge with one or more other career theories?" We urged them to go beyond surface similarities and cite aspects of their theories that significantly converge with or complement other career theories. We also encouraged them to consider areas for potential convergence and to identify innovative constructs or frameworks from other areas of psychology that might be used to bridge the various career theories. In short, we asked the theorists themselves to write chapters that discuss how their theories intersect, complement, or supplement one another.

In part 2, the attention shifts from conceptual to empirical convergence. In particular, we selected core constructs in the career literature that may offer the potential to bridge the theories. We then invited prominent researchers in vocational psychology to consider how these theoretical constructs and their accompanying empirical literature could be used to converge career theories and unify vocational research. The researchers—Robert W. Lent and Gail Hackett, Louise F. Fitzgerald and Nancy E. Betz, Arnold R. Spokane, David L. Blustein, and Susan D. Phillips—were selected because of their inquiry and writing on the variables considered to be potential *unification constructs*.

In preparing their chapters, we asked them to address the following question: "How can these constructs serve as a fulcrum for theory integration?" We encouraged them to consider how, conceptually and empirically, a particular construct or set of constructs (a) crosses two or more theories and (b) can be used to bridge existing theories.

In part 3, the focus turns from convergence rooted in research to practitioners' views on theory convergence. Specifically, at the conference that preceded this book, we convened work groups that responded to the agenda suggested by the panel of career theorists and researchers. These work groups were composed largely of career practitioners facilitated by teams of distinguished career scientist-practitioners. The aim of these groups was (a) to react to the papers presented during the conference and (b) to suggest novel perspectives on and ideas for convergence in career theories. The five work groups corresponded with the five theories represented in part 1 of this book. The discussion leaders—Linda Mezydlo Subich and Karen M. Taylor, James Rounds and Beryl Hesketh, W. Bruce Walsh and Judy M. Chartrand, Steven D. Brown and C. Edward Watkins, Jr., and Fred W. Vondracek and Nadya A. Fouad—were selected to represent the diversity of scholars involved in theory construction and research in career psychology.

In preparing their chapters, we asked these respected colleagues to address the following question: "What views did practitioners express during your discussion about theory convergence and its relevance to practice?" In addition to summarizing the practitioners' real-world concerns about theory convergence, the chapter authors were encouraged to share their own views on theory convergence.

In part 4, three discussants—Samuel H. Osipow, Lenore W. Harmon, and Mark L. Savickas—each reflect on the ideas presented during the convergence conference and in the foregoing three sections of this book. They were selected to represent the vantage points of theory, research, and practice, and were asked to form conclusions about the potential outcomes of the convergence project. In particular, the discussants were invited to consider how the chapter authors defined the problems thwarting theoretical convergence, the possibilities for resolving these problems, and areas in which the authors agreed and disagreed. The discussants were also asked to share their own views on the problems and possibilities for integrating career choice and development theories, and to identify future directions.

CAVEATS

The convergence project did not advocate the creation of a single, monolithic theoretical approach to career psychology. Historians and philosophers of science have shown that science is well served by a diversity of viewpoints rather than a monopolistic paradigm. Neither did the project advocate a "theory-building by consensus or committee" approach. Rather, keeping with the unification zeitgeist in psychology, the project merely sought to nurture consideration of cross-theoretical linkages in the career literature. Specifically, it aimed to examine converging themes among major career theories, to consider the maintenance of important and useful distinctive features and applications of each theory, and to convey the importance of an agenda for future research on theory integration.

CONCLUSION

We view this book as an initial step toward promoting a more unified scientific base for career psychology. Although career psychology has enjoyed a vigorous renaissance and important advances in recent years, this book represents the first attempt to foster rapprochement among career theories. Given the recognition that unification efforts are receiving in the larger psychological arena, we see this as an excellent time to examine the prospects that convergence holds for theories of career choice and development.

REFERENCES

Borgen, F. (1991). Megatrends and milestones in vocational behavior: A 20-year counseling psychology retrospective. *Journal of Vocational Behavior, 39,* 263–290.

Dawis, R., & Lofquist, L. (1984). *A psychological theory of work adjustment.* Minneapolis: University of Minnesota.

Ford, D. (1987). *Humans as self-constructing living systems: A developmental perspective on personality and behavior.* Hillsdale, NJ: Erlbaum.

Goldfried, M. R., & Padawer, W. (1982). Current status and future directions in psychotherapy (pp. 3–49). In M. R. Goldfried (Ed.), *Converging themes in psychotherapy.* New York: Springer.

Hackett, G., Lent, R., & Greenhaus, J. (1991). Advances in vocational theory and research: A 20-year retrospective. *Journal of Vocational Behavior, 38,* 3–38.

Holland, J. (1985). *Making vocational choices: A theory of vocational personalities and work environments* (2d ed.). Englewood Cliffs, NJ: Prentice-Hall.

Krumboltz, J., & Nichols, C. (1990). Integrating the social learning theory of career decision making. In W. Walsh & S. Osipow (Eds.), *Career counseling: Contemporary topics in vocational psychology* (pp. 159–192). Hillsdale, NJ: Erlbaum.

Mitchell, A., Jones, G., & Krumboltz, J. (Eds.). (1979). *Social learning theory and career decision making*. Cranston, RI: Carroll.

Osipow, S. (1990). Convergence in theories of career choice and development. *Journal of Vocational Behavior, 36,* 122–131.

Staats, A. (1991). Unified positivism and unification psychology: Fad or new field? *American Psychologist, 46,* 899–912.

Super, D. (1992). Toward a comprehensive theory of career development. In D. Montross & C. Shinkman (Eds.), *Career development: Theory and practice* (pp. 35–64). Springfield, IL: Charles C. Thomas.

Super, D., Starishevsky, R., Matlin, N., & Jordaan, J. (1963). *Career development: A self-concept theory.* New York: College Entrance Examination Board.

PART ONE

EXPLORATION OF THEORY CONVERGENCE

IN THIS SECTION, major career development theorists who represent the five most influential conceptual positions in career psychology—John Krumboltz, René Dawis, John Holland, Edward Bordin, and Donald Super—undergo a theoretical self-examination and consider how their own approaches converge with, or could be made to bridge, other career theories. In preparing their chapters, each theorist was urged to go beyond superficial similarities and to consider aspects of their theories that complement other career theories. They were also asked to identify innovative constructs or frameworks from other areas of psychology that might facilitate theory unification in career psychology.

In chapter 2, Krumboltz begins the section by expressing concern about theory convergence as a goal for career psychology. Pointing to inadequacies in current career theories, he recommends that each of them be improved, abandoned, or surmounted by new theories. He also notes that theories, like maps, necessarily emphasize particular phenomena while ignoring others; hence, the choice of a career theory depends on one's purposes at the time. Krumboltz compares his social learning theory of career decision making with the theories of Donald Super, John Holland, and Linda Gottfredson, noting the important commonalities and differences between them. He also considers five criteria for improving career theories.

Dawis distinguishes theory unification from theory convergence in chapter 3, suggesting that the latter represents a more attainable—yet still immensely challenging—goal. He notes two general approaches to demonstrating theory convergence: (a) observing the ways in which various theories overlap or are equivalent and (b) establishing linkages among them, possibly by creating an overarching framework. After overviewing the theory of work adjustment, Dawis considers its points of convergence, and divergence, with the theories of Holland, Krumboltz, Super, and Bordin. He concludes by observing four "iron laws" that pose steep obstacles to theory integration or unification efforts.

Like Krumboltz, Holland questions the value of theory convergence in chapter 4, proposing that renovation of existing theories offers a much more promising alternative. He argues that current career theories are actually quite diverse, with only "a very weak" convergence evident among them. For instance, the theories share certain broad background principles, for example, person-environment congruence, and concepts, but differ importantly in how they conceptualize and define such elements. Holland highlights specific reasons why theory synthesis should not be pursued and offers some suggestions for improving existing theories, including his own.

In chapter 5, Bordin notes an important, emerging area of consensus exposed by the convergence project, namely, that individuals are active agents in their own career development. They construct self-images such as identity that influence their response to the environment. Bordin advocates that career theorists should focus to a greater degree on the intrinsic motives (e.g., nurturance, curiosity) that help guide individuals' career choice and development. He also highlights the interrelation of work and play roles, the importance of self-expression within the vocational sphere, and the potential of the family system to serve as a platform for career theory convergence.

Finally, in chapter 6, Super views convergence within the context of his own theory and professional writings. He suggests that his theoretical propositions can be coded into four broad categories--trait and factor/person-environment, psychodynamic, social learning, and life span development—and that his publications are also distributed among these categories. While developmental and person-environment themes predominate in his work, Super argues that his theory be seen as an eclectic, segmentalist position, encompassing a broad array of theoretical elements and influences.

CHAPTER TWO

Improving Career Development Theory From a Social Learning Perspective

John D. Krumboltz
Stanford University

W<small>E ARE ENGAGED</small> in career theory convergence because we sense some fundamental inadequacies in the theories we use in career counseling.

The word *theory* is an abstraction that has many different meanings. As we use it here, a theory is a way of explaining what we observe. It is a way of making sense of our experiences. It is a way of summarizing a large number of facts and observations into a few general propositions. Basically, we are trying to construct some general rules, principles, diagrams, and/or formulas to explain career-related behavior.

THE MAP METAPHOR

In other contexts (Krumboltz, 1991b; Krumboltz & Nichols, 1990), I have argued that theory construction is like map making; that is, a psychological theory is an attempt to represent some aspect of behavior, much in the same way that a map is an attempt to represent some geographical territory. It may be instructive to see how maps and theories are similar.

A Representation of Reality

Both a map and a theory are intended to give us the big picture about a certain area of interest. They both help us understand the most essential characteristics of that area. Both attempt to represent some portion of reality using words, symbols, numbers, colors, and/or figures. The various symbols are selected to represent various aspects of that reality in an understandable way.

Purpose

Maps vary in their purpose. A roadmap is useful for a motorist but not particularly valuable to a railroad engineer or pilot. A map depicting average annual rainfall in various parts of the world might be more useful to an agronomist than a sociologist. A map is constructed to serve the particular purposes of its users.

Similarly, a theory is constructed to serve the specific purposes of its users—understanding a complex phenomenon, making predictions about the future, or choosing courses of action. Just as a map can be good for one purpose and not for another, so a theory can be good for one purpose and seemingly useless for another.

Omission of Nonessentials

Consider a typical roadmap. It depicts and labels major highways, streets, cities, rivers, and lakes. It does not depict houses and trees, factories and stores, swimming pools and racetracks, or flower beds and pipelines. It deliberately omits certain realities because the map maker believed them to be nonessential for its users.

In a similar way, theories ignore large areas of psychological experience. Some theories call attention to some aspects of experience, say, countertransference, whereas others completely ignore events associated with the therapist's feelings toward the client. That does not necessarily mean that cognitive therapists do not have any feelings for their clients; it just means that their theoretical constructs do not pay attention to that particular event. Each theory is an attempt to depict some part of reality and does so by deliberately ignoring other complexities.

Behavioral theories emphasize positive reinforcement that the therapist gives to the client. Client-centered theories do not discuss positive reinforcement, but that does not mean that client-centered therapists do not, in fact, reinforce some statements more than others. They do; they simply do not label it as such. Every theory is a deliberate oversimplification.

Distortion

To make the features of a certain territory clear, a map exaggerates and distorts those features. For example, a major highway may be depicted in red ink on the map, whereas in reality the highway is a dirty gray color. The width of the highway is exaggerated on the map so that it is easily visible to the unaided eye.

Maps distort reality in order to emphasize a particular point. Likewise, theories may stress the importance of certain variables by calling special attention to them—by giving them special names and by emphasizing their importance in words, figures, and formulas.

If we were to interpret certain theories literally, we would expect to be able to dissect a human body and find therein an ego, an id, and a super ego. Unless, of course, the victim were a transactional analyst, in which case we would find a child, a parent, and an adult. The concepts in our theories do not necessarily represent anything real. They are simply ways of depicting some aspect of behavior to which the theorist wishes to call attention.

Representation of the Unobservable

Just as a map may include invisible political boundaries, such as a county or state line, so a theory may include unobservable constructs and ideas believed to be important for understanding a particular phenomenon. The reality of some constructs is in the minds of the theory's adherents, just as a political boundary is in the minds of those who respect it.

Positive reinforcement itself is simply a concept, not a reality. Even behaviorists are not sure whether a given event can be called reinforcing until they see what kind of effect it has had on the client.

Scale

Maps differ in the size of the territory they represent. One inch on a map can represent 1,000 miles, 10 miles, or 10 feet. Theories also vary in scale, depending on the scope of the phenomenon they are attempting to explain.

Accuracy

Are all theories equally valid? Certainly not. Theories can be inaccurate in the same way that maps can be. In 1625, map makers thought that California was an island. Even as late as 1719, California was still represented as an island on maps. A person using these maps to travel directly from California to Philadelphia would expect to cross the Sea of California in a large sailing vessel. We know now that such an expectation would have been false, but these early maps represented reality to the best of the cartographers' knowledge.

Our psychological theories are as good as we know how to make them so far, but in all probability they are far short of being the accurate representations of psychological reality that we would like them to be. Still, they may be better than nothing. A partially accurate map can be useful part of the time, though it may mislead us at others. So it is with our psychological theories—better than nothing but not worth fighting over. The scientific ideal is to continue improving theoretical formulations to better represent reality. Over time, errors get corrected. Einstein once said that a theory should be simple enough but not too simple. In new sciences like psychology, much exploring and surveying lie ahead.

Usefulness

A good map enables us to answer all sorts of different questions. A roadmap of California is very useful if we want to know how far it is from Sacramento to Fresno, which freeway goes from Bakersfield to Los Angeles, or how to get to San Jose. If we wanted to know what location in California was the hottest in July, then a temperature map would be useful. If we wanted to locate concentrations of deciduous trees, a map of vegetation would help us. If we wanted to know where the heaviest rainfall occurred in the state, a precipitation map would give us some answers. But the precipitation map would not tell us how far it was from Sacramento to Fresno. Which map is the correct one? No one map enables us to answer every question.

Similarly, a good psychological theory enables people to derive answers (right or wrong) to innumerable questions. What are the major types of career interest? Why do some people choose a career of crime? How should I raise my children so that they can make their own career decisions? What is the best treatment for zeteophobia (the fear of career exploration and decision making)? How do people develop preferences for different occupations? What interventions are best to help young people make wise career decisions? No one theory is equally useful for every question.

So you can see that a theory is a distorted, inaccurate oversimplification of reality with unpredictable usefulness. It is a picture, a vision, an image, a description, a representation of reality. It is not reality itself. It is a way we can think about some part of reality so that we can comprehend it. Reality is too complex to understand. We need some way of simplifying those complexities. A good theory is simple enough to be comprehensible but complex enough to account for the most crucial variables. An operational definition might read something like this: *A good theory is a simplified representation of some domain constructed so that users can ask questions about that domain with an increased probability of receiving valuable answers.*

THE VALUE OF ANOMALIES IN IMPROVING THEORY

Scientists have been building theories for centuries. One of the major steps in improving scientific theories lies in the identification of anomalies. An anomaly is a fact that is difficult to explain using the current theory. According to Lightman and Gingerich (1992), "the word anomaly has a venerable astronomical usage, going back to the Greek, meaning a celestial motion that deviates from simple uniformity" (p. 690). They quote Thomas Kuhn (1970): "Discovery commences with the awareness of anomaly, that is, with the recognition that nature has somehow violated the preinduced expectations that govern normal science" (pp. 52–53). These preinduced expectations are generated from our theory. When an anomaly is detected, the theory that makes it an anomaly is weakened. Given clear evidence of an anomaly, scientists eventually discard the theory, revise it, or replace it with a better theory.

A Geographical Anomaly

To follow through on our map metaphor, let's see how a new theory now enables us to understand an old anomaly (Lightman & Gingerich, 1992). Recall how South America and Africa look on a map—almost like two jigsaw puzzle pieces waiting to be fit together. How can we explain this strange anomaly? The old theory decreed that it had to be just an odd coincidence because the location of continents was fixed. Changes in elevation could occur, but horizontal movement was outside the realm of possibility. The continental fit anomaly had been noted by scientists since 1800, but no other satisfactory explanation could be offered, as Lightman and Gingerich (1992) have noted:

> Belief in the fixity of continents held fast.... Then, in the late 1960s, the theory of plate tectonics was developed. This theory, for the first time, provided a persuasive mechanism by which the continents could move horizontally, namely, the existence of a series of 'plates' on which the continents sit. The slow, convective flows within Earth's mantle force neighboring plates apart, carrying along the continents piggyback. Given the mechanism provided by the theory of plate tectonics and the evidence for that theory, the framework of continental drift has become accepted and has replaced the previous framework of the fixity of continents. (p. 692)

We now understand that South America and Africa split apart from a common landmass millions of years ago. The closely fitting coastlines are no longer seen as an anomaly but are the logical consequence of the subsequent drifting apart. The new theory explained the old anomaly.

Career Counseling Anomalies

We have some strange anomalies in career counseling, too.

Lack of Prestige. Career counseling stands at the bottom of the prestige hierarchy among counseling psychologists. Counseling pyschologists themselves increasingly turn to more exotic, more profitable specializations such as health, aging, and addictive behaviors.

What is wrong? Is career counseling unimportant? Certainly not. One can imagine no more important set of problems than those associated with helping people find success and happiness in an activity that occupies most of their waking hours and influences where they spend their sleeping hours. Compared with career counseling, the counseling dealing with fears, sexual dysfunction, and stress pales in significance. How can such an important activity be regarded as undeserving of our highest regard?

Associated Boredom With the Work. Graduate students in counseling psychology programs find career counseling boring. They tend to shun it to the extent possible.

But the stories of people's lives, the struggles they engage in, the internal and external obstacles they overcome (or succumb to), and the interrelationships of career goals to desires for love, revenge, and domination are all grist for the most fascinating tales. Savickas (1992) and Jepsen (1992) have presented some interesting accounts of how narratives can be analyzed to detect commom themes in people's life stories. Studs Terkel (1974) has been able to describe the working lives of ordinary people in a spellbinding manner. How can career counseling possibly be viewed as boring?

Perceived Low Skill Requirements. Career counseling is perceived to require less skill than other types of counseling. Career counseling is often performed by paraprofessionals or those trained at the master's degree level, while other types of counseling require doctoral degrees. Yet career counseling requires all the skills of every other type of counseling, plus the skills in career assessment, a knowledge of the world of work, and a command of employment resources. How is it possible that we would allow people with the least training to engage in an activity that requires the highest level of skill?

Perceived Lack of Fit. Career counseling, and counseling psychology in general, is under constant scutiny and attack for not being an integral part of either education or psychology. We are constantly being asked to justify our existence, and in some locations we get shoved out of the nest. We are seen as a "support service" in more compatible environments, but seldom are we seen as essential to the central purpose of our parent organizations. How can such a strange anomaly exist when we are dedicated to human learning?! Our activities are educational from start to finish. We help our clients learn how to plan their lives. Isn't that at least as central to the educational enterprise as learning how to punctuate a sentence?

Absence of Input in Educational Reform. There is a growing demand in the current educational reform movement that education develop employability skills and prepare young people for the workplace. How many counseling psychologists have been asked for their input into this process? Should not counseling psychologists, whose major interest in life is career development, be seen as an essential part of the team working on the integration of education and work? Why are we overlooked? It does not make sense. Another strange anomaly!

Anomalies Due to Trait-and-Factor Theory

These five interrelated anomalies, and many others, exist because the theory under which most career counseling operates is grossly inadequate. Most of our activities are still governed by the three-part theory outlined by Frank Parsons (1909): (a) know yourself, (b) know the job requirements, and (c) exercise "true reasoning" to fit the first two together.

Now, of course, we are much more sophisticated in the way we apply this theory. We can help clients know themselves by administering any combination of thousands of possible assessment devices. Our knowledge of the world of work is enhanced by a flood of information emanating from the Department of Labor and other sources. And our ability to integrate all this knowledge is now markedly facilitated by the power of modern computers. Nevertheless, we are still applying Frank Parsons' trait-and-factor theory—matching personal characteristics with job environments to create some optimal congruence. And although this step is important, trait-and-factor theory nonetheless paints a picture, creates an image, and draws a map that oversimplifies the complexities of helping people with a wide range of career problems. Trait-and-factor theories lead us to overlook crucial anomalies, to short circuit our responsibilities, to leave our clientele underserved, and to convey to our colleagues a false image that our task is boring, unskilled, and irrelevant to more essential educational endeavors.

Trait-and-factor theory enables us to answer only a small fraction of the questions brought to career counselors. The test of any theory is the extent to which it enables people to formulate useful answers to their questions. Let's take a look at what trait-and-factor theory can do.

A Fictitious Died-in-the-Wool Trait-and-Factor Counselor

In comes client Alice to see career counselor Bob. Alice doesn't know what she wants to do. Bob administers some inventories and discusses her characteristics and preferences. He then puts her in contact with a variety of information resources about the world of work. Finally, he helps her determine which occupations seem to match her characteristics and preferences most closely. If the counseling is successful, Alice is able to summarize her conclusion in the last interview: "Eureka, that's it then—I'm going to be a petrochemical statistician."

"Wonderful," says Bob, "you have successfully matched your qualities to the work environment. Counseling is now completed. That will be three hundred dollars, please."

"But wait a minute," says Alice. "How do I get trained as a petrochemical statistician?"

"I don't know," says Bob. "I'm a trait-and-factor career counselor. My job was finished when you made a successful match. Maybe someone less skilled than I can help you with that minor detail."

"And if I do get training, how do I find a job?"

"That's not part of Frank Parsons' model," says Bob.

"I have a real fear about looking for jobs. Maybe I'm afraid of rejection. Can you help me get over that?"

"No, we don't deal with zeteophobia. You discovered the name of your future occupation, so my job is finished."

"Suppose I do get a job and the boss sexually harasses me. What should I do?"

"Nothing in my trait-and-factor training program covered that eventuality."

"And what if I like my job at first but then get burned out on it after several years. What should I do then?"

"Gosh, I don't know. Maybe we could go through the same three steps again."

"Jobs are constantly changing. My job tasks could be redefined, my job could be eliminated, a new job could be created that I would like better. How can I adapt?"

"Parsons says to exercise true reasoning."

"What if I get a job in one town and my husband finds a job somewhere else? How shall we handle that problem?"

"Well, let's see. Step 1 is know yourself, Step 2 is...."

"Yes, you've said that before. But then when I get ready for retirement, would you help me plan my retirement years?"

"Only if you want to find a new job," replies Bob.

Shortcomings of Trait-and-Factor Theory

This exaggerated account of fictitious career counseling was constructed to make some serious points. We have many more anomalies that need to be explained. Trait-and-factor theories do not help us understand the emotional and skill acquisition tasks required for a job search, they do not inform us about overcoming job-related phobias, they do not address problems associated with handling sexual harassment, job burnout, the constantly changing employment environment, dual career families, or retirement planning. All of this, plus much more, is involved in career counseling.

We need to draw a different map. The root of the problem is inadequate theory. That is why theory convergence is so important—we have a chance to examine and compare existing theories, point out their weaknesses and strengths, and begin to generate some ideas about ways to improve them or abandon them. We need to see ourselves as career cartographers. Our theories are about as accurate as the maps of the world drawn by cartographers 500 years ago. We already have some data that we can use to redraft our theories. We need to send out our Columbuses and our Magellans to collect further data to revise our maps.

Whatever the end product, I hope it is not the result of a political compromise. Theories are not designed by committees, though the contributions of many are required. Perhaps the best outcome will be that someone will start over and create a new theory from scratch.

THE SOCIAL LEARNING THEORY OF CAREER DECISION MAKING

Some years ago, with the able help of G. Brian Jones and Anita Mitchell, I proposed the social learning theory of career decision making, also known as SLTCDM (Krumboltz, 1979, 1981; Krumboltz, Mitchell, & Jones, 1976, 1978, 1980). This summary of SLTCDM and its relationship to the theories of Holland, Super, and Gottfredson is based heavily on a chapter written by Krumboltz and Nichols (1990).

The purpose of SLTCDM is to explain how people come to be employed in a variety of occupations and to suggest possible interventions that might help people make satisfactory career decisions. It is related to trait-and-factor theory in that it attempts to explain the process by which people find congruent occupations.

The theory's most essential concept is the concept of learning. People acquire their preferences for various activities through a multitude of learning experiences. They make sense of their activities because of ideas they have been taught. They acquire beliefs about themselves and the nature of their world through direct and indirect educational experiences. They then take action on the basis of their beliefs using skills that they have developed over time. Let's take a closer look at the process.

Why Do People Prefer Certain Activities?

People learn their preferences by interacting with their environment in a long and complex series of experiences. Two kinds of learning experience are identified in the SLTCDM: instrumental and associative.

Instrumental Learning Experiences. Imagine Fred standing at home plate. Fred swings and hits a home run. His teammates cheer. Now imagine Sam coming up to bat next. Sam swings and misses. He misses the second pitch and then the third. Sam is out. His teammates say nothing. Which of these two boys is most likely to entertain dreams of becoming a professional baseball player?

If you said "Fred," then you are thinking along the same lines as SLTCDM, which states that preferences are developed through the consequences of repeatedly trying a variety of activities. Through instrumental learning experiences, people develop a preference for activities in which they succeed or for which they are rewarded, and they tend to lose interest in activities in which they fail and for which they receive no reward or are punished.

Associative Learning Experiences. Images are flashed before our eyes in a dazzling array. Television commercials associate mundane products with glamorous images. Television programs also depict certain occupations as glamorous and exciting. Influential people talk about certain industries as "hot": plastics, computers, or genetic engineering (depending on the year). Attractive pictures and words, when associated with certain industries and occupations, can create desirable images in the minds of observers. Negative words and pictures can represent other occupations as dull and boring.

Over the years, each individual is exposed to millions of ways that various occupations and activities are associated with positive or negative values. The associations are not necessarily consistent. Some are contradictory, and some are far too complex to fit a simple description of good or bad. Complex combinations of values involving prestige, financial reward, masculinity, variety, economic security, and altruism may be represented in various ways and to different degrees.

What Are the Consequences
of These Learning Experiences?

Learning experiences do not have an automatic outcome, and they are interpreted by each individual differently. People try to make sense of what they observe by constructing *schemata,* beliefs about themselves and about the world around them. They then use their beliefs to formulate their goals and guide their choices. Self-observation generalizations and task approach skills are two consequences of these learning experiences that can be assessed with the *Career Beliefs Inventory* (Krumboltz, 1991a).

Self-observation Generalizations. When Fred observes himself successfully hitting a home run, he may very well say to himself, at that time or later, I'm good at hitting a baseball. When Sam strikes out more frequently than most of his teammates, he is likely to say to himself, I'm terrible at hitting a baseball. Each such statement is a self-observation generalization, a summary belief constructed by each individual based on a large number of prior learning experiences. It might be relatively accurate, or it could be harmfully mistaken.

Task Approach Skills. Through cognitive processes, people are able to relate their observations of themselves to their environment. They make inferences about how they might apply their skills in the real world. They develop work habits and problem-solving skills for coping with the world. They estimate the degree to which their emotional reactions would enable them to deal with certain real-world tasks. These relationships between the self-observation generalizations and the outside world are called *task approach skills.* Such skills include work habits, mental sets, perceptual and thought processes, performance standards and values, problem orientations, and emotional responses.

Some day Fred might relate his self-observation generalizations to his observations of the world around him in a task approach skill something like this: "I enjoy hitting a baseball and I think I'm pretty good at it—but probably not good enough to be a professional player. I think I'll look into some other possibilities."

Action Over Time. Over time, this incredibly complex series of instrumental and associative learning experiences enables individuals to generate ever-changing self-observation generalizations and task approach skills that provide the basis for career-relevant action. Young people apply for and obtain part-time jobs. They develop new skills and habits. They get paid for their efforts. They learn which activities they dislike. Each job provides a learning experience for future jobs. Each experience builds on prior experiences.

In What Context Do These
Learning Experiences Take Place?

Each society and culture has a particular set of environmental conditions, economic opportunities, institutions for learning, and political and social conditions that influence the nature of learning experiences. Self-observation generalizations and task approach skills depend on the environment in which one is raised. The availability of schools and libraries, the quality of teachers, the presence or absence of war, the attitude of society toward differential sex roles for males and females, the societal birthrate, labor market conditions, political stability, and many other such factors create the context in which various types of learning experiences take place. Fred might aspire to be a baseball player if he grew up in the United States, but he might have been inclined to be a cricket player if he had grown up in England.

What Predictions Can Be Derived From This Theory?

A number of testable propositions have been advanced so far, including the following:

People will tend to prefer an occupation if

- they have succeeded at tasks they believe are like tasks performed by members of that occupation
- they have observed a valued model being reinforced for activities like those performed by members of that occupation
- a valued friend or relative stressed its advantages to them and/or they observed positive words and images being associated with it

A converse set of propositions can be stated as follows:

People will tend to avoid an occupation if

- they have failed at tasks they believe are similar to tasks performed by people in that occupation
- they have observed a valued model being punished or ignored for performing activities like those performed by members of that occupation
- a valued friend or relative stressed its disadvantages to them and/or they have observed negative words and images being associated with it

Evidence relevant to the SLTCDM may be found in a number of references (Krumboltz, 1983; Krumboltz, Kinnier, Rude, Scherba, & Hamel, 1986; Krumboltz & Rude, 1981; Mitchell & Krumboltz, 1984a, 1984b, 1987).

SIMILARITIES WITH OTHER CAREER DEVELOPMENT THEORIES

Now let's see how SLTCDM is similar to a few other theories. For all practical purposes, career development theories are not as different as most descriptions of them would have us believe. Certainly, they use different terms, but to what extent are those terms synonyms for the same basic concepts, and to what extent do they represent different terrain?

There are certainly differences between theories, but let's risk the charge of oversimplification in emphasizing similarities and minimizing differences here. There are more serious dangers in the belief that each career development theory is distinct. Some counselors seem to believe that they must subscribe to one theory or another. They believe that by advocating one theory, they deny the validity of others. Other counselors like to maintain an eclectic position, picking and choosing concepts from different theories—sometimes apologetically, sometimes not—to suit their particular purposes.

In the next few pages, the SLTCDM will be compared with the theories proposed by Super, Holland, and Gottfredson. Because of space restrictions, I will drastically abbreviate the discussion of each theory while providing references to their more complete descriptions.

Super's Self-concept Theory

Super (1953, 1955, 1957, 1963, 1964) and Super, Starishevsky, Matlin, and Jordaan (1963) maintained that the occupational choice of an individual is a function of the self-concept of that individual at the time the decision is made. Super has posited that people go through a series of stages in which the self-concept is successively refined.

In Super's view, the similarity of a person's interests and abilities to the interests and abilities of people in a particular occupation increases the likelihood that a person will enter that occupation and will be happily employed there. Super does not specifically describe the ways in which learning experiences create differential interest and differential skills, as does SLTCDM. Nor does he describe how people learn how similar their abilities and interests are to those of people in different occupations. However, Super (1949) has discussed the possible origins and development of interests quite extensively, and he summarized his view quite some time ago in words that are congruent with SLTCDM:

> Interests are the product of interaction between inherited aptitudes and endocrine factors, on the one hand, and opportunity and social evaluation on the other. Some of the things a person does well bring him the satisfaction of mastery or the approval of his companions, and result in interests. Some of the things his associates do appeal to him and, through identification, he patterns his actions and his interests after them. (p. 406)

The differences in the two theories are as follows: (a) SLTCDM sees the evolution of interests occurring throughout an individual's entire lifetime, whereas Super (1949) stresses the early years ("Most of the change which does take place with maturity is complete by age 18"; p. 393) and (b) SLTCDM extends the influence of learning beyond interests to the acquisition of attitudes, emotions, work habits, skills, personality traits, beliefs, and behavior.

Super's notion of the self-concept is similar to SLTCDM's notion of the self-observation generalization. Super recognizes that the self-concept changes and develops throughout people's lives as a result of experience. The SLTCDM version posits a large number of self-observation generalizations, not necessarily a single self-concept. The two theories agree on the basic notion of people successively refining their self-concept(s) over time and applying it (or them) to the world of work.

Regardless of the specific language used, however, both theories recognize that a growing and changing self-concept results from a series of learning experiences. These learning experiences can include identification with models, in Super's terms, or vicarious learning experiences, in the terms of SLTCDM. They can result from direct experience or, in SLTCDM's terms, instrumental learning experiences. Super discusses the influence of role playing, while SLTCDM discusses the influence of positive and negative reinforcement over innumerable direct performance trials. Super also discusses the notion of reality testing, another variation of the same process.

Stages of development are a part of Super's theoretical notion, and he has suggested six developmental tasks beginning with the crystallization of a vocational preference and ending with readiness for retirement and old age. SLTCDM depicts a continuous passage of time in which learning experiences occur but does not break time down into discrete, labeled stages.

The notion of stages implies that there is some invariant sequence of behaviors that occurs at a certain period of one's life, that this sequence always occurs in the same order, and that rather rigid boundaries can be identified to distinguish the stages from each other. Super probably would not claim that the stages are all that sharply delimited and would certainly recognize the porous nature of the stages he has proposed. Indeed, in the fluid economy of the present decade, people at age 45 or 50 may well need to crystallize a vocational preference again if their present jobs have become obsolete. So at any given age, the same process may need to begin anew. For this reason, SLTCDM does not delimit the passage of time by specifying discrete stages.

However, if I were asked whether there are certain patterns of behavior that tend to occur more often with 14- to 18-year-olds than with 25- to 35-year-olds, I would certainly agree. On average, there are indeed certain common developmental tasks that occur more often at one age than at another. The absence of stage specifications in SLTCDM is a way of recognizing the fluid nature of learning experiences and the changing requirements of the occupational world. Stages are simply handy labels that could be attached to the time line in SLTCDM, if someone wanted to think in those terms.

Vocational exploratory behavior is a key concept in both formulations. Jordaan (1963) was most articulate in emphasizing the way in which vocational exploration designed by the individual can produce learning experiences that either confirm or deny the present self-concept. The same general notion is advocated by SLTCDM, which suggests that career beliefs need to be identified, examined, and subjected to testing by the person who holds them.

The distinction between self-observation generalizations and task approach skills in SLTCDM is parallel to the distinction between *psychtalk* and *occtalk* in Super's theory, as described by Starishevsky and Matlin (1963). *Psychtalk* refers to the tendency of individuals to think about themselves, for example, "I am a good baseball player," "I always tell the truth," or "I work well with others." *Occtalk* concerns the relationship between the psychtalk and the occupational and educational world. An occtalk statement might be something like, "I plan to become an accountant because I like numbers and because I work diligently and precisely and prefer to avoid excessive contact with people."

The term *incorporation* was used to indicate the degree of similarity between the psychtalk and the occtalk and the degree to which there is a realistic congruence. While not using a term such as incorporation, SLTCDM enables people facing career decisions to test the adequacy of their conceptualizations with the real world. Thus, both theories posit that (a) the career decider makes statements about the nature of the educational and occupational world, (b) these statements may be more or less accurate, (c) there are ways of testing the adequacy of these statements, and (d) actions and decisions to enter a particular occupation are based on the perceptions the individual holds.

Holland's Hexagon

Holland (1959, 1963, 1966, 1971, 1973) has generated a theory, instrumentation, and procedures that have had a powerful influence on career counseling. As a result of extensive factor analytic studies, Holland identified six orientations to describe people's interests: Realistic, Investigative, Social, Conventional, Enterprising, and Artistic. These six orientations can be represented in the form of a hexagon, with the most different orientations being at opposite sides of the hexagon and the most similar orientations being adjacent to each other.

Holland did not describe in any detail how people come to develop the interests that characterize their particular orientation. However, if we were to ask Holland how interests were generated, he would undoubtedly indicate that people acquire their interests as a result of interacting with their environment. The general learning model proposed by SLTCDM could be used to explain how people come to develop any combination of these six orientations. By the same token, SLTCDM does not specifically posit the existence of six orientations but does not deny the validity of these constructs, either. If I were asked about the usefulness of these six orientations, I would express my admiration for the research work that led to the hexagon model but would point out that there are sharp differences and distinctions within each orientation that must not be overlooked.

Holland posited a *level hierarchy* that is a function of one's general academic aptitude and self-evaluation. The self-evaluation in Holland's conception is similar to the notion of the self-observation generalization in SLTCDM and differs from it only in its degree of specificity. Self-evaluation in Holland's conception refers to a more general assessment, while SLTCDM's self-observation generalization pinpoints the self-evaluation of specific behaviors or characteristics.

Holland also posited that occupational environments are characterized by these same six general orientations and that people attempt to match their own orientation profile to the orientation of particular occupations. The more similar the fit, the higher the congruence. SLTCDM specifically describes the influence of cultural, economic, and social influences on the opportunity structure and the availability of resources. It points out how the availability of schools and libraries, for example, can influence people's eventual occupational choice. Holland represented the same idea in a more macro manner by categorizing people and environments into six orientations and then calculating the degree of congruence.

Holland also contributed the concept of *self-knowledge,* which refers to the extent to which individuals possess accurate information about their own interests and abilities. Self-knowledge to Holland is similar to the self-observation generalizations of the SLTCDM, which, in turn, is similar to the self-concept of Super.

According to Holland, a good occupational choice depends on accurate self-knowledge as well as accurate occupational knowledge. Again, he does not describe exactly how this knowledge is acquired, but we must certainly assume that it is acquired through learning and is not genetically imprinted. Some of his research (e.g., Holland, 1962) involved checking the similarity between the attitudes of students in the National Merit sample and those of their parents. He found some similarities between the attitudes held by the mothers and the students' personal orientations. He also found that the fathers' stated goals for their children were related to the basic orientation of their sons and, to a somewhat lesser degree, to the basic orientation of their daughters. Clearly, Holland recognizes the transmission of values from parents to children, though he does not specifically describe the mechanisms by which such attitudes and values are transmitted.

As a result of extensive research by Holland and his associates as well as that of independent investigators, it has become quite clear that there is indeed a relationship between the orientations of individuals and the occupations that they choose. The correlations are far from perfect, however, and there is still much to be learned about the influences that affect career choice.

Holland's primary method of gathering data is to ask people about their preferences for named occupations. Subjects seem to have relatively stable stereotypes about occupations. One might well ask how occupational stereotypes are learned, but Holland's theory is not concerned with this question. SLTCDM would suggest that stereotypes are learned primarily through associative learning experiences and the pairing of occupational names with images received through direct and vicarious experiences.

While emphasizing different features of vocational development, SLTCDM and Holland's theory do not basically disagree. Both would recognize that people develop characteristic ways of viewing themselves and the world around them as a result of learning experiences. Both stress that individuals seek to find a fit between the real world and their view of themselves. The better the fit, the happier the individual.

Gottfredson's Theory of Occupational Aspirations

A more recent theory on occupational aspirations has been proposed by Linda Gottfredson (1981). Gottfredson suggested that occupational aspirations are created in a four-stage manner:

1. Orientation to size and power at ages 3 to 5
2. Orientation to sex roles at ages 6 to 8
3. Orientation to social valuation at ages 9 to 13
4. Orientation to the internal unique self at ages 14 and over

Basically, she posited that certain aspects of the self and environment are more salient at some ages than at others. In contrast, SLTCDM does not divide the time line of development into distinct stages because learning experiences of different types can be influential at any age. Nevertheless, both theories clearly describe the increasing refinement of discriminations and conceptions that occur with increasing age.

The most creative contribution of Gottfredson's theory is the notion that the attraction of a particular occupation is primarily a function of what she called its *sextype rating* and *prestige level*. Gottfredson drew a grid in which the sextype ratings of occupations are displayed along a horizontal axis, from the most masculine occupations (e.g., miner) at the left to the most feminine occupations (e.g., manicurist) at the right. The prestige ranking of each occupation is displayed along a vertical axis, with the least prestigious occupations (e.g., groundskeeper) rated toward zero at the bottom and the most prestigious occupations (e.g., federal judge) rated toward 100 at the top. Every occupation can then be placed on the grid.

Gottfredson proposed that each individual develops a "zone of acceptable alternatives" on this grid—a subset of occupations that are within the range of masculinity-femininity desired by the person and also within upper and lower limits of prestige deemed acceptable. The more idealistic aspirations are at the top of the zone, while the more realistic aspirations are toward the bottom of the zone. Vertical boundary lines separate occupations that may be deemed by the person to be either too masculine or too feminine. Subsequent research (e.g., Leung, Ivey, & Scheel, 1991) has not supported the salient impact claimed for these two factors, especially for the gender factor.

Gottfredson did not describe how people learn about these masculine or feminine characteristics of occupations, nor did she attempt to describe how people learn what prestige levels are ascribed to each occupation. SLTCDM describes the mechanisms by which such learnings are acquired, but has not gone so far as to categorize the specific factors that influence most people at each age level. SLTCDM lists the social factors that infringe on the choices of young people, for example, labor market conditions, availability of libraries and industries, quality of education, neighborhood, and family background. This environmental context creates the conditions from which learning experiences are developed. SLTCDM describes how the learnings are acquired, while Gottfredson's theory describes how the products of that learning are organized. Each theory focuses on different aspects of the process.

Gottfredson emphasized the importance of the *self-concept*, which is similar to SLTCDM's concept of the self-observation generalization. Gottfredson stressed the importance of the *gender self-concept*, which she described as the "most strongly protected aspect of self" (p. 572). She went on to describe the gender self-concept as most important in influencing occupational aspirations, followed by social class and ability self-concept. Thus, there is a strong need to pick an occupation that fits one's gender self-concept (suitably masculine or feminine) and social class (prestige level). These primary requirements for a job take precedence over interest level, which essentially fine-tunes preferences within the zone of acceptable alternatives decreed by the gender and prestige grid. According to Gottfredson, interest inventories that ask about expressed preferences in specifically named occupations are as effective as they are in predicting occupational placement because the names of occupations include connotations of sextype and prestige as well as interests.

Gottfredson pointed out that individuals must compromise their aspirations with the reality of the job market, a process that SLTCDM designates as a task approach skill. Gottfredson describes a hierarchy of self-concepts that are important—first gender, then social valuation: "The theory proposes that when people have to compromise—as they often do—between sextype, prestige, and field of work, they will most readily sacrifice field of work" (p. 575). Gottfredson also described the "effort-acceptability squeeze," in which demands for performance may exceed one's ability to satisfy them—again, a variation of what SLTCDM categorizes under the label of task approach skill.

In summary, both theories present a picture of people developing increasing sophistication and finer discriminations over a period of time. As a result of learning experiences, people generate a set of acceptable occupational aspirations, some of which may or may not be realized due to the socioeconomic and cultural conditions existing at the time their choices are to be made. Compromises must be made between self-conceptions that may be ideal and the realistic workplace. Gottfredson argued that sacrifices are made first in the field of interest, second in the prestige level, and third in sextype, while SLTCDM leaves open the possibility that different individuals may sacrifice on a different basis, depending on specific circumstances. Both theories clearly recognize the role of self-concepts, presuppositions, and stereotypical beliefs that influence the career decision process. Both advocate that counselors need to access such beliefs.

Application of Gottfredson's theory in a society that is trying to eliminate sexism seems difficult. Strenuous efforts are being made to help young people consider nontraditional career paths and open up all occupations to both men and women.

Counselors would have to rank order every occupation on the basis of its masculinity-femininity to begin the choice process. Occupations outside the acceptable zone would be automatically excluded from consideration unless a separate rank ordering were constructed on the basis of the idiosyncratic perceptions of masculinity-femininity that each person making a career choice holds.

Gottfredson's theory also promotes occupationism—discrimination against individuals on the basis of their membership in an occupation. A linear prestige scale is proposed, and it becomes mandatory to make prestige ratings a major factor in occupational choice regardless of how important it is to the individual decider. As Krumboltz (1992) has observed, "I am troubled by the notion that every client should be encouraged to identify some zone of acceptable alternatives on the basis of some linear prestige hierarchy—as well as on the basis of its masculinity or femininity. Choosing occupations by these criteria promotes both occupationism and sexism" (p. 515).

CHOICE OF A THEORY

Three theories of career choice and development have been analyzed in an attempt to highlight their congruence with SLTCDM. While significant overlap exists, each of these four theories also describes different aspects of the career choice and development process not covered by the others. In terms of our map analogy, each theory covers the same geographic area (i.e., career development), but each highlights some parts of the terrain while leaving other parts unspecified.

In some graduate courses, students are asked to choose the theory they wish to adopt. There is an expectation that everyone should subscribe to one theory. Eclecticism is forbidden. It may be useful to consider this policy using the map metaphor.

Suppose you were asked to choose one kind of map that you would use from now on. You could choose a roadmap, a rainfall map, a vegetation map, or a population density map. How would you react? You might well say, "The choice depends on my purpose at the time. If I wanted to know where to find Monterey pines, I'd choose the vegetation map. Why should I have to choose one map for all possible purposes?"

The same argument might well apply to career development theories. Why choose one theory when each one might suit different purposes? If you want an outline of how careers evolve over a lifetime, Super's stage model might be useful. If you want to help people choose an occupation congruent with six categories of interest, take a look at Holland's theory. If a client wants an appropriately masculine high-prestige occupation, Gottfredson could help. Or, if you want to help people of any age acquire the skills, attitudes, and understandings necessary to adapt to a changing environment, SLTCDM may be worth considering. Our ability to help people traverse the morass of career planning is far from perfect because there is still a significant portion of the terrain not covered adequately by any of these theories.

A BETTER THEORY

All the career development theories we are considering, including SLTCDM, attempt to account for the placement of people in occupations, though each draws on a somewhat different, though partially overlapping, set of constructs.

The anomalies I have described are due to the narrow focus of trait-and-factor theories. We need to describe the process of career counseling in a way that incorporates the complexities of human beings struggling to satisfy their most basic instincts while striving to make a significant impact on their world. Career counseling involves much more than locating a congruent occupation for a person.

While SLTCDM in its current manifestation does not address all the issues that need to be considered, I believe that it does include the most crucial components: (a) recognition that a genetic influence can be important in career planning, (b) a description of the powerful impact the cultural environment has on human development, and (c) a learning component that makes it possible for people to take charge of their own destiny.

Qualities of a Better Theory

I have defined a theory as a set of explanatory propositions that enable us to find useful answers to our questions. A useful theory must meet the following criteria and motivate us to seek answers to a large number of practical questions, a few of which are illustrated below.

- *Accurate: It must permit us to describe occupational behavior accurately.*

    How can we classify occupations to aid people in discriminating among them?

    What factors determine which people will enter which occupations?

    What factors govern mobility between occupations?

    Given an individual with defined characteristics, what is the probability that that individual will be successfully employed in a named occupation?

    Given a job description for a specific occupation and a list of applicants with defined characteristics, which applicant will have the highest probability of performing the job successfully?

- *Responsible: It must empower people to take responsibility for their own lives.*

    How can educational institutions be reformed to develop employability skills and attitudes so that young people can shape their own career paths?

    If an individual with defined characteristics states a career-related goal, what actions can that individual take to increase the probability that the goal will be attained?

    If conditions or characteristics change in defined ways, what modifications in the individual's actions will increase the probability of goal attainment?

What types of educational experiences increase or decrease the probability that students will aspire to pursue any given occupation?

- **Comprehensive:** *It must address the full range of circumstances that affect career satisfaction.*

    How can an individual acquire the skills and emotional fortitude required for a job search?

    How can job-related phobias be overcome?

    How can sexual harassment be prevented and/or remedied?

    How can individuals be helped to deal with job burnout?

    What interventions best help families learn how to deal with dual career issues?

    What interventions best help people prepare for and adjust to retirement?

- **Integrative:** *It must be related to theories in other domains.*

    How does the process of acquiring confidence in one's ability to perform a job relate to the process of acquiring confidence in dealing with members of the opposite sex?

    How is the origin of job burnout similar to the origin of clinical depression?

- **Adaptive:** *It must change and evolve in response to newly discovered anomalies.*

    How does a new reward structure of an organization affect the motivation of employees to do their best work?

    How does the emphasis on cooperative teamwork in the modern workplace affect individual achievement?

CONCLUSION

Career counselors have defined their responsibilities too narrowly because of the dominant theory in the field, trait-and-factor theory. As a result, career counseling is perceived as simplistic, boring, and requiring relatively little training. This perception is a strange anomaly, since, in fact, career counseling requires all the skills of regular counseling plus special skills and knowledge about career development.

Trait-and-factor theory, in any of its present manifestations, addresses only one problem out of the hundreds of possible problems dealt with by career counselors, namely, matching an individual to the name of an occupation. In fact, career counselors do deal with most of these other problems, but they do so without the guidance of a generally accepted theory.

A better theory would permit us to generate questions and answers to a vastly wider range of practical issues. In particular, a better theory would meet five criteria: accuracy, responsibility, comprehensiveness, integrity, and adaptability.

Some variation of learning theory could be the foundation for the theoretical descriptions we seek. A learning theory could describe accurately how occupationally relevant skills, beliefs, and emotions are acquired and organized. It could empower both clients and counselors to construct educational experiences that would move them toward their goals. It could easily encompass the entire range of career-related activities, since all of them are learned. It would integrate career development with the fields of education and psychology, where learning theory has its base. And it could evolve and change easily as new facts and anomalies are revealed.

Present career theories are not necessarily incompatible with a learning theory approach. The wisdom we have already acquired will not be lost as we redraw our maps to incorporate the larger world before us.

REFERENCES

Gottfredson, L. (1981). Circumscription and compromise: A developmental theory of occupational aspirations. *Journal of Counseling Psychology, 28,* 545–579.

Holland, J. (1959). A theory of vocational choice. *Journal of Counseling Psychology, 6,* 35–45.

Holland, J. (1962). Some explorations of a theory of vocational choice: I. One- and two-year longitudinal studies. *Psychological Monographs, 76,* 26 (Whole No. 545).

Holland, J. (1963). Explorations of a theory of vocational choice and achievement: II. A four-year prediction study. *Psychological Reports, 12,* 547–594.

Holland, J. (1966). *The psychology of vocational choice.* Waltham, MA: Blaisdell.

Holland, J. (1971). A theory-ridden, computerless, impersonal, vocational guidance system. *Journal of Vocational Behavior, 1,* 167–176.

Holland, J. (1973). *Making vocational choices: A theory of careers.* Englewood Cliffs, NJ: Prentice-Hall.

Jepsen, D. (1992, April). *Understanding careers as stories.* Paper presented at the annual convention of the American Association for Counseling and Development, Baltimore.

Jordaan, J. (1963). Exploratory behavior: The formulation of self and occupational concepts. In D. Super, R. Starishevsky, N. Matlin, & J. Jordaan, *Career development: Self-concept theory.* New York: CEEB Research Monograph No. 4.

Krumboltz, J. (1979). A social learning theory of career decision making. Revised and reprinted in A. Mitchell, G. Jones, & J. Krumboltz (Eds.), *Social learning and career decision making* (pp. 19–49). Cranston, RI: Carroll Press.

Krumboltz, J. (1981). A social learning theory of career decision making. Reprinted in D. Montrose & C. Shinkman (Eds.), *Career development in the 1980's: Theory and practice* (pp. 43–66). Springfield, IL: Charles C. Thomas.

Krumboltz, J. (1983). *Private rules in career decision making.* Columbus, OH: National Center for Research in Vocational Education, Ohio State University.

Krumboltz, J. (1991a). *Career Beliefs Inventory.* Palo Alto, CA: Consulting Psychologists Press.

Krumboltz, J. (1991b). The 1990 Leona Tyler Award Address: Brilliant insights—Platitudes that bear repeating. *The Counseling Psychologist, 19,* 298–315.

Krumboltz, J. (1992). The dangers of occupationism. *The Counseling Psychologist, 20,* 511–518.

Krumboltz, J., Kinnier, R., Rude, S., Sherba, D., & Hamel, D. (1986). Teaching a rational approach to career decision making: Who benefits most? *Journal of Vocational Behavior, 29*, 1–6.

Krumboltz, J., Mitchell, A., & Jones, G. (1976). A social learning theory of career selection. *The Counseling Psychologist, 6*, 71–81.

Krumboltz, J., Mitchell, A., & Jones, G. (1978). A social learning theory of career selection. Reprinted in J. Whiteley & A. Resnikoff (Eds.), *Career counseling* (pp. 100–127). Monterey, CA: Brooks/Cole.

Krumboltz, J., Mitchell, A., & Jones, G. (1980). A social learning theory of career selection. Reprinted in T. Wentling (Ed.), *Annual Review of Research in Vocational Education, 1* (pp. 259–282). Urbana, IL: University of Illinois.

Krumboltz, J., & Nichols, C. (1990). Integrating the social learning theory of career decision making. In W. Walsh & S. Osipow (Eds.), *Career counseling: Contemporary topics in vocational psychology* (pp. 159–192). Hillsdale, NJ: Erlbaum.

Krumboltz, J., & Rude, S. (1981). Behavioral approaches to career counseling. *Behavioral Counseling Quarterly, 1*, 108–120.

Kuhn, T. (1970). *The structure of scientific revolutions.* Chicago: University of Chicago Press.

Leung, S., Ivey, D., & Scheel, M. (1991, August). *A systematic approach to test Gottfredson's theory.* Paper presented at the annual convention of the American Psychological Association, San Francisco.

Lightman, A., & Gingerich, O. (1992). When do anomalies begin? *Science, 255*, 690–695.

Mitchell, L., & Krumboltz, J. (1984a). Research on human decision making and counseling. In S. Brown & R. Lent (Eds.), *Handbook of counseling psychology* (pp. 238–280). New York: Wiley.

Mitchell, L., & Krumboltz, J. (1984b). Social learning approach to career decision making: Krumboltz theory. In D. Brown & L. L. Brooks (Eds.), *Career choice and development: Applying contemporary theory to practice* (Chapter 9). San Francisco: Jossey-Bass.

Mitchell, L., & Krumboltz, J. (1987). The effects of cognitive restructuring and decision-making training on career indecision. *Journal of Counseling and Development, 66*, 171–174.

Parsons, F. (1909). *Choosing a vocation.* Boston: Houghton Mifflin.

Savickas, M. (1992, April). *Career counseling using the narrative paradigm.* Paper presented at the annual convention of the American Association for Counseling and Development, Baltimore.

Starishevsky, R., & Matlin, N. (1963). A model for the translation of self-concept into vocational terms. In D. Super, R. Starishevsky, N. Matlin, & J. Jordaan, *Career development: Self-concept theory* (pp. 33–41). New York: CEEB Research Monograph No. 4.

Super, D. (1949). *Appraising vocational fitness by means of psychological tests.* New York: Harper & Row.

Super, D. (1953). A theory of vocational development. *American Psychologist, 8*, 185–190.

Super, D. (1955). Personality integration through vocational counseling. *Journal of Counseling Psychology, 2*, 217–226.

Super, D. (1957). *The psychology of careers.* New York: Harper & Row.

Super, D. (1963). Self-concepts in vocational development. In D. Super, R. Starishevsky, N. Matlin, & J. Jordaan, *Career development: Self-concept theory* (pp. 1–16). New York: CEEB Research Monograph No. 4.

Super, D. (1964). A developmental approach to vocational guidance. *Vocational Guidance Quarterly, 13,* 1–10.

Super, D., Starishevsky, R., Matlin, N., & Jordaan, J. (1963). *Career development: Self-concept theory.* New York: CEEB Research Monograph No. 4.

Terkel, S. (1974). *Working.* New York: Pantheon.

CHAPTER THREE

The Theory of Work Adjustment as Convergent Theory

René V. Dawis
University of Minnesota

Uɴɪꜰɪᴇᴅ ᴛʜᴇᴏʀʏ ɪꜱ the Holy Grail of science. Since Galileo and Newton, scientists have been seeking the theory to unify all theories. Like the quest for the Holy Grail, the search for unified theory has been a most powerful motivating force despite grave doubts that such a goal can be attained. The goal of this volume is more modest and more attainable: not unified theory, but rather, theory convergence among five major theories of career choice and development.

Setting limited goals may make the task easier, yet not necessarily easy. To begin with, there is the inescapable criterion problem: What exactly do we mean by theory convergence? How can we tell when concepts and theories converge? Theories, being incomplete pictures of reality, focus on only those aspects of special interest to the theorists. Thus, Bordin may focus on early development, Holland on choice, Krumboltz on decision making, Super on lifelong development, and Lofquist and Dawis on adjustment. Although each focus has its "spread of effect," theories are not unlike the seven blind beggars' differing descriptions of the elephant.

There are at least two approaches to demonstrating convergence: first, showing equivalence or similarity or overlap, and second, showing linkage, which could include superimposing a larger framework on the linkages. But before convergence with other theories of career choice and development can be discussed, I must set the stage by describing the theory of work adjustment (TWA; Dawis & Lofquist, 1984; Lofquist & Dawis, 1969).

THE THEORY OF WORK ADJUSTMENT

TWA began as an attempt to integrate several concepts derived from the literature (Scott, Dawis, England, & Lofquist, 1960). The theory that eventually emerged was founded on four basic psychological concepts: ability, reinforcement value, satisfaction, and person-environment correspondence. These concepts came from different theoretical traditions—in some respects, the same traditions from which the other four theories discussed in this book are derived.

The Basic Concepts

Ability was derived from the individual differences tradition (Anastasi, 1937; Tyler, 1947). The individual differences study of abilities was itself an offshoot of experimental psychology, which even today studies such abilities as psychophysical judgment, sensory perception, motor skills, linguistic skills, and memory. The study of individual differences in ability anticipated contemporary cognitive psychology (Carroll, 1976, 1992; Spearman, 1923; Sternberg, 1977), yet at the same time remained moored to behaviorist psychology or the psychology of learning. As Ferguson (1956) put it, the end product of learning is ability—abilities being behavioral attributes that have attained some stability or invariance through a typically lengthy learning process. The concept of ability, then, is a common point of convergence for different areas of psychology, and it can be a point of convergence for theories of career choice and development.

In TWA, *skills* are distinguished from *abilities*. *Skills* are the component units of the response repertoire that constitute the response capability of a person. Using the factor analysis model, TWA views skills as the observed, zero-order variables, and abilities as the inferred factors (or reference dimensions) with which skills may be described more parsimoniously. There are a very large number of human skills—cognitive, perceptual, psychomotor, physical, social, and affective—so that it would be advantageous if a relatively few ability dimensions can be used to describe (or reference) a multitude of skills. One point of confusion is that ability measures (i.e., ability tests) are, in fact, skill measures. Such confusion can be minimized if we limit the term *ability tests* to mean tests measuring established reference dimensions of ability (as, e.g., in French, Ekstrom, & Price, 1963), and identifying all other tests of behavior capability as *skill tests*. Another point of confusion is that, whereas having a particular skill implies having the requisite abilities (as defined here), having the requisite abilities does not necessarily imply having the particular skill. People with the same abilities may not have the same skills if their experience and learning are different. However, abilities can be used to predict the level on a particular skill that a person can attain if given the opportunity to learn the skill. Such predicted skill level is what TWA means by *aptitude*. Abilities, as indicators of aptitude, can be used to predict (or help predict) socially significant future behavior, such as school or job performance.

Reinforcement value, meaning the potential of a putative reinforcer to reinforce behavior, was derived from the learning theory tradition (see especially Tolman, 1932). This concept lies at the core of the TWA concept of *psychological needs.* Using reinforcement theory as its rationale, TWA defined psychological needs as the person's requirements for reinforcers. The strength or intensity of a reinforcer requirement is a function of that reinforcer's reinforcement value to the person. Thus, through the concept of reinforcement value, psychological needs are defined in TWA not only in behavioral terms but also in idiographic terms (Allport, 1961).

Psychological needs are inferred from a person's preferences for reinforcers. Over time, such preferences tend to stabilize, thereby allowing needs to be measured as a stable dispositional attribute of the person. Reinforcer preferences may be expressed in terms of the reinforcers' importance to the person. Considerations of importance inevitably lead to the concept of values. To distinguish between needs and values, the factor analysis model is again invoked, with needs being viewed as zero-order variables and values as factors. It is in this sense that one can say that values inform needs and needs reflect values.

Skills, abilities, needs, and values, then, are key variables in TWA. They are conceptualized as dispositional variables (traits) and are used in TWA to characterize the person (hence, personality). Following Cattell (1965), skills and needs might be thought of as *surface traits,* and abilities and values as *source traits,* of personality. As source traits, abilities and values are seen as providing the *structure* of personality. Thus, the operative set of skills and needs may change with time or with a given situation, but the source—personality structure—remains essentially the same.

Satisfaction, the third concept on which TWA is based, was derived from the human relations tradition, courtesy of Hoppock (1935). During that time (the early 1960s), we had observed that the research literature was oriented too much toward the employer, whereas work adjustment should be oriented toward the employee, hence, the central role TWA gave to satisfaction. Satisfaction is defined as affect—or feeling or emotion—resulting from one's evaluation of the situation. As affect, the generic concept satisfaction includes both positive affect (satisfaction) and negative affect (dissatisfaction), following two-factor theory (Herzberg, 1966; Watson & Tellegen, 1985).

Initially in our thinking, satisfaction was conceptually linked only to needs. Then we realized that the performance ratings being predicted by skill/ability variables were actually a form of satisfaction—the employer's or superior's satisfaction with the employee. The satisfaction concept could therefore be rendered in two forms: the person's satisfaction with the work environment, for which we reserved the term satisfaction, and the work environment's satisfaction with the person, for which we adopted the term *satisfactoriness,* courtesy of British occupational psychology (Heron, 1954). Note that in either of its forms, the satisfaction concept requires an evaluator as well as the evaluator's criteria for evaluating. Moreover, in addition to the person's satisfaction with the environment and the environment's satisfaction with the person, two other satisfactions are logically conceivable: the person's satisfaction with the person (i.e., satisfaction with self) and the environment's satisfaction with itself. The first must undoubtedly relate to *self-esteem,* and the second could refer to something that might be called *organizational esteem.*

The fourth concept, *person-environment* (P-E) *correspondence,* was derived from the vocational psychology tradition, which from the beginning had focused on vocational fit or vocational match (Parsons, 1909). We adopted the term *correspondence* because (a) it was novel, (b) its root word *respond* denoted behavior and co-denoted mutual interaction, and (c) it was a mathematical concept, which perhaps might open up new possibilities in analysis. If one focused on the social or human environment, one could say that the P-E correspondence concept is consonant with the humanist tradition, which holds human interrelationships to be of overarching importance. A plausible case could even be made that the idea of P-E correspondence is descended from ancient Chinese tradition, with its ideal of personal harmony with the environment. Incidentally, we also came to realize that the vaunted empirical scaling approach—so vigorously championed by Minnesota—was but an instance of P-E correspondence.

The Working Theory

The concept of P-E correspondence provided us with both a predictive model and a process model. The predictive model cast P-E correspondence as the complex independent variable, and satisfaction and its consequence, tenure, as the dependent variables. To depict the work adjustment process, the components of the predictive model were recast into a systems model (Powers, 1973) in which the driving force is achieving and maintaining correspondence and the parameter value on which the system converges is satisfaction. Dissatisfaction, then, is deviation from parameter value, which triggers the mechanism, adjustment behavior, that restores the system to its original state. Thus, in this model, dissatisfaction—whether of the person or of the environment—plays a central motivational role in work adjustment.

Work adjustment viewed from a systems (or interactive) perspective led logically to variables that characterize the features of the person's interaction with the environment, which we called *personality style variables.* TWA identified four personality style variables: celerity, or the speed of initiating interaction with the environment; pace, or the intensity (activity level) of interaction; rhythm, or the pattern of the pace of interaction (whether steady or cyclical or erratic); and endurance, or the sustaining of interaction. Thus, people with the same personality structure, that is, the same abilities and values, can still differ in their behavior and therefore in their behavioral outcomes as a function of differing personality style. Furthermore, different environments, not just persons, have different styles.

The TWA predictive model revealed four targets for adjustment behavior to operate on: response requirements, response capability, reinforcer requirements, and reinforcement capability. Because two of these targets refer to person and two to environment, two modes of adjustment were identified: (a) the active mode, when change is effected in the environment, and (b) the reactive mode, when change is effected in the person. But locus of change is not the same as locus of initiative for change, wherein initiating change is the active mode of adjustment and responding to initiatives for change is the reactive mode of adjustment. If we cross locus of change with locus of initiative for change, that is, whether person or environment initiated the change, we have four modes of adjustment (Hesketh, 1985).

The concept of adjustment mode required two additional concepts to explain when adjustment behavior starts and when it stops. The idea of dissatisfaction as the motivational force suggested two variables: flexibility, to designate initial tolerance for dissatisfaction, and perseverance, to designate continuing tolerance for dissatisfaction beyond the flexibility threshold. Like the personality style variables, these adjustment style variables—flexibility, activeness, reactiveness, and perseverance—moderate the relation of personality structure to behavior and behavior outcomes.

POINTS OF CONVERGENCE

With that description of TWA as a backdrop, we can now specify several points of convergence with the other theories.

Holland's Theory

TWA's convergence with the Holland (1985) theory is the most apparent and arguably the closest. Both theories use a person-environment fit model. Both emerged from the trait-and-factor or individual differences tradition. The outcome or dependent variables are similar, although the independent variables are different. Holland's independent variables are types rather than traits. However, the Holland types can be differentiated on traits such as abilities and values as well as on interests. For Holland (1985), types are "behavioral repertoires" (p. 18). Furthermore, the mechanisms of adjustment, the adjustment style and personality style variables of TWA, can be incorporated in Holland's theory (e.g., the types have distinctive coping styles, p. 17). Likewise, the Holland concepts of consistency and differentiation can be incorporated in TWA (e.g., consistency between ability pattern and value pattern). I have yet to find an instance where Holland's theory and TWA make contradictory assertions or predictions.

Krumboltz's Theory

Next closest in convergence to TWA would be Krumboltz's (1979; Mitchell & Krumboltz, 1990) social learning theory. Both theories are derived from learning theory, and both use the concepts of skill and reinforcement. The convergence mapping may not be one-to-one, but overlap is considerable. For example, Krumboltz speaks of abilities and values, although not as the constituents of personality structure as TWA does. Values play a key role in Krumboltz's prescriptive career decision-making model, both in the decision-making process and in the evaluation of its outcomes, just as they do in TWA. The dichotomy of personal versus environmental cuts through Krumboltz's list of "categories of influencers"; that dichotomy is basic to TWA. TWA differs somewhat from Krumboltz's theory in that it focuses on higher-order, disposition-type variables such as abilities and values, whereas Krumboltz uses lower-order, ongoing behavior variables such as task approach skills. That is, the two theories operate at different levels of abstraction.

Super's Theory

As with Krumboltz's theory, Super's (1990) developmental theory and TWA differ in that they emphasize different levels of abstraction, as well as different degrees of comprehensiveness or inclusiveness. TWA mentions development but describes it at a coarse-grained level, whereas Super's account is more fine grained. For example, TWA compresses Super's growth and exploration stages into an individuation stage, and his establishment and maintenance stages into a stability stage. TWA's personality structure is more restricted and includes only abilities and values, whereas Super's personality characteristics more comprehensively encompass needs, values, interests, intelligence, abilities, and special aptitudes. Furthermore, environment for Super includes one's family, peer group, school, and community, as well as co-workers, the work organization, the labor market, and the economy, whereas TWA confines it to the work environment.

One of Super's main concepts, the self-concept, can be linked to the TWA concept of satisfaction. Satisfaction entails evaluation, which requires an evaluator, an object of evaluation, and evaluation criteria. In earlier TWA, the object of the person's evaluation was the environment, and the evaluation criteria were the person's values. In its most recent version (Lofquist & Dawis, 1991), TWA includes the idea of the person as object of evaluation, that is, the person evaluating self. Self, then, refers to the person's perception of "person" in the P-E correspondence context, and it is this class of perceptions that is the basis for the self-concept, from a TWA point of view.

One might view the self-concept as the centroid of a distribution of perceptions of person (self-perceptions) in numerous P-E correspondence contexts. Such self-perceptions depend on one's cognitive abilities as well as on one's response and reinforcement history. Perception of "person" includes perception of one's skills and abilities or lack thereof. Self-estimation of one's skills and abilities may be seen as the basis for feelings of "self-efficacy." The evaluation of one's self-efficacy, in turn, contributes to "self-esteem." Self-esteem, or lack thereof, is thus the result of self-evaluation. In other words, self-esteem results from satisfaction (or dissatisfaction) with self or with aspects of self, such as one's abilities and one's achievements. Because context is a ubiquitous determinant, we can have high self-esteem in one context and low self-esteem in another. Similarly, self-concept can change with context, although it is customarily thought of as being stable. Through the concept of satisfaction, then, TWA can link up with Super's self-concept.

With regard to the concept of values, another important Super concept, the overlap between Super and TWA is rather substantial. Our instruments even have the same look and feel. We both went through paired comparison forms and Likert forms, although Super now favors the latter, whereas we have remained with the former. But the overlap in content is great from a linguistic-semantic viewpoint, although I am not aware of any empirical equivalence studies. In any event, Super and TWA both consider values as critical variables in career choice and development.

Bordin's Theory

Finally, what about convergence with Bordin's (1990; Bordin, Nachmann, & Segal, 1963) psychodynamic theory? The major difference between our theories, to borrow again from Cattell, is that to Bordin, TWA's source traits are no more than surface entities; his source traits lie deeper. But there are points of convergence. For example, the motivation to achieve satisfaction can be linked to earlier experiences with play and the person's need to experience joy and self-satisfaction in his or her activity. The motivation to achieve satisfactoriness (to be a satisfactory worker) can in part reflect compulsion or the pressure to satisfy others, especially authority figures. Abilities are used by the ego to formulate plans for the satisfaction of needs. Reinforcer requirements reflect needs or wishes that, in turn, originate from drives. The person's perception of P-E correspondence will be influenced by defense mechanisms, which can be viewed as manifestations of the reactive adjustment mode. However, nothing in TWA corresponds to the psychosexual stages.

Larger Frameworks

Actually, the individual differences (ID) model can link all five theories. The ID model consists of three axes or facets: individuals, variables, and time points. Thus, different individuals are observed (measured, if you will) on different variables at different time points. Grouping individuals yields types; grouping variables yields traits (which could include drives); and grouping time points yields learning curves over the short run and developmental stages over the long run. Figure 1 depicts the ID model.

Another way of linking the five theories is by using two orthogonal axes: developmental time line as the horizontal axis and level of abstraction as the vertical axis. Holland, TWA, and Krumboltz would not differ horizontally, but they would differ on level of abstraction, with Holland being the most molar, Krumboltz the most molecular, and TWA being somewhere in between. Bordin would differ from Super horizontally in that Bordin's focus would be early development and Super's later development. Super would encompass all three levels of abstraction represented by Holland, TWA, and Krumboltz, but Bordin would differ from the rest by

Time points

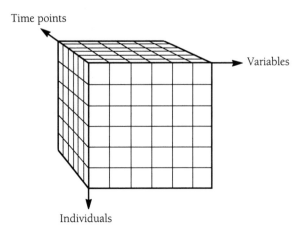

Variables

Individuals

FIGURE 1   The Individual Differences Model

having concepts found at a deeper level of abstraction. These relationships are depicted graphically in figure 2.

CAREER CHOICE

Although it has been used in the context of career counseling, TWA was not intended as a theory of career choice. It might be informative at this point to try briefly to sketch out such a theory from TWA concepts. To begin with, we might distinguish between two "outcome types" according to the outcome maximized: those who tend to maximize satisfactoriness (and therefore focus on satisfying the environment's requirements) and those who tend to maximize satisfaction (and therefore focus on satisfying their own requirements). Of course, most people will be mixed types, emphasizing one or the other outcome to varying degrees or even vacillating from one to the other. Satisfactoriness maximizers will tend to be more concerned about their skills and abilities, be more susceptible to the powerful influence of social forces, such as family, friends, class, and culture, and be more motivated to achieve goals set by others. Satisfaction maximizers will tend to be more concerned about their needs and values, be more self-directed, and be more driven to achieve self-set goals.

Next, we would assume that, as a function of both ability and opportunity (and therefore of history or experience), individuals will differ in the amount of information they have about person (self) and about environments (occupations and jobs). Information about person will influence people's perception of self, especially how capable they feel they are. Perception of self will combine with

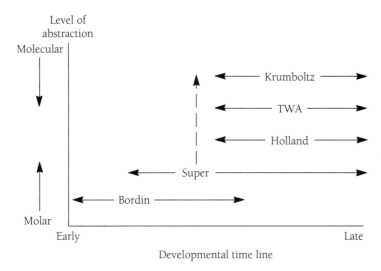

FIGURE 2   Relations Among Theories by Level of Abstraction and
Developmental Time Line

information/misinformation about work environments to yield perception of self-environment correspondences, which in turn becomes the basis for perception of career opportunity. Borrowing from Gottfredson (1981), TWA sees the process of circumscription as being dependent on perception of opportunity, and the compromise on choice as being governed by outcome type.

CULTURAL DIVERSITY

It might also be instructive at this point to address briefly the question of cultural diversity. On this question, TWA stands by its individual differences tradition (Dawis, 1992). This means (a) that TWA views people as individuals and not as members of groups; (b) that gender, ethnicity, national origin, religion, age, sexual orientation, and disability status are seen as inaccurate and unreliable bases for estimating the skills, abilities, needs, values, personality style, and adjustment style of a particular person; and (c) that present status is seen as a function of response and reinforcement history—in other words, of opportunity or of its absence. Thus, two people may have the same abilities but manifest different sets of skills because of differential opportunity. Two people may manifest the same level of skills, but this may mask different ability levels because of differential opportunity. In a similar manner, two people may have the same values but differing needs, or the same needs and need levels but different value levels—all because of differential opportunity, that is, differential exposure. According to TWA, the fullest development of a person can only occur when person-environment correspondence is maximal. This means that both work and training environments will have to be made flexible enough to accommodate culturally diverse, or experientially diverse, groups of workers. Ironically, it also means that people in identical or objectively equivalent environments cannot be validly compared and evaluated unless it can be shown that correspondence is maximal or at least comparable for all parties. Identical or objectively equivalent environments may not have the same degree of correspondence for different people, and the more correspondent person will have the (unfair? or lucky?) advantage.

CONCLUSION

Let me end as I began with a comment about unified theory. Although theory convergence and even some degree of theory integration is possible, unified theory is a will-o'-the-wisp. Even if it is achieved—a very long shot indeed—theory will not remain unified for long because of four "iron laws." The first is the *iron law of ability*, which states that the ability curve is asymptotic to the baseline. In other words, no matter how far you can see theoretically, someone else who sits on your shoulders will be able to see farther than you. The second is the *iron law of reinforcement value*, which states that reinforcement value is two-valued, positive and negative. In other words, one person's theoretical preference may be another's theoretical aversion. The third is the *iron law of satisfaction*, which states that satisfaction has a very short half-life. In other words, theory consumers are never satisfied for long. And the fourth is the *iron law of correspondence*, which states that discorrespondence is the natural, normal condition. In other words, unified theory, like correspondence, is a peak experience that is rare and fleeting. But, like correspondence, it can happen!

REFERENCES

Allport, G. (1961). *Pattern and growth in personality*. New York: Holt, Rinehart and Winston.

Anastasi, A. (1937). *Differential psychology*. New York: Macmillan.

Bordin, E. (1990). Psychodynamic model of career choice and satisfaction. In D. Brown & L. Brooks (Eds.), *Career choice and development: Applying contemporary theories to practice* (2d ed., pp. 102–144). San Francisco: Jossey-Bass.

Bordin, E., Nachmann, B., & Segal, S. (1963). An articulated framework for vocational development. *Journal of Counseling Psychology, 10*, 107–116.

Carroll, J. (1976). Psychometric tests as cognitive tasks: A new "structure of intellect." In L. Resnick (Ed.), *The nature of intelligence*. Hillsdale, NJ: Erlbaum.

Carroll, J. (1992). Cognitive abilities: The state of the art. *Psychological Science, 3*, 266–270.

Cattell, R. (1965). *The scientific analysis of personality*. Chicago: Aldine.

Dawis, R. (1992). The individual differences tradition in counseling psychology. *Journal of Counseling Psychology, 39,* 7–19.

Dawis, R., & Lofquist, L. (1984). *A psychological theory of work adjustment.* Minneapolis: University of Minnesota Press.

Ferguson, G. (1956). On transfer and the abilities of man. *Canadian Journal of Psychology, 10,* 121–131.

French, J., Ekstrom, R., & Price, L. (1963). *Kit of reference tests for cognitive factors* (Rev. ed.). Princeton, NJ: Educational Testing Service.

Gottfredson, L. (1981). Circumscription and compromise: A developmental theory of occupational aspirations. *Journal of Counseling Psychology, 28,* 545–579.

Heron, A. (1954). Satisfaction and satisfactoriness: Complementary aspects of occupational adjustment. *Occupational Psychology, 28,* 140–153.

Herzberg, F. (1966). *Work and the nature of man.* New York: World Book Publishing.

Hesketh, B. (1985). In search of a conceptual framework for vocational psychology. *Journal of Counseling and Development, 64,* 26–30.

Holland, J. (1985). *Making vocational choices: A theory of vocational personalities and work environments.* Englewood Cliffs, NJ: Prentice-Hall.

Hoppock, R. (1935). *Job satisfaction.* New York: Harper & Row.

Krumboltz, J. (1979). A social learning theory of career decision making. In A. Mitchell, G. Jones, & J. Krumboltz (Eds.), *Social learning and career decision making* (pp. 19–49). Cranston, RI: Carroll Press.

Lofquist, L., & Dawis, R. (1969). *Adjustment to work.* New York: Appleton-Century-Crofts.

Lofquist, L., & Dawis, R. (1991). *Essentials of person–environment–correspondence counseling.* Minneapolis: University of Minnesota Press.

Mitchell, L., & Krumboltz, J. (1990). Social learning approach to career decision making: Krumboltz's theory. In D. Brown & L. Brooks (Eds.), *Career choice and development: Applying contemporary theories to practice* (2d ed., pp. 145–196). San Francisco: Jossey-Bass.

Parsons, F. (1909). *Choosing a vocation.* Boston: Houghton Mifflin.

Powers, W. (1973). *Behavior: The control of perception.* Chicago: Aldine.

Scott, T., Dawis, R., England, G., & Lofquist, L. (1960). *A definition of work adjustment* (Minnesota Studies in Vocational Rehabilitation: X). Minneapolis: University of Minnesota, Industrial Relations Center.

Spearman, C. (1923). *The nature of "intelligence" and the principles of cognition.* London: Macmillan.

Sternberg, R. (1977). *Intelligence, information processing, and analogical reasoning: The componential analysis of human abilities.* Hillsdale, NJ: Erlbaum.

Super, D. (1990). A life-span, life-space approach to career development. In D. Brown & L. Brooks (Eds.), *Career choice and development: Applying contemporary theories to practice* (2d ed., pp. 197–261). San Francisco: Jossey-Bass.

Tolman, E. (1932). *Purposive behavior in animals and men.* New York: Century.

Tyler, L. (1947). *The psychology of human differences.* New York: Appleton-Century-Crofts.

Watson, D., & Tellegen, A. (1985). Toward a consensual structure of mood. *Psychological Bulletin, 98,* 219–235.

CHAPTER FOUR

Separate But Unequal Is Better

John L. Holland
Professor Emeritus, Johns Hopkins University

THEORETICAL RESTORATION OR renovation looks like a productive strategy with relatively few barriers, but integration looks like a strategy with many barriers. Therefore, I had some difficulty preparing this chapter. The conference goal to facilitate theory integration and stimulate theory unification research appeared ill-advised. I resolved my conflict by preparing a paper about the futility of convergence attempts and the virtues of renovating existing theories and strategies.

CONVERGENCE AND INTEGRATION

The background papers by Krumboltz and Nichols (1990), Osipow (1990), and Super (1992) and a recent review by Borgen (1991) imply a very weak convergence. It would take an active and persistent imagination to envision how this divergent collection of theories and strategies might be integrated. The most promising integration would be to insert the Krumboltz learning theory into every other vocational theory. Alternatively, almost any learning theory might be appropriated and inserted whenever learning is implied. Likewise, satellite theories like self-efficacy could also be patched in.

The background papers point to some similarities among theories that are simply background principles that have been assumed by all theories for more than 80 years. For example, person-environment congruence has been labeled "suitable choice," "correspondence," or "a good match" when some assessment appears to imply a P-E fit. At the same time, some theories define these terms only vaguely, and definitions have not always been empirically tested.

Similarly, concepts such as vocational adjustment, vocational maturity, career adaptability, and identity suggest a common core of desirable cultural attitudes, interpersonal competencies, and extroversion, but these concepts are far from identical in their measurement and in the way they are imbedded into different theories.

These and other resemblances—for instance, does Super's self-concept equal Holland's personality types?—have stimulated some authors to believe that it is time to put it all together as a disciplinary vocational platform. As I say in my letters to the IRS—I disagree! There are at least 10 good reasons why integration is a poor strategy at this time.

First, different theories have different goals. Mine is aimed primarily at practitioners and their clients, so I have tried to develop a statement that is relatively simple to comprehend and apply.

My biases about a desirable theory grew out of my experience using the old *Strong* and the *Dictionary of Occupational Titles* (DOT). Those magnificent publications seemed to cry out for simplification. I soon realized that if I wanted people to use my work, I had to comply as much as possible with the ambiguous and shifting criteria for a good theory. Here I was influenced by two fortuitous events—taking a philosophy of science course as a student and, at a much later time, being tutored by a philosopher who told me about the shortcomings of my theorizing and how they might be alleviated. Consequently, I have tried to make revisions from time to time that would be both scientifically sound and would not confuse clients, practitioners, or researchers.

Theories have different audiences and goals. Some are oriented to practitioners; others are oriented to psychologists, sociologists, or other groups. It's hard to do both, for practitioners want help and psychologists want perfection or scientific respectability. Vocational theories are also oriented to different human problems—field or kind of work, occupational level, satisfaction, involvement, vocational adjustment, and so on. To summarize, integration requires agreement about goals, but different goals are weighted differently by different people.

Second, we have divergent beliefs about development, learning theory, and vocational problems.

Third, we have divergent beliefs about philosophy of science research strategies and criteria for a satisfactory theory.

Fourth, we have divergent beliefs about vocational assistance for different groups of people in our society. These beliefs are accompanied by political agendas that occasionally make civil discussion and research planning difficult.

Fifth, we have divergent beliefs about human resources, especially research resources. The cost of writing a theory that is a literary venture is minimal, but the long-term cost of researching theoretical ideas for clarification, revision, or replication is great. We do not have the human and financial resources to examine every career outcome in the growing shopping list of desirable or peripheral outcomes.

Some outcomes are more important than others. The identification of satisfaction and satisfactoriness by Dawis and Lofquist (1984) as primary outcomes provides a helpful beginning. Some industrious researcher should organize all the things a good theory should do and perhaps sort outcomes according to degree of importance for different populations and different interest groups, such as client versus employer and other special groups.

Sixth, any attempt at a theoretical synthesis would benefit from clear support from background fields such as psychology, cognitive psychology, and sociology, but those fields also have their own differences, so you can easily find support for contradictory ideas.

I will not explicate reasons seven through 10. They include such ideas as you cannot assemble theoretical constructs like Tinkertoy materials or that theory construction is not a literary project. The reader can easily think of other barriers.

RESTORATION AND RENOVATION

In contrast to the problems of theoretical integration, the restoration or renovation of current theories is a much more promising enterprise for many reasons.

First, the consensus of a group of authors with different orientations is unneeded. Second, the scientific and practical deficiencies of all theories are so gross that they can easily be improved by following a few simple strategies. Third, more useful theoretical statements would sharpen differences and similarities as well as make individual theories more researchable and testable. My opinions about some potential revisions of present theories are presented below.

Bordin's Theory

The early attempts to test analytic ideas by studying the life histories of accountants, social workers, lawyers, writers, and engineers are persuasive and contribute some useful ideas about the origins of vocational interests and the interpretation of person-occupation interactions. They also imply some therapeutic strategies. At the same time, the labor-intensive requirements of that early work soon made it apparent that the resources needed to assess large occupational samples using extensive case histories would not be forthcoming.

Because the analytic orientation brings some insights about vocational decision making and personality that are special, if not unique, it appears desirable to continue this early research effort by exploring the use of recent tests such as the *Defense Mechanism Inventory* (DMI; Ihilevich & Gleser, 1986) to hasten the assessment of representative occupations.

More recently, Silver and Spilerman (1990) have developed an inventory to link character structure (based on Axis II of the DSM-III-R) to occupational plans using six short scales to assess personality styles. This work is in progress, but preliminary studies indicate that choice of major field is predictable from character structure variables. In a related article, Lowman (1987) has suggested how to link

occupational knowledge to therapeutic strategies and analytic concepts. His specu-
lation merits research. Finally, Cramer (1991) has reviewed 58 different empirical
measures that have been developed to assess defenses. Her book is another
promising starting point.

These recent developments imply that Bordin's ideas could have a productive
renewal. For instance, if Silver's work were combined with almost any occupational
classification scheme, then the task of tying analytic ideas and signs of pathology to
occupations should become an achievable goal.

Lofquist and Dawis' Theory

The work adjustment theory exemplifies many features of a useful theory. It has an
explicit statement with clear hypotheses and empirical definitions for the main
constructs. It has been revised several times in response to data, and the inventories
designed to measure the key constructs have desirable properties. In contrast, the
research and practice that would be helpful to evaluate the theory have lagged far
behind the amount of skilled developmental work. The theory also has an
occupational classification that parallels its personal assessment variables.

The structure of the Minnesota theory—using different variables and starting
with vocational adjustment rather than vocational choices—parallels my theory in
its major outline. For instance, the personal assessment constructs have parallel
environment constructs, and "correspondence" equals "congruence."

Although this theory has a forbidding complexity, its main ideas are easily
grasped. I see no need for revision. So far, this theory has an impressive research
record. Instead, I would find a new publisher to stimulate more widespread research
and use of the assessment materials in counseling and applied work. Professionals
take the easy way out: They use materials that they know; they do not actively search
out new inventories or pursue a passive publisher, such as a university press. In
short, the authors and their sponsors should consider more active public relations
activities.

Krumboltz's Theory

As Krumboltz and Nichols (1990) have summarized, "The purpose of the social
learning theory of career decision making is to explain how a person's learning
experience influences his or her career decisions and to suggest possible interventions" (p. 162). The Krumboltz theory accomplishes these goals by outlining the
learning processes that lead to different vocational preferences. Because all career
theories explicitly or implicitly invoke learning, his theory supplements all other
theories by providing more explicit accounts of how types, self-concepts, or work
personalities might come about over the life span.

This theory does not organize or structure existing evidence about kinds of
preferences, occupations, or personalities or what particular learning experiences

are associated with particular occupations. Instead, it provides an organization or structure for comprehending and examining the learning processes that lead to a variety of career decisions or outcomes. It could also be used as an outline to study the impact of different environments or the kinds of learning they would be expected to stimulate. In one sense, the social learning theory is a more diffuse and flexible theory than the other theories because it is not tied to existing career knowledge, or its scope is much wider or greater than the other theories. Parenthetically, self-efficacy theory looks like a small piece of the Krumboltz social learning theory.

The future of social learning theory has many possibilities. They include finding a hospitable host theory, remaining as an independent entity to stimulate relevant research, or devising more effective career interventions. I see the last two goals as its most productive applications. The *Career Beliefs Inventory* (CBI; Krumboltz, 1991) illustrates one important practical outcome of this kind of theorizing. It begins to organize kinds of destructive learning outcomes.

Like the Minnesota theory, the Krumboltz theory needs use more than revision. In conjunction with other theories, it can be used to specify unspecified learning experience. Aside from its diagnostic value, the CBI could be used to identify life histories that lead to particular destructive beliefs. A new inventory following the Krumboltz theory could also be constructed to provide standard life histories; such histories would make it possible to relate many career outcomes to special life histories.

As it now stands, this theory does not structure current knowledge, but serves instead as a powerful heuristic for exploring—after the fact—how a person's particular preference or vocational behavior may have developed or originated.

Super's Theory

I see Super's theory as a set of useful strategies for understanding career development. These have stimulated much research over many decades, but because the segments—self-concept, life stages, life rainbow, and career temple—often lack explicit definitions and statements, it is hard to link research outcomes to explicit hypotheses. The theory is rarely tested, but the strategy is. In recent years, Super has developed several inventories to assess some of his concepts. These also need revision. Some data in the relevant manuals contradict the theory.

My ideas for renovation consist of three strategies. One would be to produce a single volume—a festschrift, consisting of the theoretical segments—so that researchers would have a convenient volume for reference. A second strategy would be to review the segments for missing empirical definitions of key concepts and fill in definitions or suggest several for the same concept. Finally, the segments might benefit from some attempts to show how the different segments might be articulated and organized. Super has occasionally begun this task, but this suggestion is like asking someone to develop a useful theory—easier said than done.

Holland's Typology

I have been renovating the internal structure of my own theory (Holland, 1992) to give it more explanatory power. This goal needs clarification.

In general, the strengths of typologies lie in their ability to organize information. In contrast, the weaknesses of typologies lie in their neglect of the processes entailed in change and development. At the same time, typologies often provide powerful explanations of stability in personality and vocational behavior.

After five years of sporadic effort, the internal structure of the types, environments, and their interactions has been elaborated to include life goals and values, self-beliefs, and problem-solving style as well as vocational and avocational preferences. The developmental nature and learning experiences of the types over the life span have also been elaborated. Unfortunately, it has been necessary to perform some research and review activity to find support for the revisions. Last but not least, I, along with others, have reconsidered the goals of this typology and in so doing discovered that I should do a better job of linking the typology to vocational interventions.

SO NOW WHAT?

In short, it appears more productive to renovate old theories or strategies than to stitch together an integrated theory. I have outlined some low- and high-level activities and strategies for theoretical restoration. These include reviewing theories for their obvious scientific deficiencies and making a concerted effort to fix them and devising research strategies for testing key ideas or neglected hypotheses. My review of the current theories is that they are only partially explored in any empirical way. Much more clarifying research is required before we can rely on their integration. An intermediate and traditional scientific strategy is to see if a particular theory can be used or revised, without destroying its integrity, to explain a broader range of career processes, behaviors, and outcomes. I prefer this strategy.

I am indebted to Travis Hirschi, whose paper with the same title as this chapter dealt with a flawed proposal to integrate theories of delinquency. I am also grateful to Gary D. Gottfredson for his counsel.

REFERENCES

Borgen, F. (1991). Megatrends and milestones in vocational behavior: A 20-year counseling psychology retrospective. *Journal of Vocational Behavior, 39,* 263–290.

Cramer, P. (1991). *The development of defense mechanisms: Theory research, and assessment.* New York: Springer.

Dawis, R., & Lofquist, L. (1984). *A psychological theory of work adjustment.* Minneapolis: University of Minnesota Press.

Holland, J. (1992). *Making vocational choices* (2d ed.). Odessa, FL: Psychological Assessment Resources.

Ihilevich, D., & Gleser, G. (1986). *Defense mechanisms: Their classification, correlates, and measurement with the Defense Mechanisms Inventory.* Owosso, MI: DMI Associates.

Krumboltz, J. (1991). *Career Beliefs Inventory.* Palo Alto, CA: Consulting Psychologists Press.

Krumboltz, J., & Nichols, C. (1990). Integrating the social learning theory of career decision making. In W. Walsh & S. Osipow (Eds.), *Career counseling: Contemporary topics in vocational psychology* (pp. 159–192). Hillsdale, NJ: Erlbaum.

Lowman, R. (1987). Occupational choice as a moderator of psychotherapeutic approach. *Psychotherapy, 24,* 801–808.

Osipow, S. (1990). Convergence in theories of career choice and development. *Journal of Vocational Behavior, 36,* 122–131.

Silver, C., & Spilerman, S. (1990). Psychoanalytic perspectives on occupational choice and attainment. *Research in Social Stratification and Mobility, 9,* 181–214.

Super, D. (1992). Toward a comprehensive theory of career development. In D. Montross & C. Shinkman (Eds.), *Career development theory and practice* (pp. 35–64). Springfield, IL: Charles C. Thomas.

CHAPTER FIVE

Intrinsic Motivation and the Active Self

Convergence From a Psychodynamic Perspective

Edward S. Bordin
Professor Emeritus, University of Michigan

THIS CONTRIBUTION WILL be directed toward one emerging consensus of the convergence project, namely, that the individual must be viewed as more than a passive participant with the pushes and pulls exerted by the environment. If individuals are to become independently identifiable factors in the interaction with their situational contexts, they need to construct self-images of what it is that they possess that influences their responses. This self-image requires a view of human motives that distinguishes those that are inherent in the pressures on the individual and those that arise out of these hypothesized inner structures. The most likely candidates for inclusion in such a personal construct include self, identity, and personal style or lifestyle.

In the first half of this chapter, I will treat these inner originating motives from the framework of work and play. In the second half of the chapter, I will address work and personality from the perspective of intrinsic satisfactions, a view of identity that features an individual's unique contribution. The chapter ends with my idea for an agenda for future work on the convergence project.

WORK AND PLAY

Most theories of career choice and development and a preponderance of research on them have concentrated on the goal of the individual fulfilling a productive social role. Super (1990) has made a great integrating contribution toward pulling together the varieties of both external and internal factors. But he is still tied to the metaphor of the gate or archway in entering the world of work. I propose a somewhat broader perspective. I believe that our preoccupation with the material necessities has narrowed our view of the imperatives of being human. We may pay lip service to the idea that a person does not live by bread alone, but, for example, much of our concerns about the process of career choice centers on the necessity of being realistic and of avoiding being overtaken by dreams or wishes. Our emphasis on tests, assessment, and occupational information seems to reflect a conviction that dreams and aspirations are intrinsically unrealistic and therefore need to be corrected.

We direct much attention to factors that influence the individual's capacity to earn a livelihood, such as climate and geography, societal and productive organizations, and the aptitudes and accumulated learning the person possesses. When we examine his or her history, we look at how family, educational, and social experience have fashioned the person for particular productive roles.

I do not deny that work or earning a living is one of the imperatives that humans face, but I think we must not overlook another vital imperative, that is, the need for a playful attitude. Human nature is such that when the work imperative leaves no room for playfulness and self-expression, people become wage slaves engaged in alienated toil. Charlie Chaplin's classic movie *Modern Times* captures the way the alienation created by the assembly line can be converted to a playfulness that sabotages the productive process.

It is not enough to include an interest inventory in our test battery. We must give deeper attention to the psychological meaning of work and play. There has been a tendency to fall into a Maslovian relegation of play and self-expression as a luxury to be afforded after more basic needs are met. Let me remind you that the Dutch historian Huizinga (1955) reads history as being pervaded by play and the playful spirit. He documented how societies in all times have created institutional practices in connection with law, economics, and religion that had elements of contests as vehicles of self-expression and even aesthetic experience. In these contests, especially the military ones, he found evidence that self-expression was more important than staying alive.

If we pay attention to observing the current scene, we see plenty of evidence that meeting the demands of selfhood can be more powerful than the need to stay alive. People choose the highly dangerous life in search of selfhood.

I conclude that a fuller understanding of human action is obtained when we assume two powerful imperatives, those of work and play. Once we take this route, we notice all kinds of seeming anomalies. Is a professional athlete working or playing? One person takes time off from work to play golf. Another person works during a period designated as vacation time. The simple idea that work is what you do for a living is no longer as simple as it once was.

The popular usage of the terms work and play can be supplemented by further explicating the different aspects encompassed by them. I refer to the elements of spontaneity, effort, and compulsion. Spontaneity and compulsion, especially when the latter is felt as coming from outside oneself—capture a major part of the juxtaposed spirit conveyed by work versus play. There is an inner versus outer quality in that pairing. When we speak of a person acting spontaneously, we refer to the person being moved from within to act. When a person is being moved by some control of rewards and punishments outside of self, we speak of the person being forced or compelled to act. Under the latter circumstance, the assembly line worker refers to self as a wage slave, and the child driven to practice a musical instrument by an ambitious parent complains of drudgery.

Spontaneity denotes the free expression of self, the wish to soar. Compulsion connotes being a prisoner of someone else, or even an impersonal system forcing one by threat to give up one's self. Effort, the physical, intellectual, and emotional energy demanded by a specific action, makes for a volatile mix. As play takes on subtlety and complexity, achieving the satisfaction it offers can require a great deal of energy. Such expenditures create increasing pressures against continuing (the need to rest), and what has begun in the spirit of spontaneity takes on the flavor of compulsion. The musician who reaches for the joys of playing Bach or Mozart may begin to feel the slave of a compulsion in trying to master the skills required.

Another way of referring to this inner-outer quality in work and play is to distinguish between intrinsic and extrinsic rewards, satisfactions, and motives. On the one hand, if we engage in some kind of activity because performing at some standard will win us a prize—say, a monetary reward or even social respect—that constitutes performance under extrinsic motivation. On the other hand, if engaging in the activity is satisfying in itself, irrespective of prizes, money, or the like, we have an example of intrinsic motivation. That is, if I jog regularly because I enjoy the rhythm of movement and being outdoors, then I am intrinsically motivated to jog. But if I jog because I have decided it is good for my health, then I'm extrinsically motivated.

By now you are likely to have concluded, as I have, that it is natural for individuals to seek a maximum fusion of work and play, the fusion of inner and outer pressures, and the maximum coincidence of inner and outer motives. Achieving such an ideal permits us to convert the feeling of being a slave to circumstance into a sense of freedom of self-expression. We have all heard our clients express the almost stereotypic statement, "I want to find an occupation that I can make a good living at and that I would be happy doing."

Not all people who say that find it an easy goal to set for themselves, much less achieve. Earlier I saw only the natural obstacles toward fusing work and play and thought that the wish for fusion was a reflection of an immature unwillingness to accept reality. But this judgment applies only to difficulties inherent in the opportunities available. Those difficulties arising within the person, seeming to stand in the way of even wishing for fusion of the intrinsic and extrinsic, are quite a different set of obstacles. During the 1960s, a time marked by generational alienation between parents and children, I could not help observing frequent instances in which work and play were seen as unconnected, even incompatible, and when the normal path toward productive work was referred to as "joining the rat race." Frequently, the standard response to incorporating a recreational activity into a vocation was, "Oh, no! That would take the fun out of it." Later, while discussing family systems and dynamics, I will speculate on how the way chores are treated may contribute to obstacles in fusing work and play.

Recapitulating, individual differences in response to reconciling the imperative in work and play requires that we look to history, the context of individual experience, and vicissitudes in the expression of spontaneity, effort, and compulsion. We must be sensitive, whether in research or in counseling, to the inhibitions and freedoms the person feels in self-expression, how much this person feels able to expend great effort, and how much he or she feels vulnerable or dependent on outside pressures, whether they be personal or impersonal.

This perspective can be particularly useful in understanding and supporting women and racial/ethnic minorities in their struggles with career decisions. These are individuals who have experienced the pressures of institutional racism and societal stereotypes. These external pressures complicate the fusing process. This also brings us to the concept of identity formation, which I will be discussing further under the topic of personality and work.

Before summarizing this topic, I would like to call your attention to another arena for examining the relationship between work and play. I have already touched lightly on how a child can respond to chores. Under the most favorable conditions, the progression from infancy into the various stages of childhood are marked by movement from almost total dependence on both the care and demands of others to the flowering of a full sense of self and the testing of self-expression. In my view, educators, as well as society as a whole, keep moving between the extremes of treasuring and working from the child's intrinsic interests to the opposite extreme, which features a concentration on mastery of instrumental skills and knowledge. If there is any doubt of my position, it is one that seeks to bring together the benefits of the intrinsic and extrinsic without falling victim to either.

To sum up this section, I have sought to add the perspective of work and play to Super's metaphor of the gate for entering the world of work, which already attends to the social, economic, family, and psychological-personological factors involved in choosing paths and living within this world. I hope that my explication of the underlying elements that this dichotomy encompasses has provided enough illustration to point to the kinds of experiences in family and school that can be expected to shape how a person deals with the imperatives of work and play.

PERSONALITY AND WORK

I remind you that I have proposed that the degree to which a person succeeds in fusing work and play is an important determinant of the degree to which career choice is determined and expressed by personality (Bordin, 1990). This proposition takes me beyond Holland's "birds who flock together" explanation of personality differences that distinguish members of specific occupational groups. What follows from my assertion is a requirement of a new kind of occupational analysis. Instead of classifications based on the aptitudes and education and training required to perform the tasks and carry out the responsibilities included, we need to examine job performance as a way of life. For instance, what intrinsic satisfactions are inherent in the life associated with being a secondary school English teacher, an engineer, a carpenter, or a lawyer?

To engage in this new kind of occupational analysis, which is geared to personality, lifestyles, and intrinsic motives, we need a taxonomy of motives with supporting definitions and examples. I will give a brief explication of what such a taxonomy requires, then turn to a brief discussion of identity formation as another facet of personality in work.

Mapping Occupations in Terms of Intrinsic Motives

My first approximation of a list of intrinsic motives that can act as a scaffold for mapping occupations will contain many echoes of Darley and Hagenah's (1955) and Holland's (1985) interest patterns, both of which are founded in exhaustive analyses of interest inventory data. I emphasize that no single one of these motives is expected to correspond to a given occupation or grouping. I view occupations as containing opportunities for various mixes of the indicated satisfactions. To the extent that an occupation is more malleable, meaningful versions of it are available to fit diverse mixes of intrinsic motives. In this sense, the person can shape the occupation to fit his or her personal requirements rather than select the occupation as a good fit. It might be good social policy to modify jobs so as to introduce more opportunities for intrinsic satisfaction to minimize the creation of an underclass of workers whose sole stake in their work is the external rewards it offers.

The challenge of this approach to mapping occupations is to identify a set of intrinsic motives that can be found somewhere in the range of productive work. My first approximation of such a list is as follows:

- *Precision.* This is a satisfaction in neat, clear, error-free thought and action. Aspects of it are caught in record keeping, and in identifying and following fully stated rules of thought, such as in mathematics or law. It is contained in the action of the carpenter or the tool and dye maker.

- *Nurturance.* This motive refers to the investment made in caring for and fostering the growth of living things. Thus, it is part of being a teacher, a social worker, or a psychotherapist, yet also is included in being a farmer, a florist, or an animal herder.

- *Curiosity.* The complexity of this wish to know and understand what is behind what we observe is shown by the many forms it can take. It can take an impersonal form in our interest in the physical world, such as in physics or geography. Then there is the personal form expressed as curiosity about events, actions, thoughts, and feelings that represent the secret life of other people to which the obligations of counselors, lawyers, and the clergy provide a privileged access.

- *Power.* This is another complex motive. It refers to building up one's physical power, such as in heavy labor, the augmenting of human power through the use of machines, the actual designing and building of such machines, and the harnessing of the powers of the universe. It can also be expressed through psychological, social, and legal skills that exert personal power over other people.

- *Aesthetic expression.* This motivation refers to the sensory and rhythmic satisfactions found in the whole range of the arts—from the visual through the performing arts—including composition, writing, and choreography.

- *Ethics and concern with right and wrong.* The inescapable social aspect of being human and dealing with the sense of self as distinguished from others carries with it an intrinsic investment in right and wrong, the definition, justification, and enforcement of both the spirit and the letters of laws. We have jobs such as police officer, lawyer, and clergy that are concerned with various facets of this ethic motive.

Theoretical and Research Impetus

This approach to mapping intrinsic motives opens the door to deeper and broader theoretical and research questions than the mere question of their distribution and their statistical relations. In my mind, questions about the developmental course and nature of each of these motives brings our career development concerns into the mainstream of psychology, correcting the reductionistic stereotype foisted on the field from outside and lamented by Krumboltz.

I will illustrate my point by commenting on the theoretical and research questions embedded in each of my six proposed intrinsic motives that can map the world of work.

Precision. With regard to the intrinsic satisfactions associated with precision in thought, action, and expression, I am not aware that we have gone beyond the point of seeking social conformity, which is too focused on a pathology-centered approach to intrinsic motives. I suspect that the important leads to deeper understanding of intrinsically motivated precision can be found increasingly in the theory and research on cognitive development and cognitive psychology. There may be a connection with the aesthetics of good form.

Nurturance. When I think about the satisfactions associated with nurturing, I realize that I and probably many others have taken an oversimplified view. Our shared social heritage contains prescribed nurturant responses. Parenting, usually gender differentiated, contains specific expectations mediated through play and other preparatory and shaping experiences. In this sense, every individual is being prepared to gain satisfaction through nurturing another person. But we must not ignore the uniqueness of individual experience with nurturance and the fact that the person who chooses an occupational role that features nurturance is transcending the more generally shared expression of this kind of motive. Over the years I have noticed that the inventoried need patterns of people in this field have not only included elevation of the need to nurture but also of the needs for succorance and autonomy. Another line of thought we ought to be pursuing is the interest of social and developmental psychologists in altruism (e.g., Krebs, 1970; Macaulay & Berkowitz, 1970; Mussen & Eisenberg-Berg, 1977).

Curiosity. It is my impression that the general interest in curiosity, sparked by Berlyne (1960), was not long lived. Perhaps it was because too much attention was given to comparative animal models and not enough was given to humans, both children and adults. Thus, concern was reduced to the qualities of attention grabbing and novelty. Some of this is grantedly a first step to understanding the general nature of human curiosity. Our needs for understanding, however, require us to examine the ecology of human development that can channel curiosity into the variety of directions that it can take in human work. Galinsky's (1962) comparison of physicists and clinical psychologists, whose work involved very different forms of curiosity, found differences in family atmospheres and intellectual interests that corresponded to the differences in curiosity expressed in the occupation. If there does not already exist a body of child development research centered on family influences on curiosity, there surely ought to be such enterprises.

Power. The attractiveness of seeking the intrinsic satisfactions in augmenting one's physical power is called to our attention by the uproar over the use of steroids. The extrinsic and intrinsic satisfactions are combined when the professional athlete resorts to these chemicals, but when it is taken up by hoards of adolescents of both sexes, it is more clearly an example of the search for intrinsic satisfactions. McClelland (1975) has broken ground in the examination of this motive, but many facets bear further examination. If physical power is only one facet of interpersonal power, and if these two are seen as functionally related, it opens the door to examining the power of words and intellect, and of physical attractiveness. Beyond the givens of one's physical attributes, there is the need to account for choices of satisfactions in the use of words, tractors and cranes, or bombs as the means for expressing power. What are the kinds of shaping experiences, starting in the family and extending out to the world, that influence the direction of choice?

Aesthetic Expression. The aesthetic satisfactions in life have such strong qualities of clearly expressed spontaneous sensuality that one is always fearful of losing their essential quality in the process of analytical examination. In successful art, there are subtle conceptions and a skillful use of a well-known mastery that is the result of much effort and practice. But in thinking about this kind of satisfaction, I am by no means confining myself to the formally designated artist-performers. I am thinking of the opportunities for aesthetic expression or performance that may accompany the work of the teacher, the lawyer, the executive, or the carpenter. Are these satisfactions tied to inborn talents? How much are they influenced by models within or outside of the family? How much are they nourished by the willingness of key family members to offer encouragement?

Ethics and Concern With Right and Wrong. Both Nachmann (1960) and Gilligan (1979) have offered two conceptions of right and wrong—one based on a rational analysis of the letter of the law (i.e., rules), and the other centered more on the spirit of law (i.e., relationships). Nachmann thought that the differences between the rule and relationship orientations differentiated male lawyers from social workers and offered evidence to fit that belief. Gilligan saw these two orientations as differentiating the way that men and women think about morality. During Penner's (1990) replication of Nachmann, he was able to add a comparative sample of female lawyers, dentists, and social workers. Although methodological complexities undermined the firmness of his findings, it was interesting that he reported evidence that the rule versus relationship orientations also differentiated female lawyers from social workers. Even accepting Penner's results does not negate Gilligan's contention that men are socialized toward the rule orientation whereas women are socialized toward the relationship orientation, but it does suggest that the gender factor is not monolithic (although I am not certain that she intended to make that assertion).

A PERSPECTIVE FOR
THE CONVERGENCE PROJECT

As I reconsidered the viewpoints expressed regarding the possibility of convergence of career theory and my own contribution to it, I was drawn to the old story of the three blind beggars and the elephant. As you may recall, limited to the sense of touch and the particular part of the beast that they grasped, each blind person was left with a concept of the whole beast based only on the part of the animal that was grasped: the tail, the trunk, or the leg.

No! I am not about to describe career theorists as a group of people with limited vision whose efforts have resulted in ludicrous oversimplifications. On the contrary, we have profited from Super's (1990) prodigious synthesis of our diverse preoccupations with various more limited aspects of career choice and development. Thus, Super has allowed us to see our connections in the context of a larger perspective. Moreover, this larger view establishing the overall concept of the beast allows each theory, through more intensive attention, to contribute an enrichment of the common understanding.

My contribution to the convergence project is to suggest the use of an even broader perspective than Super's synthesis, namely, the view offered by looking from the vantage point of the family as a system. The enlarged perspective offered by the family system can encompass all theories. The family system can provide a source for understanding the transmission of social influences that are reflected in both Krumboltz's social learning theory and Super's operational social development theory. At the same time, we can use the view from the family system to understand the development of personality types and traits described by Holland and by Dawis as well as use it to blend in my views on intrinsic motives and the role of work and play in one's life. The family system perspective offers a wide vista from which to conceptualize constructs and foster research that contributes to convergence of career theories.

REFERENCES

Berlyne, D. (1960). *Conflict, arousal, and curiosity*. New York: McGraw-Hill.

Bordin, E. (1990). Psychodynamic model of career choice and satisfaction. In D. Brown & L. Brooks (Eds.), *Career choice and development* (2d ed., pp. 102–144). San Francisco: Jossey-Bass.

Darley, J., & Hagenah, T. (1955). *Vocational interest measurement*. Minneapolis: University of Minnesota Press.

Galinsky, M. (1962). Personality development and vocational choice of clinical psychologists and physicists. *Journal of Counseling Psychology, 9*, 299–305.

Gilligan, C. (1979). In a different voice: Women's conceptions of self and morality. *Harvard Education Review, 49*, 431–435.

Holland, J. (1985). *Making vocational choices: A theory of vocational personalities and work environments* (2d ed.). Englewood Cliffs, NJ: Prentice-Hall.

Huizinga, J. (1955). *Homo ludens: A study of the play-element in culture*. Boston: Beacon Press.

Krebs, D. (1970). Altruism—An examination of the concept and a review of the literature. *Psychological Bulletin, 73*, 258–302.

Macaulay, J., & Berkowitz, L. (Eds.). (1970). *Altruism and helping behavior*. New York: Academic Press.

McClelland, D. C. (1975). *Power: The inner experience*. New York: Wiley.

Mussen, P., & Eisenberg-Berg, N. (1977). *Roots of caring, sharing, and helping: The development of prosocial behavior in children*. San Francisco: Freeman.

Nachmann, B. (1960). Childhood experiences and vocational choice in law, dentistry, and social work. *Journal of Counseling Psychology, 7*, 243–250.

Penner, E. (1990). *Childhood determinants of adult vocational choices: A study of lawyers, dentists, and social workers* (Doctoral dissertation, University of Michigan). *Dissertation Abstracts International, 51*, 2323A.

Super, D. (1990). A life-span, life-space approach to career development. In D. Brown & L. Brooks (Eds.), *Career choice and development* (2d ed., pp. 197–261). San Francisco: Jossey-Bass.

CHAPTER SIX

A Life Span, Life Space Perspective on Convergence

Donald E. Super
Professor Emeritus, Columbia University

I₅ YOU HAVE taken or taught a course in career development using Brown and Brooks' (1990) current text, the substance of what I write here will be already familiar to you. I do, however, trust that you will gain some new and highly relevant ideas, for I shall approach my topic with convergence in mind. But please do not expect me to draw any conclusions or to start with any preconceived notions of who is converging on whom; instead, in the tradition of dust-bowl empiricism, I shall do something that too few people, in my experience as an aviation psychologist in World War II and in business and industry since then, know how to do: I shall count! If you want to personalize convergence and draw conclusions about who is converging on whom, perhaps my counting will be of some help.

AT FIRST COUNT

Knowing *what* to count does, of course, help. So let me take a few moments to describe my method. I went through my chapter in Brown and Brooks (1990), concentrating first on the 14 propositions (pp. 206–208), then on the further treatment (pp. 219–226) that occurs in the same text. I encoded the material in the propositions separately and analyzed the discursive treatment of career development. I used four categories to do my encoding: trait-and-factor theory and person-environment theory (merging these on the grounds that the latter is actually an updating of the former), psychodynamic theory, into which I think one can place Anne Roe's choice theory (although some may disagree), social learning theory, and life span development theory. The question here is to what extent has convergence already taken place in my own work and about when did it happen? The extent to which it is evident in other theories is, of course, best left to their exponents.

In the 14 propositions in my Brown and Brooks (1990) chapter, there are 11 trait-and-factor or congruence statements, 22 of which represent life span-developmental, four of which represent social-experiential learning, and two of which represent psychodynamic. The score is thus 11 to 22 and 4 to 2 in this complex game. I think that I can therefore ask not to be so easily labeled as I have usually been. In the book edited by John Whiteley and Arthur Resnikoff (1972) that was based on a series of symposia at Washington University, Florida State University, and elsewhere in the late 1960s, I ended my basic presentation with the following statement:

> If, then, my approach must be labelled, let it be a *differential-developmental-social-phenomenological psychology*. For it is only as we make use of all of these fields, and also of aspects of sociological, and economic theory, that we will eventually construct a theory of vocational development that deals adequately with the complex processes by which people progress through the sequence of positions constituting a career. (p. 38)

THE LIFE SPAN, LIFE SPACE PERSPECTIVE ON CONVERGENCE

In approaching the topic of convergence from the vantage point offered by a life span, life space perspective, I use a set of five figures that illustrate and integrate important aspects of career development. These five figures serve as heuristic devices that facilitate thinking about convergence among career development constructs and theories. In turn, I will explain the Life Career Rainbow, the Archway of Career Determinants, the Ladder Model of Life Career Stages, the Cycling and Recycling Model for Career Tasks, and the Web Model for Bases of Career Maturity.

Life Career Rainbow

The Life Career Rainbow, reproduced in black-and-white here as figure 1, tells a complex story. This figure is labeled "Life Career" to emphasize the fact that it deals with both the life span and the life space, that is, with the course of life and with the major life roles. It also shows the timing of the entry into and exit from each of these roles by one person, a person not atypical of Americans who go to four-year colleges, to graduate school and internships, and (either then or after starting a family) to work. Like most schematic drawings, it oversimplifies, making the transitions sometimes seem more abrupt than they usually are, but illustrates with its shading greater or lesser involvement in each role.

Notice that for some time after entering the work force and after marriage, this person devoted less time to work than at certain other periods; during this period,

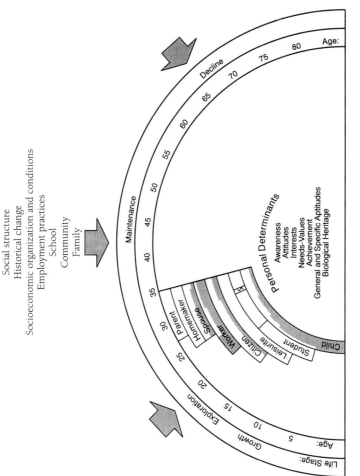

FIGURE 1   The Life Career Rainbow

From "A Life-Span, Life-Space Approach to Career Development" by Donald E. Super, 1990, *Career Choice and Development: Applying Contemporary Theories to Practice*, p. 200. Copyright 1990 by Jossey-Bass. Reprinted by permission.

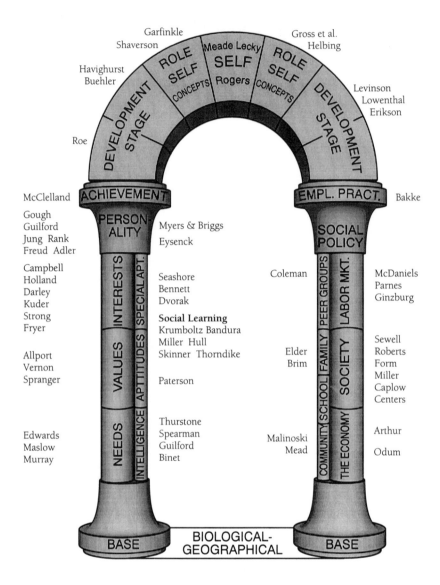

FIGURE 2   The Archway of Career Determinants

dating and homemaking made inroads into evening and weekend work. In one colorized version of the illustration, in which the roles of spouse, parent, and homemaker were separated, the arc for spouse was colored purple—a deep purple during the couple's courtship and early marriage, a paler purple while they experienced marriage difficulties, and a deeper purple again after they had undergone a genuine reconciliation. Similarly, the arc for the worker was colored blue—dark blue at times when the individual's occupation was emotionally involving, paler blue when it was less so.

Archway of Career Determinants

One deficiency of the rainbow is that, in seeking to deal adequately with the life span and life space, it merely *suggests* the situational and personal determinants of careers. The Archway of Career Determinants seeks to remedy this limitation (see figure 2). It reflects the segmental nature of my theory, for here each stone in the composite columns depicts a determinant, with those that are more basic nearer the base of the structure. Those that are the outcomes of these determinants form the arch that rests on the pillars and capitals portraying the amalgam of the individual's determining qualities and of the society's characteristics that have an impact on them. In a complete figure, these forces or vectors would be shown by arrows—a few single-headed but primarily double-headed ones. To give just one example, peer groups in the right-hand column have real effects on the needs, values, and interests in the left-hand column, and vice versa, and thus have real effects on the achievement and career maturity in the capital of that column. The omission of the vectors makes it possible to include the names of many of the theorists and researchers who have illuminated each determinant of occupational choice and career development. For example, E. K. Strong (1943) is a contributor to the study and assessment of interests as well as to experiential or social learning theory, as is evidenced in his brief discussion of how aptitudes come to be related to occupational choice (pp. 11–13; 682–683). I derived a more developed treatment of this topic from Strong's work, which appears in my *Appraising Vocational Fitness* (Super & Crites, 1962, p. 402–411).

Some of the names in figure 2 are those of people interested not so much in occupational choice or career development as in, for example, the nature and effects of social class (e.g., Centers, 1949) or of personality (e.g., Maslow, 1954). But the archway is important in illustrating the ways in which the qualities of the individual and his or her society contribute in systematic rather than chaotic ways to career development. It emphasizes, too, that it is the individual who, in his or her own way, synthesizes the effects of these determinants: It is the person, the self—the keystone of the arch—who is the decision maker. This is not to say that each individual has a free and undetermined choice; he or she does choose between whatever possibilities and pressures are known or sensed when facing a choice.

Retirement	Death
Specialization? Disengagement	Decline
Deceleration?	
Innovating? Updating? Stagnation?	
Holding	Maintenance
Advancement? Frustration? Consolidation	
Stabilizing? Trial (Committed)	Establishment
Trial (Tentative)	
Tentative	Exploration
Capacities	
Interests Fantasies Curiosity	Growth Birth

FIGURE 3   The Ladder Model of Life-Career Stages, Developmental Tasks, and Behaviors

From "A Life-Span, Life-Space Approach to Career Development" by Donald E. Super, 1990, *Career Choice and Development: Applying Contemporary Theories to Practice*, p. 214. Copyright 1990 by Jossey-Bass. Reprinted by permission.

Ladder Model of Life Career Stages

The rainbow and the archway are both necessary for an understanding of career development. As in a set of house plans, no one drawing is sufficient, for builders need both floor plans equal in number to that of the floors, and elevations equal to the number of exterior walls, be they the usual four or the less common six or eight. As Roe (1976) has demonstrated, hexagons and octagons need to be conical. And now we come to derivatives of my two models, the Ladder Model of Life Career Stages and Tasks and the Cycling and Recycling of Developmental Tasks Throughout the Life Span.

The ladder model portrayed in figure 3 is another way of depicting the classical sequence of life stages (in the right hand column), their characteristic tasks and in some instances their outcomes, the ages at which these typically occur, and the ages of the transitions from one stage or substage to another. It may be worth noting that the *Career Development Inventory* (Super, Thompson, Lindeman, Jordaan, & Myers, 1981; Thompson, Lindeman, Super, Jordaan, & Myers, 1984) assesses the qualities relevant to the earlier stages, while the *Adult Career Concerns Inventory* (Super & Thompson, 1988) addresses late adolescence and adulthood. Both play important roles in my developmental model of career assessment and counseling, and both are highlighted in my test manuals and in the case of the client J.C. in Brown and Brooks (1990, pp. 250–257; see also Super, Osborne, Walsh, Brown, & Niles [1992]).

As the ladder model seems to imply climbing, it is important to note that, as was discovered years ago in the career study of Miller and Form (1951), climbing is *not* inevitable. The sample of adult men in Ohio that they studied had essentially three types of careers: stable, unstable, and multiple-trial. Stability/instability in this sociological context refers not to a personality characteristic, but rather to the constancy or change characterizing a career. For example, my own career has been stable in that since the age of 25 I have always been an applied psychologist, whether engaged in teaching, counseling, test development, or industrial and organizational consulting and studies. One of my sons has since graduate school worked as a developmental psychologist working with children. My other son has pursued an emerging career, beginning first in the fine arts, then moving to architecture, then to architectural photography, then to work as a buyer and restorer of Victorian homes and office buildings, and finally to computers and computer graphics. There is psychological continuity here, in what Miller and Form (1951) would call a sociologically discontinuous career—that of design.

Havighurst (1953) has made the point that if the developmental tasks of any one stage (e.g., exploration) are bypassed, dissatisfaction is likely to result in later years from this premature foreclosure. A case in point is one of the ninth graders in my Career Pattern Study (CPS), one of the cases in a study that followed the career patterns of people from age 14 to age 50. This particular youngster had known since childhood that he wanted to be a lawyer, and he moved directly toward that objective. He became very successful, but when interviewed at age 35 and again when in his fifties, he was quite unsure of the wisdom of his choice. At age 35, he was merely unsure of this choice, but by age 55, he was both unsure and unhappy, thinking he might have been more satisfied as a stamp dealer, or wealthier had he been a real estate developer. He had been very successful in both his hobby and his law practice, yet the pursuit of law had led to much domestic unhappiness and, in time, to outright failure.

	Age			
	Adolescence 14–25	Early Adulthood 25–45	Middle Adulthood 45–65	Late Adulthood 65 and over
Decline Developmental tasks at each age	Giving less time to hobbies	Reducing sports participation	Focusing on essentials	Reducing working hours
Maintenance Tasks at each age	Verifying current occupational choice	Making occupational position secure	Holding one's own against competition	Keeping what one enjoys
Establishment Tasks at each age	Getting started in a chosen field	Settling down in a suitable position	Developing new skills	Doing things one has wanted to do
Exploration Tasks at each age	Learning more about more opportunities	Finding desired opportunity	Identifying new tasks to work on	Finding a good retirement place
Growth Tasks at each age	Developing a realistic self-concept	Learning to relate to others	Accepting one's own limitations	Developing and valuing nonoccupa- tional roles

(left margin label: *Life Stage*)

FIGURE 4   Cycling and Recycling of Developmental Tasks Throughout the Life Span

From "A Life-Span, Life-Space Approach to Career Development" by Donald E. Super, 1990, *Career Choice and Development: Applying Contemporary Theories to Practice*, p. 216. Copyright 1990 by Jossey-Bass. Reprinted by permission.

Cycling and Recycling Model for Developing Tasks

Figure 4 stems from the ladder and is designed to show how one cycles and recycles through the life stages, or, more accurately, how one faces essentially the same developmental tasks in different forms as one travels through life. Starting at the top, and moving from left to right, we see that there is declining behavior even in adolescence, for during the late teens and early twenties, less time is devoted to hobbies and more time is devoted to dating, courtship, and establishing a home, community, and work life. In the next age stage, early adulthood (ages 25–45), sports participation declines, reduced so as to allow more time for the working and homemaking roles, and often also because of changes in physical capacities.

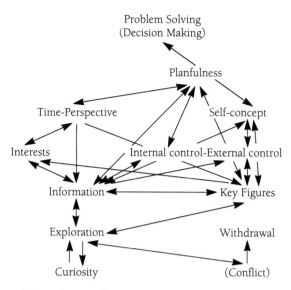

FIGURE 5   Psychological Bases of Career Development and Maturity

From "Report to the Board of Education of Charles County, Maryland" by Donald Super and JoAnn Bowlsbey, unpublished, and A. G. Watts, D. E. Super, and J. M. Kidd, 1981, *Career Development in Britain*. Copyright 1981 by Hobson's Press. Reprinted by permission.

Studies by Margaret Fiske Lowenthal et al. (1975), Daniel Levinson (1978), and others have documented the changing nature of the major developmental tasks as people age, and also the minicycles within the maxicycle of life. For example, one of the developmental tasks faced by many octogenarians is that of accepting physical limitations and developing nonoccupational roles as their professional lives diminish.

Web Model for Bases of Career Maturity

Figure 5 has an interesting history. Caroline Graham, the Director of Guidance and Career Education for Charles County, Maryland, was not satisfied with the district's program in career education in the upper grades. She asked JoAnn Bowlsbey and me to clarify what career education should do and how it should go about doing it. John Lin (a doctoral candidate at Columbia) and I did a review of the literature on career development in childhood (two literatures, in fact—one, that of career education, was easily done, as there was no such literature; the other, that of child development, was fortunately quite extensive).

The result was essentially the spider web model shown in figure 5. It served as the basis for an interview outline for the collection of data from children in grades 4 through 8. Twelve Charles County elementary school counselors were trained to

TABLE 1   Publications of Donald E. Super by Category

Quinquennium	Person-Environment	Life Span Development	Social Learning	Self-concept	Psycho-dynamic
1939–1943	10	4			
1944–1948	5	1			
1949–1953	4	3	1	1	
1954–1958	4	8			1
1959–1963	7	4	1	1	
1964–1968	2	5			
1969–1973	3	12			
1974–1978	9	5			
1979–1983	5	9			
1984–1988	3	8			
1989–1992	1	2			

From "A Life-Span, Life-Space Approach to Career Development" by Donald E. Super, 1990, *Career Choice and Development: Applying Contemporary Theories to Practice*, p. 216. Copyright 1990 by Jossey-Bass. Reprinted by permission.

use this outline, with live participants, videotaping, and critiquing. The literature-based model stood the trials very well and data were soon collected. Two doctoral candidates were then trained to analyze the protocols under my supervision. With these data, some minor modifications were made in the model shown in figure 5, a model of the early years of person-environment interaction that may be less confusing than some (e.g., Vondracek, Lerner, & Schulenberg, 1986) and which shows development as Holland's (1985) hexagon cannot. Vondracek and Holland managed with just one figure, while here five are needed to tell the complex story of career development. Each researcher and practitioner now has a choice between Vondracek's complexity, Holland's simplicity, and this multiplicity of simplicities! One important fact highlighted by figure 5 is that information is not enough: Time perspective, a sense of autonomy, and other elements are essential to the proper use of information.

A FINAL COUNT

Believing in quantifying data, in counting, I have analyzed, encoded, and counted my publications in such a way as to show the extent to which I have been constant in an orthodoxy of eclecticism (which here means comprehensiveness and therefore segmentalism), or in inconstancy due to shifting loyalties. Doing this has been a demanding task, for it called for a difficult decision about whether to classify a test or inventory of career development as a person-environment (P-E) or as a life span development (LSD) instrument. Not at all convinced that the logic was sound, I considered all career development measures to be P-E tests because they place people on trait scales (career maturity) in the context of their age groups.

Using five-year periods from the date of my first relevant publication (1939) to 1992, we have 11 quinquennia constituting my professional career. These publications fall into five categories: person-environment, life span development, social learning, self-concept, and psychodynamic. The "score" of how these publications break down into categories is shown in table 1.

It is perhaps noteworthy that my publication scores seesaw back and forth largely from person-environment to life span development, with person-environment dominating in the earlier years and leading in five quinquennia, and life span development ahead in the later years and leading in six time brackets. Meanwhile, social learning, self-concept, and psychodynamic items are few and scattered. There are, importantly, notable exceptions in this cyclical trend. It should be remembered also that the items are not all easily grouped into one category and are not weighted (e.g., a minor journal article is weighted as much as a major book or inventory). The important point here is that this analysis reveals essentially both a P-E and a developmental theorist, a straddle that seems appropriate in a segmentalist who also published a scattering of social learning, self-concept, and psychodynamic items. The rainbow, archway, and web models show consideration of traits over time as well as in context. Traits are developmental and, developing with experience, they are learned. As I claimed more than 20 years ago, I am a "differential-developmental-social-phenomenological" psychologist (Whiteley & Resnikoff, 1972).

REFERENCES

Brown, D., & Brooks, L. (Eds.). (1990). *Career choice and development: Applying contemporary theories to practice*. San Francisco: Jossey-Bass.

Centers, R. (1949). *The psychology of social classes*. Princeton, NJ: Princeton University Press.

Fiske Lowenthal, M., Thurnher, M., & Chiriboga, D. (1975). *Four stages of life*. San Francisco: Jossey-Bass.

Havighurst, R. J. (1953). *Human development and education*. New York: Longman's.

Holland, J. L. (1985). *Making vocational choices: A theory of vocational personalities and work environments*. Englewood Cliffs, NJ: Prentice-Hall.

Levinson, D. (1978). *The seasons of a man's life*. New York: Knopf.

Maslow, A. (1954). *Motivation and personality*. New York: Harper & Row.

Miller, D., & Form, W. (1951). *Industrial sociology*. New York: Harper & Row.

Roe, A. (1976). *A classification of occupations by group and level*. Bensonville, IL: Scholastic Testing Service.

Strong, E. (1943). *Vocational interests of men and women.* Stanford, CA: Stanford University Press.

Super, D. (1990). A life-span, life-space approach to career development. In D. Brown & L. Brooks (Eds.), *Career choice and development: Applying contemporary theories to practice* (2d ed., pp. 197–261). San Francisco: Jossey-Bass.

Super, D., & Bowlsbey, J. *Report to the Board of Education of Charles County, Maryland.* Unpublished manuscript.

Super, D., & Crites, J. (1962). *Appraising vocational fitness.* New York: Harper & Row.

Super, D., Osborne, W., Walsh, D., Brown, S., & Niles, S. (1992). Developmental career assessment and counseling: The C-DAC model. *Journal of Counseling and Development, 71,* 74–80.

Super, D., & Thompson, A. (1988). *Adult Career Concerns Inventory.* Palo Alto, CA: Consulting Psychologists Press.

Super, D., Thompson, A., Lindeman, R., Jordaan, J., & Myers, R. (1981). *Career Development Inventory.* Palo Alto, CA: Consulting Psychologists Press.

Thompson, A., Lindeman, R., Super, D., Jordaan, J., & Myers, R. (1984). *Career Development Inventory: Technical manual.* Palo Alto, CA: Consulting Psychologists Press.

Vondracek, F., Lerner, R., & Schulenberg, J. (1986). *Career development: A life-span developmental approach.* Hillsdale, NJ: Erlbaum.

Watts, A. G., Super, D. E., & Kidd, J. M. (1981). *Career development in Britain.* Cambridge, UK: Hobson's Press..

Whiteley, J., & Resnikoff, A. (Eds.). (1972). *Perspectives on vocational development.* Alexandria, VA: American Association for Counseling and Development.

PART TWO

CRITICAL CONSTRUCTS TO BRIDGE THEORIES

In Part 2, convergence is explored at the level of research constructs. In particular, this section highlights several core constructs in the career literature that might provide the basis for bridging, or tying together, various theories. Career psychology researchers identified with each set of constructs (e.g., identity, cultural variables, sociocognitive factors) consider how the constructs, and their accompanying empirical literatures, could be used as a fulcrum for theory and research unification.

In chapter 7, the opening chapter of this section, Lent and Hackett trace the impact of the "cognitive revolution" on contemporary conceptions of human development and change. Cognitive-constructivist approaches, emphasizing the active means by which people construe and shape their experiences, have begun to influence inquiry on counseling and career development. Lent and Hackett overview one integrative theory-building effort that attempts to explain, from a social cognitive perspective, central mechanisms and processes giving rise to career interest, choice, and performance. They also note ways in which this emergent framework complements, yet is distinct from, existing career theories.

In chapter 8, Fitzgerald and Betz note an ironic basis upon which career theories generally converge, namely, that they lack relevance to large segments of the working population. Fitzgerald and Betz question common assumptions about the very concept of career development, pointing out that career theorists and researchers have focused disproportionately on white, middle class, heterosexual individuals—and have understudied the vocational experiences of other groups. Moreover, they contend that the available career theories do not devote sufficient attention to the effects of structural and cultural factors on vocational behavior. They advocate that these factors be employed as an overarching perspective for enhancing the utility of career theories.

In chapter 9, Spokane considers the notion of person-environment fit, or congruence, as a conceptual bridge among the foundational career theories. Although noting that congruence is a common focal point of the theories, Spokane highlights important underlying differences among the trait, developmental, and social learning positions that constrain efforts to unite them at a substantive—rather than superficial, semantic—level. He also poses several questions that may require greater study as a prelude to theory convergence. In particular, does career choice involve personal change? And what role do cognitive processes play in mediating person-environment congruence?

In chapter 10, Blustein acknowledges that self mechanisms are of universal importance to career theories. However, the theories use different constructs to define the essential self attributes that influence career development. For example, Holland emphasizes vocational identity; Super, self-concept; and Krumboltz, self-observation generalizations. These constructs differ along important dimensions, such as their level of abstraction. Blustein proposes that the construct of embedded identity, based on psychodynamic theory and research on adolescent development, be used as a fulcrum for career theory convergence. He also highlights the role of relational and contextual variables in identity formation and career development.

Phillips views theory convergence from a decision-making perspective in chapter 11. She argues that our major theories generally converge on the view of career decision-making as a rationally driven enterprise wherein deciders systematically gather and integrate self and career information, arriving at a "best course of action." Yet, as Phillip points out, there is ample evidence to question this view. For instance, people's information searches are often less than thorough, and their capacity to process data about the self and career alternatives is subject to various biases and limitations. Phillips raises a number of issues for future inquiry—for example, the roles of affect, subjectivity, consultation, and provisional commitment in career decision making.

CHAPTER SEVEN

Sociocognitive Mechanisms of Personal Agency in Career Development

Pantheoretical Prospects

Robert W. Lent
Michigan State University

Gail Hackett
Arizona State University

The cognitive revolution has quietly overtaken vocational psychology, leaving the field ripe for more explicit integration.

—F. H. Borgen (1991)

IN MANY WAYS, career development can be seen as a cognitive enterprise. People selectively perceive, weigh, and incorporate information about themselves and the world around them in considering various career paths. They frame personal goals that help motivate their academic and occupational behavior. They craft and revise career plans based on beliefs about their capabilities and other self-attributes, the resources afforded by their environment, and the likely outcomes of different courses of action.

At the same time, it is well known that people's career trajectories are not just the result of their cognitive activity. For instance, emotional reactions may overrule rational thought. People possess varying achievement histories regarding different school or work-related activities. Social and economic conditions may promote or inhibit particular career ambitions for given individuals. In short, a multitude of factors—such as culture, gender, genetic endowment, social context, and unexpected life events—may interact with or supersede the effects of career-related cognitions.

Certainly, any truly comprehensive approach to career development should account for the complex connections between the person and his or her context, between intrapsychic and interpersonal mechanisms, and between volitional and nonvolitional influences on the career development process. In the face of all of this complexity and, in particular, the sociocultural forces that may circumscribe the pursuit of career options, one may reasonably wonder whether the concepts of career choice and development hold much meaning for a large segment of the American work force (see Fitzgerald & Betz, this volume). Although we acknowledge that extrapersonal factors can and do powerfully affect career possibilities, we nevertheless believe that much can be gained from exploring the role of cognitive variables. Our view is that certain cognitive mechanisms play a crucial, though by no means exclusive, role in shaping people's career realities—and that these mechanisms offer a potentially fruitful arena for convergence in theories of career behavior.

This chapter consists of four parts. First, we will note some larger trends in psychology and the cognitive sciences that are altering contemporary conceptions of human development and change. After a long period of behaviorist-imposed exile, there has been, in Borgen's (1992) words, a "reemergence of the mind" (p. 114) as a legitimate topic for psychological inquiry. The "cognitive revolution" of the past several decades has spawned constructivist approaches that emphasize the active means by which humans construe and shape their experiences. These cognitive-constructivist perspectives are, increasingly, informing models of counseling (Mahoney & Patterson, 1992).

Second, we will note how cognitive trends in the larger psychological and psychotherapeutic literatures are being expressed in current inquiry on career choice and development. Borgen (1991) has argued that such currently popular topics as cognition, personal agency (e.g., the capacity to direct one's own behavior), and empowerment have long been implicit within the major models of vocational psychology. Nevertheless, recent years have seen a dramatic increase in cognitively focused career theory and research (Hackett, Lent, & Greenhaus, 1991). While many conceptual and measurement challenges remain (cf. Chartrand & Camp, 1991; Pryor, 1985), this area of inquiry represents an important medium for theoretical convergence.

In the third section of this chapter, we will overview one recent model-building effort, based largely on Bandura's (1986) general social cognitive theory, that attempts to complement, and build conceptual linkages with, existing career development models. This emergent model, resting on certain constructivist assumptions, emphasizes the dynamic processes through which career-related interest, choice, and performance are forged and reshaped over time. It deals with key learning and cognitive phenomena that may help "cement" the various "segments" of career development (Super, 1990). Finally, we will note several specific points of convergence and divergence between the social cognitive career framework and the four dominant theories of career development identified by Osipow (1990).

THE COGNITIVE REVOLUTION
AND CONCEPTIONS OF THE SELF

Mahoney and Patterson (1992) identified four forces within psychology that reflect historical changes in views of the self. The first force was psychoanalytic theory, which viewed the self as being molded largely through unconscious forces and biological impulses, and as being relatively impervious to change beyond early childhood. In response to this heavily intrapsychic and deterministic view, behaviorism emerged as the second force in psychology. In the classic behavioral view, the self and other mental processes were eliminated from the realm of scientific scrutiny, and the self was seen as merely the repository of environmental learning experiences.

According to Mahoney and Patterson (1992), both psychoanalytic and behavioral theories shared a "linear, unidirectional model of causality" (p. 667). In psychoanalytic theory, human action was propelled by intrapsychic forces; in behavioral theory, it was propelled by environmental events. In neither theory was the reciprocal interaction of the self and environment considered to any great extent. The third force, existential and humanistic theories, highlighted the potential for personal agency, placing the self at center stage. Although the third force theories adopted a less deterministic view of behavior than did their psychoanalytic or behavioral forebears, they were generally influenced by psychodynamic conceptions and, thus, largely emphasized the role of intrapsychic factors.

In contrast, the fourth force in psychology, the "cognitive revolution" (Dember, 1974), has emphasized the self in interaction with the environment, and has prompted renewed interest in the self as an active agent and constructor of meaning (Borgen, 1991). Although this force has produced important developments in conceptions of the self, it is important to note that the "cognitive revolution" does not represent a cohesive, homogeneous movement. Rather, the fourth force, like its predecessors, has been marked by different waves or trends. The first wave introduced information processing models, the "first scientific alternatives to the mediational models based on classical learning theories" (Mahoney & Patterson, 1992, p. 670). These models, drawn mainly from mechanistic computer metaphors of cognitive processes (Gardner, 1985), allowed for the empirical study of mental operations.

In the second wave, early cognitive information processing models were modified to reflect biological (versus mechanistic) models of the nervous system. However, these "connectionist" models "only partially abandoned the computer metaphor" (Mahoney & Patterson, 1992, p. 671). The first two waves of the cognitive revolution have had a pervasive influence on the psychological literature, as is illustrated by the large amount of study devoted to information processing, attributions, expectancies, human inference processes, and cognitive styles and beliefs (e.g., Fiske & Taylor, 1991; Heppner & Frazier, 1992).

The cognitive revolution is currently undergoing a third wave, characterized by constructivist and motoric conceptions of the mind and human experience. As Mahoney (1985) has described, "while the rest of psychology has been becoming energetically more cognitive, cognitive psychology has taken a dramatic step toward becoming more *motoric*" (p. 14). Information processing models stand in sharp contrast to trait and psychodynamic perspectives, yet they can also be differentiated from motor theories, which assert that the sensory and motor components of the nervous system are integrally linked and that the "mind is intrinsically a motor system" (Weimer, 1977, p. 272). Motoric conceptions involve feed-forward (as opposed to feedback only) mechanisms, highlighting the active means by which people process information and construct meaning. *Proactive cognition,* the notion that "all human knowing is active, anticipatory, and constructive" (Mahoney & Patterson, 1992, p. 671), is a hallmark of such conceptions.

Contemporary constructivist and motoric views of cognition represent the most revolutionary wave of the fourth force. In the therapeutic literature, Alfred Adler and George Kelly provide two early examples of constructivist thinking, and a number of prominent contemporary writers, such as Guidano (1987), Mahoney (1991), and Markus and Nurius (1986), have developed constructivist theoretical formulations. According to Mahoney and Lyddon (1988),

> the constructivist perspective is founded on the idea that *humans actively create and construe their personal realities.* The basic assertion of constructivism is that each individual creates his or her own representational model of the world.... Central to the constructivist formulations is the idea that, rather than being a sort of template through which ongoing experience is filtered, the representational model actively *creates* and constrains new experience and thus determines what the individual will perceive as "reality." (p. 200)

Mahoney and Lyddon have also observed that within the constructivist tradition, affect is accorded a central role as "a primitive and powerful form of knowing" (p. 218), and is not considered a mere subordinate of cognition; unconscious (or nonconscious) processes have been reclaimed from psychodynamic theory and reconceptualized as *tacit knowing;* problems are seen as resulting from a discrepancy between situational challenges and client capacities; and counseling is focused on understanding and changing meaning structures, as well as on emotional and behavioral functioning (Mahoney, 1991).

The implications of these new cognitive perspectives are far-reaching. Nurius (1986) observed that "in contrast to earlier reliance on a narrow band of traitlike descriptors...the emerging view is of a self-concept that is dynamic and future oriented, including self-knowledge about goals and motives, personal standards and values, and rules and strategies for regulating and controlling one's [own] behavior" (p. 430). Discussing trends in motivation research, Weiner (1990) noted that "the main theories today are based on the interrelated cognitions of causal ascriptions, efficacy and control beliefs, helplessness, and thoughts about the goals for which one is striving...all concern perceptions about the self as a determinant of prior or future success and failure" (pp. 620–621).

In the realm of counseling, newer cognitive-constructivist models are emerging that represent important departures from earlier cognitive-rationalist approaches. Ellis' (1962) rational emotive therapy is exemplary of rationalist approaches. Despite some emphasis on personal agency, such cognitive therapies highlight reality testing, logic, and reason. They hold that maladaptive thoughts and inaccurate beliefs cause negative affect; thus, treatment should be geared toward thinking more rationally, correcting inaccuracies, controlling thought processes, and eliminating problematic affect. In contrast, constructivist counseling approaches are concerned more with the *viability* (i.e., functional utility) than with the validity or accuracy of cognitive representations of "reality." They also highlight the "self-organizing" activities of the individual, that is, the complex developmental and dynamic processes through which people maintain a coherent sense of self and interpret their experiences (Mahoney & Patterson, 1992).

COGNITIVE AND SELF-FORMULATIONS IN VOCATIONAL PSYCHOLOGY

The concept of the self, in various guises, has been one of the most durable constructs in theories of career development. In his 1990 article on theoretical convergence, Osipow noted that personality plays a central and important role in all theories of career development. Within their conceptions of personality, each of the major career theories devotes some attention to the self or self-cognitions. Examples include Super's vocational self-concept, Krumboltz's "self-observation generalizations," and the person side of P-E fit formulations. However, these theories generally rely heavily on trait conceptions of the self and diverge considerably in their views of the specific self-mechanisms assumed to affect career development.

The Cognitive Revolution and Vocational Psychology

Although trait-oriented self-conceptions still dominate the vocational literature, there are indications that the cognitive revolution is making its mark (Borgen, 1991). Vocational researchers of all theoretical persuasions are exhibiting a greater tendency to include cognitive variables in their research and to view people as active agents in their own career development, as opposed to passive reactors to intrapsychic or external determinants (Borgen, 1991). This cognitive trend in career research has been evident in both the counseling psychology and organizational perspectives on vocational behavior (Hackett et al., 1991), as exemplified by research on vocational schemata (Neimeyer, 1988), career self-efficacy (Lent & Hackett, 1987), and work motivation (Locke & Latham, 1990).

Over the past decade or so, career development theorists have also been increasingly emphasizing cognitive and agentic mechanisms in career development. For instance, in explicating the self-concept in her theory, Gottfredson (1985) asserted that the self is "an active agent" (p. 159). Likewise, Super's (1990) incorporation of Kelly's (1955) psychology of personal constructs emphasizes personal agency. Recently, person-environment fit writers have proposed infusing older trait-and-factor models with newer, cognitively focused information processing (Rounds & Tracey, 1990) and social learning (Gottfredson, 1990) perspectives. Career development is increasingly being viewed as a process involving active agents who not only adjust to but also influence and transform their environments (Vondracek, Lerner, & Schulenberg, 1986).

Problems in Unifying Self-conceptions

Borgen (1991) has argued that an emphasis on the person as active shaper of his or her career actually represents a long-standing tradition in career and counseling theories. He has observed that "human agency has long been alive and well in the guise of Rogers' self-actualization, Kelly's personal constructs, and Super's career as implementation of self-concept" (p. 281). We agree with Borgen's assessment that vocational psychology has long dealt with agentic notions and has energetically been incorporating recent cognitive streams in its research. However, it is also important to acknowledge the key differences that remain in vocational theorists' cognitive formulations, as well as the conceptual and methodological barriers that may stymie progress in cognitively guided vocational inquiry.

Although there may be increasing convergence on the view that people are active shapers of their career development, vocational researchers have often failed to capture this constructivist, agentic perspective in their choice of measures and research designs. For example, most research on Holland's (1985) theory still defines and assesses the self and self-in-environment in global, static terms, despite the newer person-environment fit emphasis on the reciprocal interaction between an active person and a dynamic environment. Measurement devices and research designs that better capture the dynamic flow of the work adjustment process have generally lagged behind theoretical developments.

Additionally, despite career theorists' acknowledgment of cognitive person or self-mechanisms, there is continuing controversy over how self-conceptions have been conceptualized in vocational psychology (Borgen, 1991; Chartrand & Camp, 1991). Pryor (1985), for example, has advocated "exorcising" the self-concept from vocational theory, replacing it with more dynamic representations of the self and its properties. Others see the self-concept as salvageable, if we can somehow surmount the definitional and measurement problems that have sullied its reputation (e.g.,

Gottfredson, 1985). Of course, debates of this sort are not unique to vocational research; rather, they reflect theoretical and methodological controversies that stem from psychology's earliest days. For example, William James viewed the self as "the arbiter of all experience" and as representing "perhaps *the* basic problem" for psychology (Markus, 1990, p. 181).

COGNITION AS A FULCRUM
FOR THEORETICAL CONVERGENCE

In a recent review of theoretical and empirical advances in the career literature (Hackett, Lent, & Greenhaus, 1991), we suggested that the time may be ripe for constructing integrative theories that "(a) bring together conceptually related constructs (e.g., self-concept, self-efficacy); (b) more fully explain outcomes that are common to a number of career theories (e.g., satisfaction, stability); and (c) account for the relations among seemingly diverse constructs (e.g., self-efficacy, interests, abilities, needs)" (p. 28). Noting trends in the vocational literature toward theoretical convergence and the ascendance of agentic and cognitive positions, Borgen (1991) similarly concluded that "today vocational psychology has unprecedented prospects for integration" (p. 280).

In this section we will overview a theory-building project that we and our colleague, Steven Brown, have recently initiated. (For a more detailed version of this project, see Lent, Brown, & Hackett, in press.) Our model attempts to address the integrative agenda suggested above in several ways. For instance, it considers a number of person constructs (e.g., interests, abilities, expected outcomes, and goals) that are dealt with in varying degrees by other career theorists and which may be brought together under the umbrella of Bandura's (1986) unifying theory. While it incorporates a variety of person, contextual, and behavioral variables, our career-specific elaboration of Bandura's theory suggests several central mechanisms and paths through which these variables may affect career-related outcomes.

The social cognitive career framework is aimed at explaining the processes whereby (a) academic and career interests develop, (b) interests and various other mechanisms promote career-relevant choices, and (c) people achieve varying levels of performance and persistence in educational and career pursuits. By emphasizing the cognitive and experiential precursors of interest, choice, and performance, this framework may help explain certain learning and developmental phenomena implicit in, but not fully addressed by, existing career models (e.g., how interest types develop in Holland's theory or what variables promote differential role salience in Super's theory). After outlining our nascent conceptual scheme, we will cite several specific potential interconnections between it and the dominant models of career choice and development.

Social Cognitive Career Theory

In approaching our theory-bridging effort, we were influenced by several sources. First, Bandura's (1986) social cognitive theory formed the basic underpinnings for our integrative model. We adapted, elaborated, and expanded on those aspects of the general theory that seemed most relevant to the processes of career-related interest formation, choice, and performance. Second, we attempted to build connections with several domain-specific models of vocational interests (Barak, 1981), academic choice (Meece, Wigfield, & Eccles, 1990), and career choice/ decisions (Mitchell & Krumboltz, 1990) that have similar social learning or expectancy theory roots. Third, our effort was informed by cognitive theories of work motivation emanating from organizational psychology (e.g., Locke & Latham, 1990) and by inquiry in personality and social psychology (e.g., Ajzen, 1988; Watson & Clark, 1984).

Social Cognitive Mechanisms of Personal Agency. In Bandura's (1986) view of person-situation interaction, which he has termed *triadic reciprocality,* three major classes of causal factors affect one another bidirectionally: (a) person variables, such as internal cognitive and affective states, and physical attributes, (b) external environmental factors, and (c) overt behavior, as distinct from internal and physical qualities of the person. The systemic relations among this set of causal factors are seen as essential in understanding the dynamic nature of person-context transactions.

In its analysis of the personal determinants within the triadic causal system, social cognitive theory highlights a variety of cognitive, vicarious, self-regulatory, and self-reflective processes (Bandura, 1986). While each of these processes is assumed to play an important role in guiding psychosocial functioning, we believe that there are three social cognitive mechanisms that are particularly relevant to understanding career development: (a) self-efficacy beliefs, (b) outcome expectations, and (c) goal representations. These mechanisms form the basic building blocks of our model and are seen as the primary means through which people assert agency in their career choice and development.

Self-efficacy has received much empirical attention in the recent career literature (Hackett & Lent, 1992; Lent & Hackett, 1987; Locke & Latham, 1990). According to Bandura (1986), self-efficacy beliefs refer to "people's judgments of their capabilities to organize and execute courses of action required to attain designated types of performances" (p. 391). These beliefs are seen as constituting the most central and pervasive mechanism of personal agency (Bandura, 1989). In the social cognitive view, self-efficacy is not a passive, static trait but rather a dynamic aspect of the self-system specific to a given performance domain and that interacts complexly with other person, behavior, and environmental factors.

Hackett and Betz (1981) introduced this construct to the career literature, proposing that efficacy percepts might influence achievement behavior, academic and career decisions, and career adjustment processes. They emphasized that self-efficacy might be especially useful in understanding women's career development. Research has subsequently indicated that these percepts are generally predictive of academic attainments, career entry indices, and work adjustment outcomes (Hackett & Lent, 1992).

Outcome expectations, referring to beliefs about the consequences of performing particular behaviors, constitute another important social cognitive mechanism. Whereas self-efficacy beliefs are concerned with one's response capabilities (i.e., "Can I do this?"), outcome expectations involve the imagined results of a course of action ("If I do this, what will happen?"). Social cognitive theory suggests that "people act on their judgments of what they can do, *as well as* [italics added] on their beliefs about the likely effects of various actions" (Bandura, 1986, p. 231).

Although citing the dual role of self-efficacy and outcome expectations, Bandura (1986) has argued that these two forms of belief are often differentially potent, with self-efficacy serving as a more influential behavioral determinant. For example, there are many instances in which people may anticipate valuable outcomes to result from a given course of action (e.g., the common belief that pursuing a medical career will yield a high income) but avoid such action if they doubt they possess the requisite capabilities. On the other hand, a strong sense of efficacy may sustain efforts, even in instances where outcome attainment is uncertain.

Personal goals are also seen as playing an important role in the self-regulation of behavior. Although environmental events and personal history help shape their behavior, people are seen as more than just mechanical responders to deterministic forces. By formulating personal goals, people are viewed as capable of engaging in purposive, self-directed action. As Bandura (1989) has observed, "people anticipate the likely outcomes of their prospective actions, they set goals for themselves, and they plan courses of action likely to produce desired outcomes" (p. 1179). Thus, people can transcend the "indefinite but omnific 'history of reinforcement' " (Bandura, 1986, p. 468) and maintain some control over their own behavior.

A goal may be defined as the determination to engage in a particular activity or to effect a particular future outcome (Bandura, 1986). Goal setting helps people organize and guide their behavior, sustain it over time (even in the absence of external reinforcement), and increase the likelihood that desired outcomes will be attained. Social cognitive theory posits important reciprocal relations among self-efficacy, outcome expectations, and goal systems in the self-regulation of behavior. For example, by creating self-set incentives for performance, goals are assumed to influence the development of self-efficacy. Self-efficacy, in turn, may affect the subsequent behavioral goals that one selects and the effort expended in their pursuit (Bandura, 1986).

The function of personal goals is implicit, if not explicit, in all theories of career choice and decision making. Such concepts as career plans, decisions, aspirations, and expressed choices are all essentially goal mechanisms. In each case, their import derives from their presumed role in motivating behavior (or symbolizing intended behavior); the differences among these various goal terms relate principally to their degree of specificity and proximity to actual choice implementation. For example, career goals have often been referred to as occupational aspirations or daydreams when they are assessed remotely in time from actual career entry, when they do not demand commitment or carry real consequences, and when they do not require persons to factor in reality considerations, such as job market conditions. They are more likely to be dubbed expressed choices, plans, or decisions when they involve specific behavioral intentions (e.g., determination to enter a particular field), are assessed near or at career entry, and require commitment.

A Social Cognitive Analysis of Interest and Choice Processes. In our more detailed version of the social cognitive career framework (Lent et al., in press), we treat career-related interests, choices, and performances within three interlocking, segmental models—following Super's (1990) lead of dividing complex career processes into component parts. For our present purposes, we must necessarily condense our discussion of these models. Thus, we will emphasize the sociocognitive mechanisms and pathways that are hypothesized to influence the formulation of academic/career interests and choices. Figure 1, which highlights cognitive and behavioral influences during childhood and adolescence, provides a schematic view of the means by which interests may develop and differentiate over time.

It is important to note here that in keeping with social cognitive theory's complex, reciprocal view of person-behavior-situation interactions, we believe that most of the major system elements represented in figures 1 and 2 may actually affect one another bidirectionally over time. Our decision to point the causal arrows in these figures in only one direction is based on our assumptions about the predominant pathways through which interests and choices develop and change.

Over the course of childhood and adolescence, people's environments expose them to a variety of activities that have eventual career relevance, such as writing, athletics, and cooking. Not only are people exposed to such activities, but they are also differentially reinforced for pursuing certain activities from among those that are possible and for achieving satisfactory performances in chosen activities. Through repeated practice and feedback from important others, children and adolescents refine their skills, develop personal performance standards, form a sense of their efficacy in particular tasks, and acquire certain expectations about the outcomes of their performance.

We believe that perceptions of self-efficacy and outcome likelihood figure prominently in the formation of career interests. More specifically, it is likely that people form enduring interests in activities at which they view themselves to be efficacious (cf. Bandura, 1986; Lent, Larkin, & Brown, 1989) and for which they anticipate positive outcomes. These relations are illustrated by paths 1 and 2 in figure 1. Indeed, it may be difficult for robust interests to blossom where self-efficacy is weak or where neutral or negative outcomes are foreseen. Emergent interest (or activity enjoyment), in turn, promotes goals for further activity exposure (path 3), which increase the likelihood of subsequent task practice (path 4). Activity involvement or practice results in particular performance attainments (path 5; e.g.,

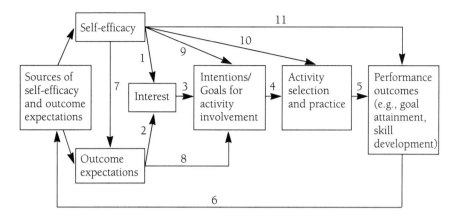

FIGURE 1   Model of How Basic Career Interests Develop Over Time

From "Toward a Unified Social Cognitive Theory of Career and Academic Interest, Choice and Performance" by R. W. Lent, S. D. Brown, and G. Hackett, in press, *Journal of Vocational Behavior.* Copyright 1993 by R. W. Lent, S. D. Brown, and G. Hackett. Reprinted by permission.

successes and failures), which then serve to revise self-efficacy and outcome expectancy estimates (path 6).

We believe that this process repeats itself continuously over the life span, though it is perhaps most fluid up until the mid-twenties, when career interests tend to stabilize (Hansen, 1984). Once interests crystallize and people come to develop characteristic patterns of career interests (Holland, 1985), it may take very compelling experiences to provoke a fundamental reappraisal of career self-efficacy and outcome beliefs and, hence, a change in basic interest patterns. Such occasions seem rare in later life, but are theoretically possible, particularly when changing life or work circumstances (e.g., job loss, accident, birth of a child, technological innovations) require or encourage the cultivation of different competencies.

In the course of interest formation, it is likely that outcome expectations will partly be determined by self-efficacy (path 7), since people presumably expect to achieve desirable outcomes in activities at which they view themselves to be efficacious (Bandura, 1986). Furthermore, outcome expectations may affect goals for activity involvement directly (path 8), as well as indirectly, through interests. That is, people develop goals for activity involvement partly because of their intrinsic interest in these activities and partly because of the extrinsic rewards they anticipate. Self-efficacy is also assumed to exert direct effects on activity goals, practice, and performance accomplishments (paths 9, 10, and 11). For instance, self-efficacy helps people interpret and organize their skills and persist despite inevitable performance setbacks.

Our model of the career/academic choice process is illustrated in figure 2. This figure actually incorporates the basic causal sequence suggested by figure 1, but differs in that the activity goal and behavior (choice action) variables in this figure specifically represent career/academic choice goals and their enactment. Thus, in one sense, this model is a developmental extension of the process of basic interest formation. It may be seen that we have conceptually divided the career choice phase into several component processes: (a) the formation of a primary career goal (or choice) from among one's major career interests, (b) efforts designed to implement the choice (e.g., enrolling in a particular training program or academic major), and (c) subsequent action outcomes (e.g., academic failures, admission acceptances) that create a feedback loop, affecting the shape of future career behavior.

Our model adopts the distinction that Krumboltz and his associates have made between career choice intentions (or goals) and entry behaviors, that is, those actions designed to implement one's goals (Mitchell & Krumboltz, 1990). We find this distinction useful for several reasons. First, subdividing the choice process in this way highlights the intermediate role of personal goals in choice making. We do not believe that choice actions are automatically implanted by the press of one's environment or personal history; rather, self-set goals arising from the interplay of self-efficacy, outcome beliefs, and interests afford a measure of personal agency in the determination of one's career future.

Second, choices do not represent static acts. Once implemented, choices are often modified by ensuing performance outcomes. For example, after arriving at the choice of engineering as a major, a student may have serious difficulty passing the necessary physics and chemistry courses. Such compelling performance data may force a revision of perceived capabilities, ultimately prompting a change in goals (e.g., the selection of a new major). Thus, the proposed scheme conceptualizes career/academic choice as a dynamic enterprise.

As indicated in figure 2, and discussed earlier within the context of the interest development model, self-efficacy and outcome beliefs jointly give rise to interests (paths 1 and 2). Interests, in turn, promote cognized career goals (i.e., intentions, plans, or aspirations to engage in a particular career direction; path 3), which increase the likelihood of choice actions (e.g., declaring a corresponding academic major; path 4). Actions (or entry behaviors) then lead to subsequent performance attainments (path 5), which may support or weaken efficacy and outcome percepts (path 6) and, ultimately, choice persistence.

In addition to affecting choice behavior indirectly through their impact on interests (paths 2 and 3), outcome expectations may exert a direct effect on the selection of career goals (path 8). The more valued the perceived outcomes, the more likely it is that people will adopt particular career goals. Self-efficacy is also seen as affecting the choice process through several paths: indirectly via outcome expectations (path 7) and interests (path 1), and directly via career goals, actions, and performance outcomes (paths 9, 10, and 11, respectively).

We should say a bit more about the manner in which interests translate into goals (i.e., choice content). As suggested by Holland's (1985) theory, some people have relatively well-differentiated interest profiles in that their primary interest lies in one particular occupational realm, while others may hold competing interests in several

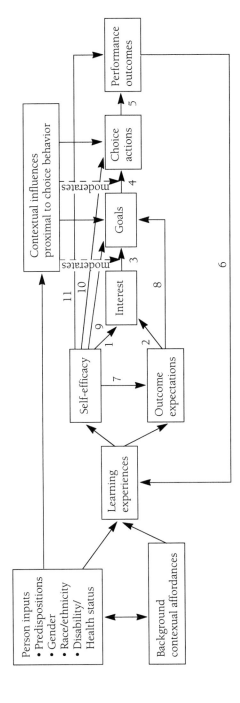

FIGURE 2   Model of Person, Contextual, and Experiential Factors Affecting Career-related Choice Behavior

From "Toward a Unified Social Cognitive Theory of Career and Academic Interest, Choice and Performance" by R. W. Lent, S. D. Brown, and G. Hackett, in press, *Journal of Vocational Behavior*. Copyright 1993 by R. W. Lent, S. D. Brown, and G. Hackett. Reprinted by permission.

broad areas or specific options at once. Transforming an interest into a goal may be a relatively straightforward process in the former case, particularly assuming there is a supportive environment. However, it is more tricky when one needs to select among several desirable alternatives or when there are extenuating (e.g., economic) considerations.

Ordinarily, we expect that people will tend to select career options that match their primary career interests or that combine their primary and secondary interest themes. In essence, this supposition recalls Holland's (1985) well-studied "birds of a feather" hypothesis (e.g., a person with dominant artistic interests will gravitate toward artistic occupations). One difference from Holland's scheme, however, is that we specify goals as forming an intermediate link between interests and choice actions. Another is that we view self-efficacy and outcome expectations as important precursors of interest. A third difference is that we see self-efficacy and outcome beliefs as potentially contributing directly to goals (paths 8 and 9 in figure 2). This independent effect of efficacy and outcome beliefs may help explain why interests and career choices do not always coincide (e.g., Williamson, 1939). For instance, interests may be compromised in the service of economic need, occupational status, or job availability.

Other Person and Contextual Influences on Interest and Choice. To this point in our analysis, we have been highlighting certain hypothesized cognitive and behavioral determinants of career/academic interest, choice, and performance. This focus stems from our effort to elaborate a (primarily) psychological account of the role of self-reflective and self-regulatory mechanisms in career development. However, as noted at the outset, comprehensive models of career development also need to reckon with the effects of a variety of other person and contextual variables on career outcomes.

Our framework deals with three broad additional sets of components: (a) *person inputs*, such as inherited affective and physical attributes; (b) features of the social, physical, and cultural *environment* that may support or limit personal development; and (c) career-relevant *learning experiences*. While acknowledging the bidirectional, interdependent relations among these elements, we envision three predominant causal paths through which person, contextual, and experiential factors may influence career-related interests and choice behavior: (a) as *precursors* of sociocognitive variables, (b) as *moderators* of interest-goal and goal-action relationships, or (c) as *direct facilitators* or deterrents (e.g., physical requirements or overt discriminatory practices that restrict access to particular choice options). Certain factors may operate through more than one influence mode. These three paths of influence are incorporated into figure 2.

While space limitations preclude a detailed discussion of these person, contextual, and experiential factors, we will briefly consider a few examples. Several theorists have envisioned career-relevant skills as having an hereditary component (e.g., Strong, 1943; Super, 1953). Our framework also assumes that certain basic skill potentialities, for example, spatial perception, manual dexterity, or symbolic manipulation, may be transmitted genetically. However, latent aptitude requires cultivation if it is to acquire career relevance. Thus, it seems crucial to consider the interplay between skill potential and learning opportunities that are jointly engineered by the person and his or her environment. Figure 2 traces the hypothetical path between inherited skill potential, included within the rubric of "person inputs," and subsequent career-related behavior.

Over the course of development, certain of the child's native skills may be perceived by parents, other socialization agents, and the self as differentially efficacious or desirable. Given suitable environmental resources, these skills may be gradually developed via goal setting, selective reinforcement, observational learning, and related processes. Skill development, in turn, fosters percepts of differential self-efficacy and outcome expectations with respect to particular skill domains.

By adolescence, most people have a sense of their competence at a vast array of performance domains, along with convictions about the likely outcomes of their participation in these activities. As hypothesized earlier, these self-efficacy and outcome beliefs, in combination with evolving abilities, may figure prominently in the development of vocational interests, choices, and performances. Thus, this analysis suggests that the effect of skill potentialities on subsequent academic/career interest and behavior operates largely through intervening learning experiences that further shape abilities and form the substrate upon which self-efficacy and outcome beliefs are based.

In addition to inheriting skill potentials, every infant is the beneficiary of a particular set of overt physical attributes, such as race and sex. These factors have long been the focus of career development research, though until recently much of this inquiry has involved documenting simple race or sex differences in particular vocational outcomes (Hackett & Lent, 1992). Study of the specific paths through which biological race and sex may affect career development has been much less common, and there is continuing controversy over whether generic career theories can adequately explain the career behavior of women and minority group members, or whether gender- and culture-specific models may be required (Hackett & Lent, 1992).

While race and sex are biological attributes at one level, few would deny their profound psychological and social significance. In fact, much of their relevance to career development derives not from their physical presence per se, but rather from the characteristic reactions they may evoke from the sociocultural environment, as well as from their relation to the structure of opportunity within which academic and career behavior is enacted. Thus, race and sex may also be viewed as socially conferred or constructed statuses, transcending their biological properties. Congenital health/disability status may also be so described, recognizing that the impact of physical disability on career development—apart from imposing potential skill limitations—is partly mediated by sociocultural forces.

Cogent arguments have been made for distinguishing between sex, a biological variable, and gender, a sociocultural construction involving the psychological ramifications of sex (Unger, 1979). Similar distinctions may be made between race and ethnicity (cf. Casas, 1984). By viewing gender and ethnicity as socially constructed aspects of experience, it is possible to emphasize those sociocultural agents that help shape the career development process—for example, by orchestrating the learning opportunities to which particular children and adolescents are exposed, as well as the nature of the outcomes they receive for performing different activities. Hackett and Betz (1981) have illustrated, for example, how the process of gender-role socialization may bias boys' and girls' access to the sources of information necessary for the development of strong efficacy percepts in particular culturally sanctioned activities. Whereas girls may be differentially encouraged to pursue female-typed activities, such as artwork or domestic tasks, boys tend to be rewarded more for engaging in male-typed pursuits, such as science or athletics. Consequently, boys and girls may be more likely to develop abilities and self-efficacy at tasks that are culturally defined as gender appropriate.

Similar psychosocial processes may help dictate the development of career-related self-efficacy and outcome expectations in people of particular racial/ethnic or disability groups. For example, certain cultures may selectively reinforce particular occupationally relevant activities; conditions of poverty or racism can bias the quality and types of learning experiences one receives; and people with a given disability may be subject to socialization processes and differential opportunities that favor the development of particular skills and the underutilization of others. Personal expectations and performance standards, forged through learning experiences, may also interact with social realities to delimit or enhance academic/career options.

In sum, as diagrammed in figure 2, we believe that the effects of gender and ethnicity on career interests, choice, and performance will be partly mediated by self-efficacy and outcome expectations—or, more precisely, by the differential learning experiences that give rise to these expectations. On the other hand, as is also illustrated in figure 2, gender and cultural factors are also typically linked to the opportunity structure within which academic/career goals are framed and implemented. We will consider this important link as we turn to the effects of contextual and experiential factors in the social cognitive model.

In their important treatise on career development from a life span perspective, Vondracek et al. (1986) argued that "the context, whether viewed in a global or specific way, from a proximal or a distal, or from a micro or a macroperspective, is an integral and necessary component of any explanatory scheme that tries to account for human development" (p. 67). In sketching out our conception of the environment, we found it useful to draw upon certain ideas and constructs presented by Vondracek et al. (1986). For example, we adapted Vondracek et al.'s "contextual affordances" construct as an organizing principle in our analysis.

According to Vondracek et al. (1986), "the concept of affordance centers on the idea that environments offer, provide, and/or furnish something to the organism as long as the organism can perceive 'it' as such" (p. 38). This emphasis on personal perceptions of the environment is quite consistent with the importance that social cognitive theory places on cognitive appraisal processes in guiding behavior. Such a view does not minimize the significance of objective features of the environment, but it does highlight the person's active, phenomenological role as the interpreter of contextual inputs.

For conceptual convenience, we have divided contextual affordance or opportunity structure variables into two subgroups, based on their relative proximity to career choice points: (a) more distal, background influences that precede and help shape interests and self-cognitions and (b) proximal influences that come into play at critical choice junctures. Figure 2 outlines the hypothesized connections of each set of contextual factors to various career development outcomes. In our scheme, contextual factors (a) help shape the learning experiences that fuel personal interests and choices and (b) comprise the real and perceived opportunity structure within which career plans are devised and implemented. Certain environmental events may also exert direct, potent effects on choice formation and implementation (e.g., discrimination in hiring).

Although much remains to be learned about environmental effects on academic and career choice behavior, we believe it is reasonable to speculate about a few potentially important causal paths. In particular, as figure 2 indicates, we suspect that features of the opportunity structure may moderate the relations of (a) interests to choice goals and (b) goals to actions. Earlier, we posited that interests will ordinarily relate positively to choice goals and, likewise, goals will increase the likelihood of corresponding choice actions. We now qualify these predictions by suggesting that interest-goal and goal-action relations will tend to be stronger among people who perceive beneficial environmental conditions (e.g., the presence of ample support and few barriers) and weaker among people who perceive less favorable conditions.

As also diagrammed in figure 2, opportunity structure variables may help mediate (i.e., explain) the effects of gender, ethnicity, and disability status on choice behavior. For example, a woman may be less likely to translate her scientific interests into a science-related academic major if she perceives little support for this option from her significant others. Thus, the interest-goal relationship will be weakened in this instance. Note, however, that it is not her gender per se that lessens this association, but rather how her gender relates to the perceived structure of opportunity.

In addition to their potential moderating and mediating roles, we recognize that certain environmental events or circumstances can directly influence the choice process or affect the relative predominance of certain cognitive determinants. For example, optimal socioeconomic and educational conditions allow people to translate their primary career interests into corresponding career goals. However, basing career choice on interests is a luxury that many people cannot afford. Where choices are constrained by such considerations as educational background or economic necessity, career goals and actions may be less influenced by interests than by outcome expectations and self-efficacy beliefs. As Bandura (personal communication, March 1, 1993) has noted, "people often choose and pursue occupations because they believe they can do them and they want the money the jobs pay. People don't choose to labor on assembly lines, in coal mines, in bureaucracies because they were driven by consuming interest in these occupations."

CONNECTIONS WITH THE "BIG FOUR" THEORIES

In this final section we will briefly consider some key points of convergence, divergence, and complementarity between our framework and other models of career development, thereby encouraging more integrative efforts at theory build-ing. Osipow (1990) identified the "Big Four" of career theories, namely, those of Super (1990), Holland (1985), Dawis and Lofquist (1984), and Krumboltz and associates (e.g., Mitchell & Krumboltz, 1990). These four have garnered varying degrees of empirical support and are generally acknowledged as the most influential models emanating from the counseling psychology perspective on career behavior (Hackett & Lent, 1992; Osipow, 1990). The theoretical linkages between our social cognitive framework and Krumboltz and associates' social learning theory of career decision making are the most forthright; the dissimilarities are crucial but less apparent.

The other major career development theories may bear little surface resemblance to the social cognitive model, but there are several points of possible convergence that deserve attention. For instance, at a broad level, the theories all consider person influences, such as interests and self-concept, on career development (Osipow, 1990). Also, despite important assumptive differences, various theorists have acknowledged the impact of learning experiences and/or self-efficacy mechanisms on the career development process (e.g., Holland, 1990; Super, 1990). We will explore here some specific ways in which social cognitive theory may inform, and be informed by, these foundational perspectives.

Krumboltz's Social Learning Theory

Like Krumboltz and colleagues' social learning theory (SLT) of career decision making, our theoretical perspective acknowledges the influence of genetic endow-ment, special abilities, and environmental conditions on career decision making. Both models also agree on the importance of learning experiences (operant, associative, and vicarious), in interaction with person and contextual factors, in guiding career development. Likewise, both approaches view interests as learned proclivities rather than innate predispositions, and both acknowledge the impact of cognitive processes on career behavior.

However, the two theories differ somewhat in the phenomena that they attempt to explain, that is, SLT is primarily concerned with choice behavior, while our framework focuses on the interlocking processes of interest development, choice, and performance. The two approaches also diverge on a number of key points, most notably on the relative prominence accorded to cognitive processes, the specific cognitive constructs included within the models, and the interactive role of cognition in regulating motivation and action. One of the key distinctions is that, within social cognitive theory, self-efficacy mechanisms are posited to be major mediators of choice and development, whereas within SLT, self-efficacy is assigned a relatively minor role. As Mitchell and Krumboltz (1990) have explained, "in the social learning theory of career decision making, self-efficacy expectations are dependent variables—the outcome of numerous learning experiences—not independent variables" (p. 171).

In contrast, the social cognitive position attempts to highlight specific theoretical mechanisms, such as self-efficacy, that may account for the relationship between past and future behavior. Simply asserting that past learning experience begets future behavior or that a cumulative "reinforcement history" is responsible for career outcomes does not provide a sufficient explanation of how prior experience exerts its impact on future behavior, let alone what factors produced the past behavior. We take the view that the effect of learning experiences on future career behavior is largely mediated cognitively. For instance, people differentially recall, weight, and integrate past performance information in arriving at efficacy appraisals; thus, such appraisals are not likely to be isomorphic with, or mechanically implanted by, past performance indicators. Research supports the role of self-efficacy as an independent predictor of performance and as a partial mediator of the effects of aptitude (or past performance) on career/academic outcomes (see Lent et al., in press).

Perhaps the key points of divergence between the two models reflect assumptive differences about self-regulation and cognition. While clearly encompassing social and cognitive phenomena, Krumboltz's SLT and recent work on career beliefs lean toward a rationalist perspective on the relationship between thought and behavior (cf. Mahoney & Lyddon, 1988). And, in attributing a primary causal role to past behavior and learning experiences, Mitchell and Krumboltz's (1990) scheme reflects a largely mechanistic view of human functioning. Bandura (1989) observed that, in such a view, "internal events are mainly products of external ones devoid of any causal efficacy. Because agency resides in environmental forces, the self system is merely a repository and conduit for them" (p. 1175).

In contrast, social cognitive theory attempts to take more of a cognitive constructivist approach to career development. As noted earlier, constructivist theories emphasize cognitive feed-forward mechanisms, highlighting the importance of anticipation, forethought, and the active construction of meaning, in interaction with environmental events. Such theories view people as proactive shapers of the environment, not merely as responders to external forces. Importantly, Krumboltz and Nichols (1990) recently suggested that Ford's (1987) living systems framework might be used to build a broader theoretical scaffolding for SLT. Pending future theoretical elaborations, this apparent move toward greater emphasis on cognitive and self-regulatory capacities within SLT signals the potential for reconciling some of its assumptive differences with the current social cognitive career perspective.

Super's Developmental Theory

Super's theory attaches primary importance to career stages, career maturity, the translation of the self-concept into a vocational identity, and life role salience (Super, 1980, 1990). Although earlier versions of Super's theory do not readily invite points of convergence with social cognitive theory, more recent reformulations, such as Super's redefinition of the self-concept, allow for the incorporation of self-efficacy percepts into the developmental model (Super, 1990).

Super's current theorizing holds that personal constructs compose an aspect of personality, and self-efficacy is afforded some notice, though it does not appear to play a significant role. Indeed, self-efficacy is regarded as one of many self-concept variables; it is on an even footing with and is not clearly differentiated from self-esteem or the multitude of other self-appraisal constructs. While Super (1990) still discusses self-concept systems largely in trait terms, his adoption of Kelly's (1955) personal constructs notion may suggest, at least to some extent, an emergent constructivist view of self-cognitions.

Super (1990) also proposes that learning theory is the "cement" binding together the various components of his archway model of career development, and he regards learning experiences as pivotal to the development of career-related personality variables such as interests. However, Super is not explicit in his explanation of learning mechanisms and, as in his discussion of self-concept systems, he appears to draw heavily from differential (trait) psychology in conceptualizing personality, interests, and values. A more adequate and faithful incorporation of social cognitive mechanisms within Super's theory may prove valuable. Such an integration could provide a useful microanalytic adjunct to Super's macroscopic view of development as well as a more precise consideration of social/ environmental influences on personal constructs. For example, social cognitive theory offers specific predictions about how self-efficacy develops and changes as a result of performance accomplishments, vicarious learning, verbal persuasion, and physiological and affective reactions (Lent et al., in press). Thus, learning experiences are explicitly related to personal constructs, in this case, self-efficacy.

Holland's Typology

There are also some important points of convergence and divergence with Holland's theory. For example, both models predict correspondence between career-related interests and choices, but social cognitive theory emphasizes important mediators (personal goals) and moderators (e.g., opportunity structures and support systems) of this relationship. Holland (1990) and his associates (Gottfredson, 1990) have begun to consider the integration of social learning and social cognitive variables into Holland's theory. For example, Holland (1990) has suggested that social learning theory may help account for the development of his six personality types.

Gottfredson (1990) singled out the self-efficacy construct as offering an important direction for advancing inquiry on Holland's formulations, though his definition of self-efficacy may be much broader and more inclusive than what is intended
by social cognitive theory. For instance, Gottfredson appeared to equate self-
efficacy with self-estimated ability, as indexed by the *Self-Directed Search* (SDS), and
argued that "self-estimates in the SDS are related to independent measures of
ability—but the correlations are small to moderate.... These self-estimates may be
stable measures of how respondents *see themselves* more than measures of ability"
(p. 3).

Leaving aside the conceptual and measurement differences between self-efficacy
and the SDS' self-estimated abilities, this statement does suggest an openness to
employing social cognitive variables within the rubric of research on Holland's
theory. Gottfredson (1990) also suggested that parental self-efficacy may be an
important factor in understanding the development of children's types. Though
promising, efforts to integrate Holland's theory and social cognitive formulations
are in their infancy, and there have been few research efforts thus far incorporating
or comparing these models (e.g., Lent, Brown, & Larkin, 1987).

In addition to helping flesh out the experiential determinants of person types and
the key mechanisms through which learning experiences may promote interests,
social cognitive theory may also be relevant to the study of P-E congruence (Holland,
1985). For instance, social cognitive mechanisms may help explain how people
resolve states of incongruence with their work environments. If congruence is partly
a matter of perception, then outcome expectations are likely to influence one's sense
of P-E fit. Coping efficacy (e.g., personal perceptions of one's ability to manage work
task or organizational challenges) may also affect one's level of perceived congruence, as well as the persistence of efforts designed to modify the work environment.
Research on such possibilities may simultaneously push the boundaries of Holland's
conceptualization of P-E fit (e.g., types as static entities) and add greater dimension
to social cognitive accounts of career change and adjustment.

Theory of Work Adjustment

There are several potential areas of convergence or complementarity between social
cognitive theory and Dawis and Lofquist's (1984) theory of work adjustment
(TWA). For instance, TWA specifies that the degree of correspondence or congruence between an individual's abilities and the ability requirements of the work
setting helps to determine important work outcomes, such as job tenure. Social
cognitive theory might further suggest that the relation of P-E ability correspondence to success or tenure may be moderated by perceived efficacy. That is, social
cognitive theory views ability as a dynamic rather than a fixed attribute, the exercise
of which depends partly on how people interpret and deploy their skills (Bandura,
1989). Thus, it may be that P-E ability correspondence is more strongly predictive
of work success/tenure when people possess strong versus weak efficacy percepts,
since robust self-efficacy may help maximize skill use.

As we noted in connection with Holland's theory, social cognitive theory may also complement TWA's view on the process by which people negotiate person-environment incongruence. We concur with TWA's view of work adjustment as a "continuous and dynamic process" of transaction between the individual and the work setting (Dawis & Lofquist, 1984, p. 55). TWA enumerates a variety of "adjustment style" variables that are used to promote or restore an adequate state of P-E fit. For example, individuals may differ in their characteristic "activeness" in trying to shape the work environment or in their ability to tolerate discorrespondence ("flexibility").

From a social cognitive perspective, the nature and persistence of one's efforts to cope with discorrespondence may depend importantly on one's sense of coping efficacy and outcome expectations. Those who doubt their ability to affect organizational change, for example, may be less likely to mount active efforts to modify their work environment; instead, they may be more likely to either tolerate discorrespondence or change environments. We do not rule out the possibility that dispositional factors such as activeness may influence responses to incongruence; however, it is likely that such factors interact with more situation- and domain-specific social cognitive mechanisms.

SUMMARY

We have sketched some recent developments in cognitive psychology that may offer valuable contributions to career development inquiry, including efforts to promote rapprochement among the major theories of career choice and development. Evolving notions about cognition and human agency—and larger shifts in our scientific paradigms (Borgen, 1992; Mahoney & Patterson, 1992)—make possible integrative models of career behavior that view people and their environments in more fluid, dynamic terms than do career models that are based exclusively on trait, psychodynamic, or behavioral conceptions.

We have also provided an overview of an evolving social cognitive career framework that attempts to build integrative linkages with existing career development models. This framework extends Bandura's (1986) general social cognitive theory to career development phenomena, endorses the constructivist view of the person as active shaper of his or her experience, and draws on findings from career/counseling, organizational, personality, and social psychology (Lent et al., in press). In particular, the theory highlights several sociocognitive mechanisms that enable the exercise of personal agency and traces key causal paths through which environmental and person factors (such as gender) may affect career interest, choice, and performance.

Finally, we have cited some ways in which this model may complement and converge with (as well as be distinct from) the "Big Four" career theories. Further refinements in, and study of, the social cognitive career model will help clarify its contribution to a larger, pantheoretic framework for understanding career behavior.

REFERENCES

Ajzen, I. (1988). *Attitudes, personality, and behavior.* Stony Stratford, UK: Open University Press.

Bandura, A. (1986). *Social foundations of thought and action: A social cognitive theory.* Englewood Cliffs, NJ: Prentice-Hall.

Bandura, A. (1989). Human agency in social cognitive theory. *American Psychologist, 44,* 1175–1184.

Barak, A. (1981). Vocational interests: A cognitive view. *Journal of Vocational Behavior, 19,* 1–14.

Borgen, F. H. (1991). Megatrends and milestones in vocational behavior: A 20-year counseling psychology retrospective. *Journal of Vocational Behavior, 39,* 263–290.

Borgen, F. H. (1992). Expanding scientific paradigms in counseling psychology. In S. D. Brown & R. W. Lent (Eds.), *Handbook of counseling psychology* (2d ed., pp. 111–139). New York: Wiley.

Casas, J. M. (1984). Policy, training, and research in counseling psychology: The racial/ethnic minority perspective. In S. D. Brown & R. W. Lent (Eds.), *Handbook of counseling psychology* (pp. 785–831). New York: Wiley.

Chartrand, J. M., & Camp, C. C. (1991). Advances in the measurement of career development constructs: A 20-year review. *Journal of Vocational Behavior, 39,* 1–39.

Dawis, R. V., & Lofquist, L. H. (1984). *A psychological theory of work adjustment: An individual differences model and its applications.* Minneapolis: University of Minnesota Press.

Dember, W. N. (1974). Motivation and the cognitive revolution. *American Psychologist, 29,* 161–168.

Ellis, A. (1962). *Reason and emotion in psychotherapy.* New York: Lyle Stuart.

Fiske, S. T., & Taylor, S. E. (1991). *Social cognition* (2d ed.). New York: McGraw-Hill.

Ford, D. H. (1987). *Humans as self-constructing living systems: A developmental perspective on personality and behavior.* Hillsdale, NJ: Erlbaum.

Gardner, H. (1985). *The mind's new science: A history of the cognitive revolution.* New York: Basic Books.

Gottfredson, G. D. (1990, August). *Applications and research using Holland's theory of careers: Where we would like to be and suggestions for getting there.* Paper presented at the annual meeting of the American Psychological Association, Boston.

Gottfredson, L. S. (1985). Role of self-concept in vocational theory. *Journal of Counseling Psychology, 32,* 159–162.

Guidano, V. F. (1987). *Complexity of the self: A developmental approach to psychopathology and therapy.* New York: Guilford.

Hackett, G., & Betz, N. E. (1981). A self-efficacy approach to the career development of women. *Journal of Vocational Behavior, 18,* 326–336.

Hackett, G., & Lent, R. W. (1992). Theoretical advances and current inquiry in career psychology. In S. D. Brown & R. W. Lent (Eds.), *Handbook of counseling psychology* (2d ed., pp. 419–451). New York: Wiley.

Hackett, G., Lent, R. W., & Greenhaus, J. H. (1991). Advances in vocational theory and research: A 20-year retrospective. *Journal of Vocational Behavior, 38,* 3–38.

Hansen, J. C. (1984). The measurement of vocational interests: Issues and future directions. In S. D. Brown & R. W. Lent (Eds.), *Handbook of counseling psychology* (pp. 99–136). New York: Wiley.

Heppner, P. P., & Frazier, P. A. (1992). Social psychological processes in psychotherapy: Extrapolating basic research to counseling psychology. In S. D. Brown & R. W. Lent (Eds.), *Handbook of counseling psychology* (2d ed., pp. 141–175). New York: Wiley.

Holland, J. L. (1985). *Making vocational choices: A theory of vocational personalities and work environments* (2d ed.). Englewood Cliffs, NJ: Prentice-Hall.

Holland, J. L. (1990, August). *Applications and research using Holland's theory of careers: Where are we now?* Paper presented at the annual meeting of the American Psychological Association, Boston.

Kelly, G. A. (1955). *The psychology of personal constructs.* New York: Norton.

Krumboltz, J. D., & Nichols, C. W. (1990). Integrating the social learning theory of career decision making. In W. B. Walsh & S. H. Osipow (Eds.), *Career counseling: Contemporary topics in vocational psychology* (pp. 159–192). Hillsdale, NJ: Erlbaum.

Lent, R. W., Brown, S. D., & Hackett, G. (in press). Toward a unified social cognitive theory of career and academic interest, choice, and performance. *Journal of Vocational Behavior.*

Lent, R. W., Brown, S. D., & Larkin, K. C. (1987). Comparison of three theoretically derived variables in predicting career and academic behavior: Self-efficacy, interest congruence, and consequence thinking. *Journal of Counseling Psychology, 34,* 293–298.

Lent, R. W., & Hackett, G. (1987). Career self-efficacy: Empirical status and future directions [Monograph]. *Journal of Vocational Behavior, 30,* 347–382.

Lent, R. W., Larkin, K. C., & Brown, S. D. (1989). Relation of self-efficacy to inventoried vocational interests. *Journal of Vocational Behavior, 34,* 279–288.

Locke, E. A., & Latham, G. P. (1990). *A theory of goal setting and task performance.* Englewood Cliffs, NJ: Prentice-Hall.

Mahoney, M. J. (1985). Psychotherapy and human change processes. In M. J. Mahoney & A. Freeman (Eds.), *Cognition and psychotherapy* (pp. 3–48). New York: Plenum

Mahoney, M. J. (1991). *Human change processes: The scientific foundations of psychotherapy.* New York: Basic Books.

Mahoney, M. J., & Lyddon, W. J. (1988). Recent developments in cognitive approaches to counseling and psychotherapy. *The Counseling Psychologist, 16,* 190–234.

Mahoney, M. J., & Patterson, K. M. (1992). Changing theories of change: Recent developments in counseling. In S. D. Brown & R. W. Lent (Eds.), *Handbook of counseling psychology* (2d ed., pp. 665–689). New York: Wiley.

Markus, H. (1990). On splitting the universe. *Psychological Science, 1,* 181–185.

Markus, H., & Nurius, P. (1986). Possible selves. *American Psychologist, 41,* 954–969.

Meece, J. L., Wigfield, A., & Eccles, J. S. (1990). Predictors of math anxiety and its influence on young adolescents' course enrollment intentions and performance in mathematics. *Journal of Educational Psychology, 82,* 60–70.

Mitchell, L. K., & Krumboltz, J. D. (1990). Social learning approach to career decision making: Krumboltz's theory. In D. Brown, L. Brooks, & Associates, *Career choice and development: Applying contemporary theories to practice* (2d ed., pp. 145–196). San Francisco: Jossey-Bass.

Neimeyer, G. J. (1988). Cognitive integration and differentiation in vocational behavior. *The Counseling Psychologist, 16,* 440–475.

Nurius, P. S. (1986). Reappraisal of the self-concept and implications for counseling. *Journal of Counseling Psychology, 33,* 429–438.

Osipow, S. H. (1990). Convergence in theories of career choice and development: Review and prospect. *Journal of Vocational Behavior, 36,* 122–131.

Pryor, R. G. L. (1985). Toward exorcising the self-concept from psychology: Some comments on Gottfredson's circumscription/compromise theory. *Journal of Counseling Psychology, 32,* 154–158.

Rounds, J. B., & Tracey, T. J. (1990). From trait-and-factor to person-environment fit counseling: Theory and process. In W. B. Walsh & S. H. Osipow (Eds.), *Career counseling: Contemporary topics in vocational psychology* (pp. 1–44). Hillsdale, NJ: Erlbaum.

Strong, E. K., Jr. (1943). *Vocational interests of men and women.* Stanford, CA: Stanford University Press.

Super, D. E. (1953). A theory of vocational development. *American Psychologist, 8,* 185–190.

Super, D. E. (1980). A life-span, life-space approach to career development. *Journal of Vocational Behavior, 16,* 282–298.

Super, D. E. (1990). A life-span, life-space approach to career development. In D. Brown, L. Brooks, & Associates, *Career choice and development: Applying contemporary theories to practice* (2d ed., pp. 197–261). San Francisco: Jossey-Bass.

Unger, R. K. (1979). Toward a redefinition of sex and gender. *American Psychologist, 34,* 1085–1094.

Vondracek, F. W., Lerner, R. M., & Schulenberg, J. E. (1986). *Career development: A life-span developmental approach.* Hillsdale, NJ: Erlbaum.

Watson, D., & Clark, L. A. (1984). Negative affectivity: The disposition to experience aversive emotional states. *Psychological Bulletin, 96,* 465–490.

Weimer, W. B. (1977). A conceptual framework for cognitive psychology: Motor theories of the mind. In R. Shaw & J. Bransford (Eds.), *Perceiving, acting, and knowing* (pp. 267–311). Hillsdale, NJ: Erlbaum.

Weiner, B. (1990). History of motivational research in education. *Journal of Educational Psychology, 82,* 616–622.

Williamson, E. G. (1939). *How to counsel students.* New York: McGraw-Hill.

CHAPTER EIGHT

Career Development in Cultural Context

The Role of Gender, Race, Class, and Sexual Orientation

Louise F. Fitzgerald
University of Illinois

Nancy E. Betz
Ohio State University

THIS BOOK AIMS to build on the observations of Osipow (1990), exploring points of potentially useful commonality, or convergence, between and among the major theories of career development and vocational adjustment. Our chapter begins by pointing out and elaborating on an ironic aspect of current theoretical convergence, namely, the general lack of utility of major career theories to large segments of the population. We proceed to discuss possible unifying constructs and associated research directions, and conclude by offering suggestions for theory expansion and theory convergence.

CURRENT CONCEPTUAL, THEORETICAL, AND EMPIRICAL INADEQUACIES

There are at least three ways in which theory or theories and their associated empirical literatures may be inadequate for large numbers of people. The first is the relevance of the concept of career development itself; the second is a lack of attention to large groups; and the third has to do with theoretical postulates that fail to take structural and cultural factors into account.

Concept of Career Development

The first point we raise has to do with the very concept of career development itself. In other words, is career development a meaningful concept in the lives of the majority of the population? As Smith (1983) noted some time ago, for millions of people in this country a permanent job will never become a reality: "Many of these individuals are grouped in what has become the underclass—that large group of people who are so removed from the mainstream of America that they are no longer considered part of the traditional class structure" (p. 163). As she noted, this underclass includes not only the *unemployed* and the *inactive*—that very poignant term for those who are not employed, not in school, and not looking for a job—but also for thousands of people who are employed, but who hold jobs that do not provide for full-time meaningful employment, upgrading, mobility, and the other factors that represent the basic underpinnings of career development as we understand it.

Rather than expanding the phenomena to which our theories can reasonably be expected to apply, we suggest that it may be more appropriate to recognize the limitations of these theories, and a first step may well be to reevaluate the notion that work is psychologically central to the lives of all individuals, and to accept the reality that many jobs are unable to provide for needs that are any more complex than those for subsistence and the structuring of time. Warnath (1975) made this point nearly 20 years ago when he wrote that

> vocational psychologists have centered their theories of vocational decision making on the individual. They have assumed an open market, the dignity of all work and the person's ability to operate free of environmental constraints. As leading advocates of populism and romantic individualism, vocational theorists have concentrated their attention almost exclusively on those characteristics of the individual that can be exploited in the search for self-realization. (p. 425)

We suggest that for much of the population, economic survival may be a far more relevant issue than self-realization, a point that most of us manage to overlook at least in part because such individuals rarely find their way into our studies (a point that we revisit below).

Particularly in these difficult economic times, grandiose ideas such as optimal career development are reduced in importance; environmental constraints, economic contingencies, and the grinding cycle of poverty that envelopes much of the urban poor (e.g., see Ferraro, 1984; Sidel, 1986) constrain the explanatory power of theoretical career development formulations, limiting their utility and relevance for many people's lives. Disregard of the constraints placed on these formulations by macroenvironmental variables appears to us to represent a major limitation of current theories.

Homogeneity and Empirical Neglect

Career development theories have always had the most to say about the smallest segment of the population, that is, white, middle class heterosexual men. Although it is true that our knowledge of women's career development has grown immensely in the last two decades, this increase has not been matched by anything approaching meaningful growth in our understanding of the vocational behavior of non-Caucasian men and women, and nonprofessional workers. Similarly, until very recently, the possibility that gay men and lesbians might face particular issues and/or unique barriers to career development was largely ignored. Such individuals continue to be relatively invisible in the vocational literature, despite the fact that by most accounts they constitute 10 percent of the population.

To be fair, this has more to do with researcher behavior than with the theories themselves; there is no intrinsic reason to assume a priori that constructs such as congruence, career stages, and so forth are necessarily less applicable to non-white or working-class individuals. The point is that we simply do not know, mainly because we have not asked.

The following data help illustrate these points. African-American and Hispanic individuals now comprise 16 percent of the population and nearly 20 percent of the labor force. Although the labor force itself was projected to increase by only 19 percent between 1986 and 1990, the increase for African-Americans was expected to be 29 percent, for Hispanics, 74 percent, and for Asian and Pacific Islanders, 70 percent. Against this backdrop, it is instructive to consider the main data base upon which the vocational behavior literature is based. For example, the entire 1987 volume of the *Journal of Vocational Behavior* included data on only 95 individuals who could be identified as non-Caucasian. Of the 32 empirical articles, less than 20 percent (or six articles) even reported participant ethnicity. Of these, two studies reported that all their participants were white; the other four studies reported a total of 95 blacks, Hispanics, and Asian-Americans. As only one of these studies analyzed the data by race, the only specific data reported on non-white individuals had to do with five African-American college undergraduates.

In the same year, the *Journal of Counseling Psychology* published seven articles that could reasonably be classified within the category of career development. Four did not report the racial/ethnic composition of their samples; the other three reported data on a total of 62 minority individuals. Again, only a single study actually analyzed the data by race—reporting information on 33 African-American college students. Simply put, of the 39 articles in the *Journal of Vocational Behavior* and the *Journal of Counseling Psychology* that appeared in 1987, 5 percent reported results for race (the same percentage that Gottfredson found in 1982)—a total data base of 38 black college students. Four years later, the results for 1991 were only marginally better. The relative representation of minority individuals in the labor market and in vocational behavior research is depicted heuristically in figure 1.

Let us consider another set of statistics. In 1989, 21 percent of the population over the age of 25 had a college degree; for African-Americans, that figure was 11.8 percent, and for Hispanics, it was 9.9 percent. In that same year, the *Journal of Vocational Behavior* published 35 empirical articles, 14 (40%) of which studied college student samples. Of the 18 samples that included working adults, nine were composed entirely of professional level, presumably college-educated adults; others

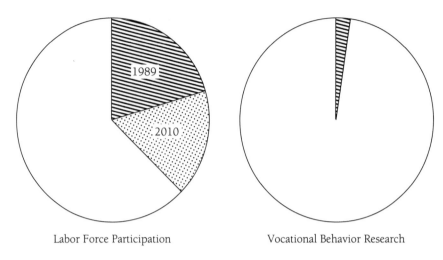

Labor Force Participation   Vocational Behavior Research

FIGURE 1   Actual and Projected Minority Labor Force Participation by Year
Versus Proportion of Vocational Psychology Research Devoted
to Ethnic and Racial Minorities

were of mixed populations; and only five (14%) could be clearly identified as other than professional-level employees. Of the 12 career development studies published that year by the *Journal of Counseling Psychology,* 75 percent examined college students or professional individuals, one study examined homemakers (predominantly middle or upper middle class), one studied vocational counseling clients, and one examined a mixed working sample.

To oversimplify a bit for purposes of illustration, less than 25 percent of the work force possesses a college degree, whereas more than 75 percent do not (Herr, 1992). However, the research base in the major career development journals is more or less reversed—approximately 80 percent of the data base is comprised of college students and individuals with college and professional degrees. These relative proportions are diagrammed in figure 2.

Such figures justify our conclusion that our knowledge of career choice is generally limited to college students and those who are college bound, individuals who are mostly white and middle class. When we do include minorities in our samples, they disappear from the data set by virtue of not being identified or analyzed. It is fair to say that we know almost nothing about the career choice process in the majority of the population: those who do not attend college, are not white, and are of lower socioeconomic status. Similarly, our knowledge of the career adjustment years is tied very closely to samples of professionals—engineers, managers, college professors, attorneys, and the like.

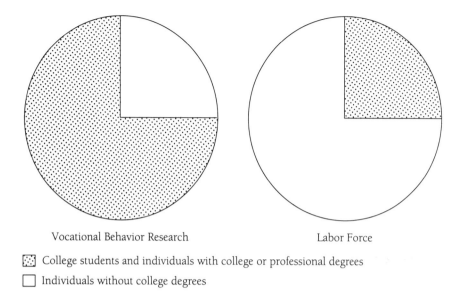

Vocational Behavior Research   Labor Force

::: College students and individuals with college or professional degrees

☐ Individuals without college degrees

FIGURE 2   Representation of Populations in Vocational Behavior Research
            Versus Their Numbers in the Labor Force

Inattention to Structural and Cultural Factors

The third problem we raise is that available theories lack systematic explanation of the role of structural and cultural factors in shaping individuals' vocational behavior, despite the fact that such factors can be shown to influence each and every unifying construct that has been suggested in the literature. Table 1 depicts a matrix of structural and cultural factors that have been demonstrated to affect vocational behavior. Four critical contextual variables are displayed as headings at the top of the table, and relevant cultural and structural factors related to each appear below the variables in columns.

Structural factors are characteristics of the society or organization, including its members, that limit access to or opportunities in the occupational and/or organizational environment. Discrimination and poverty are examples. *Cultural factors* are beliefs and attitudes commonly found among group members—often these are socialized by society (i.e., occupational gender stereotypes, internalized homophobia), but after internalization they serve as self-perpetuating barriers to the individual. Each of these factors has been found to affect vocational behavior in important, systematic, and predictable ways, yet each is generally ignored by the major theories of such behavior, a situation that limits their power for understanding much of the population. As space does not permit a comprehensive review of the effects of structural and cultural factors on career choice and development, the following is viewed as illustrative rather than exhaustive.

TABLE 1   Examples of Structural and Cultural Factors Affecting Vocational Behavior

Gender	Race/Ethnicity	Social Class	Sexual Orientation
Structural Factors			
Discrimination	Poverty	Poverty	Discrimination
Null environment	Discrimination	Discrimination	Myths and stereotypes
Home-Work interface	Lack of education	Lack of education	
Occupational stereotypes	Racial stereotypes		
Sexual harassment	Racial harassment		Harassment; "Gay bashing"
Cultural Factors			
Gender-role socialization	Collectivism vs individualism	Work irrelevance	Internalized homophobia
Motherhood mandate	Non-Eurocentric value systems	Culture of poverty	
	Acculturation Racial/Ethnic identity		
Occupational sex stereotypes	Racial stereotypes		

Gender

Beginning with gender, the focus of considerable recent research (see Betz & Fitzgerald, 1987; Walsh & Osipow, 1994), table 2 depicts some of the structural and cultural factors that have been shown to influence women's vocational behavior, relationships between each factor and specific theoretical criteria, and the process or mechanism through which each factor is thought to exert its influence. As shown in the table, women's career development is affected in specific ways by a variety of structural factors, such as discrimination and sexual harassment, as well as by such cultural constraints as occupational gender stereotypes, gender-role socialization, and the dictates of the "motherhood mandate" (Russo, 1976).

As stated by Osipow (1990), the major theories of career development all seem to adopt some type of "matching" or person-environment fit approach to career development (e.g., Holland's "congruence," Super's self-concept implementation, etc.), yet it is this matching or fit that often fails to describe women's career choices. As reviewed by Betz (1992), Kerr and Maresh (1992), and others, gifted women in particular fail to pursue occupations at a level commensurate with their intellectual abilities. Kerr and Maresh (1992) discussed the "extraordinary gap between aptitude and achievement in gifted women" and described the career development

TABLE 2   Structural and Cultural Effects of Gender on Women's Vocational Behavior

Factor	Process	Criterion
Structural		
Discrimination	Inhibition of ability/ Requirement match	Satisfactoriness Realism
Null environment	Inhibition of ability/ Requirement match	Satisfactoriness
	Truncation of range of interests	Realism
Sexual harassment	Job loss; job change; educational loss; change of field	Tenure Satisfaction Congruence Self-efficacy Self-concept
Home-Work interface	Inhibition of ability/ Requirement match	Realism Satisfactoriness Satisfaction (?) Work force participation
Cultural		
Gender-role socialization	Inhibition of interest/ Field match	Congruence Satisfaction
	Inhibition/Facilitation of ability/Requirement match	Satisfactoriness Realism

of young gifted women as the "gentle downward spiral" of self-esteem and career aspirations through adolescence and young adulthood.

An illustration of limitations of trait-and-factor theories of adult career adjustment was Fitzgerald and Rounds' (1993) analysis of the theory of work adjustment. One of the postulates of the theory is that satisfactoriness (i.e., vocational success) results from the match between individual abilities and relevant job requirements. If the match is a good one, the result is tenure, and the individual remains in that position; ability greater than that required should lead to promotion, whereas too little ability should predict job failure, demotion, transfer, or termination. We know from decades of research that the distribution of general ability is similar for women and men; thus, the theory of work adjustment would predict that the distribution of occupational level should also be similar, that is, similar numbers of men and women should be found at various occupational levels. This is not the case, in that women are much more often found in traditionally female, lower-level occupations, which reflects the pervasive underutilization of women's abilities in both educational and occupational levels attained (Betz, 1992; Kerr & Maresh, 1992). Reducing the extent to which there is an ability/requirement match, or more generally, person-environment congruence (e.g., Holland's model also predicts a match between ability and job level) are the factors proposed in table 2. Stated simply, the dictates of the interface between home and work and the motherhood mandate (Russo, 1976), along with the effects of discrimination, combine to ensure that large numbers of women are found in jobs and occupations for which they are overqualified.

An additional illustration of the failure of trait-and-factor theories to take context into account is the finding that one of the most powerful factors affecting tenure is sexual harassment. In 1981, a government study revealed that, in a two-year period alone, 36,000 women left their jobs in the federal government due to sexual harassment (U.S. Merit Systems Protection Board, 1981). In another study, 50 percent of the women who filed harassment complaints were fired (Coles, 1986). The problem is particularly severe in certain fields (science, the blue-collar trades, and other nontraditional areas), where women are routinely "driven out" (Fitzgerald, 1993). In the face of such data, assertions that women's vocational success and tenure are solely a function of the ability/requirement match are woefully unconvincing.

The other major dependent variable in the theory of work adjustment, satisfaction, is based on the correspondence between work needs and reinforcer systems. However, Fitzgerald and Rounds (1993) noted the complete absence in this equation of one set of organizational conditions that can "make or break" many women's job satisfaction, that is, the interface between home and work; this important interface can be facilitated (or not) by such conditions as flextime, on-site childcare, family leave policies, and cafeteria-style benefits packages. Thus, women's job satisfaction and, consequently, tenure, are probably not as well accounted for as would be predicted by the congruence of the 20 or so individual vocational needs measured by the *Minnesota Importance Questionnaire* (MIQ) and the reinforcer system of the occupation in which a woman is employed.

The foregoing examples are illustrative rather than exhaustive of the ways structural and cultural factors can reduce the applicability of current theory to women's career development. It is, of course, not only the theory of work adjustment that has failed to take these factors into account, but other theories of career development as well.

Although most research attention to date has been paid to structural and cultural barriers affecting women, there has also been increasing cognizance of the potential lack of applicability of career theories as a function of race and ethnicity, social class, and affectional/sexual orientation. It is to these factors that we now turn.

Race/Ethnicity

Bingham and Ward (1992) and Bowman (1992) discussed the lack of utility of current career theory and research to members of racial/ethnic minority groups. For example, theories based on individualistic values versus collectivistic value orientations fail to meaningfully include the group and family-oriented value systems predominant in many minority groups. Leong (1992) provided the following concrete example: A major tenet of Super's theory is that of self-concept implementation; however, in some minority groups, occupations are chosen based on the goals of preservation of the family and culture of origin rather than to implement one's self-concept.

More generally, examination of table 1 suggests several additional factors that may reduce the utility of career theories for members of racial/ethnic minority groups. Lack of educational opportunities oftentimes reduces the extent to which minority individuals are able to fully develop their abilities and talents, and the effects of discrimination have substantial adverse effects on minority career development (Hotchkiss & Borrow, 1990). Like occupational gender stereotypes, racial stereotypes lead to prejudice and, often, to discrimination from others. Further, it leads to self-selection into or out of occupations based on beliefs of racial appropriateness. For example, many young black women grew up believing that the only professional occupation open to them was teaching, and many Asian-Americans have been expected to pursue careers in science and engineering, regardless of individual suitability. Another important aspect of racial stereotyping, as noted by Leong (1985), is the myth of Asians as the "model minority," the idea that they have made it in society and experience no prejudice or discrimination and, thus, need no special attention from career educators or counselors.

Overlapping significantly with both minority and lower socioeconomic status groups is the large number of individuals who will not obtain college degrees. As mentioned earlier in this chapter, the vocational literature has largely ignored the 75 percent of high school graduates who will not complete college (50% will never even begin higher education). This group is the focus of a major new research and intervention effort of the Grant Foundation (1988) and the American Counseling Association (Herr, 1992). Calling these young people "work-bound youth" rather than the more often used terms "noncollege-bound" or "the forgotten half" (Grant Foundation, 1988) highlights the need for job training and programs for facilitating the school-to-job transition. The structural and cultural barriers faced by these young people (e.g., see Hotchkiss & Borrow, 1990) warrant theoretical consideration as well as extensive and appropriate intervention.

Sexual Orientation

Finally, a recent direction in career counseling research has been a focus on the unique problems faced by gay men and lesbians in their career choice and adjustment, including discrimination and negative stereotyping (Hetherington, Hillerbrand, & Etringer, 1989). For example, gays may be discouraged from pursuing teaching careers because of harmful myths and their lack of access to military occupations is the topic of much current debate. Morgan and Brown (1991) discussed areas of inapplicability of theories of women's career development to lesbians. Ironically, however, lesbians may be a group of women for whom traditional trait-and-factor theories of career choice may be more applicable (in comparison to other women) because most lesbians assume that they will need to support themselves and plan accordingly, rather than making work and career plans "contingent" on when and whom they marry, as many young heterosexual women continue to do (see *Educated in Romance*, as cited in Kerr & Maresh, 1992). The fact, though, that one-third of lesbians are mothers, and between one-fourth to one-half of gay men are natural fathers (Bozett, 1989; Fassinger, 1991), means that issues having to do with childcare and parental leave policies may be no less important to job satisfaction and tenure among gay men and lesbians than they are to heterosexual parents.

IMPLICATIONS FOR THEORY EXPLICATION

The preceding discussion illustrates the potential range of complexities of career choice and adjustment for members of underrepresented or oppressed groups. Before proceeding to a discussion of the theoretical implications of these problems, however, it is important to acknowledge that although limited in utility for many, the major career theories have had tremendous heuristic and practical utility. Fitzgerald and Rounds (1993) noted that more than 250 studies of the theory of work adjustment confirm that the theory does have important implications for career counseling. Similarly, a voluminous literature exists supporting the general utility of Holland's theory (see Hackett & Lent, 1992, for a recent review), and there appears to be continuing strong interest in the social learning theories of career behavior (Hackett & Lent, 1992). Our suggestions for theory explication and development should not be taken to imply that such theories are useless, but rather as proposals to enhance the theoretical and applied utility of the theoretical base that currently exists.

Given this, we suggest that it is important to enhance the applicability of career theories to those individuals traditionally overlooked, and that such examination could usefully begin by concentrating on major individual difference categories (we suggest gender, race, ethnicity, social class, and sexual/affectional orientation) and the structural and cultural factors and conditions that, in one way or another, influence the theoretical and applied utility of career theories. Such a project involves at least three possible approaches.

First, the applicability of a given theory to a particular group can be examined. For example, there has been some interest in examining the validity of Holland's theory for African-Americans. Walsh and his colleagues conducted a series of studies investigating the comparative validity of Holland's theory for black and white employed men and women (e.g., Greenlee, Damarin, & Walsh, 1988; Sheffey, Bingham, & Walsh, 1986; Walsh, Bingham, Horton, & Spokane, 1979). More recently, a series of articles in a special issue of the *Journal of Vocational Behavior* addressed the cross-cultural utility of Holland's postulates regarding the structure of interests (Fouad & Dancer, 1992; Swanson, 1992), suggesting that hexagonal order, although not necessarily shape, is invariant across different populations, including African-Americans and Hispanics (although, once again, even these studies focused only on college students and professionals). Holland and Gottfredson (1992) suggest that we also need research on the *effects* of interest inventories on these groups.

Second, research using individual differences and structural or cultural variables as moderator variables (Ghiselli, Campbell, & Zedeck, 1981; Zedeck, 1971) could provide information concerning groups or characteristics of people that reduce or increase the predictive validity or utility of a theory. Not only would such research be informative regarding a specific theory, but it may well be that there are commonalities across theories in the specific variables delimiting their usefulness.

For example, Wolfe and Betz (1981) examined the extent to which gender role variables moderated the congruence of Holland personality and occupational environment choice in college women. They reported that strong relationships with nontraditional choices were significantly more likely than traditional choices to be congruent with the woman's measured interests. Because the "masculinity" of gender role orientation was associated with nontraditional preferences, it, too, was strongly related to congruence. In a replication and extension of that study, Betz, Heesacker, and Shuttleworth (1990) concluded that college women high in instrumentality and those making nontraditional choices were more likely to be using their abilities in career choices. Overall, this research and similar studies reviewed by Betz and Fitzgerald (1987) suggest that available career theories may be most useful for women who have surmounted the effects of traditional gender-role socialization. Thus, the use of such indicators as degree of instrumentality or profeminist attitudes (see Beere, 1990, for an encyclopedic coverage of measures of gender role attitudes and attitudes towards feminism) would likely assist us in more clearly delimiting the utility of theoretical postulates. For racial/ethnic minority groups, the potential moderating roles of acculturation and racial identity development have been widely discussed (see Bingham & Ward, 1992; Helms, 1989; Leong, in press) but not yet incorporated into our theories of career development.

Third, and most importantly, we suggest that each career theory be subject to a careful and detailed analysis of the roles of structural and cultural factors in both the conceptualization and measurement of its important variables, both dependent and independent. Fitzgerald and Rounds (1993) have recently analyzed the applicability of the theory of work adjustment to women using this model, and their analysis leads not only to constructive suggestions for changes in the theory and measurement models but also to a reaffirmation of the basic soundness of the theory. This analysis is a beginning, but systematic attention to other "special groups" and other theories is badly needed.

What we are suggesting, then, is that the concept of structural and cultural factors provides an overlay to, or new perspective for, the consideration of career theories. It is not a theory itself, but rather a unifying perspective or context within which to examine and modify current theoretical formulations. And it is important to note that our emphasis on structural and cultural factors as a unifying integrative concept is not new, although previous discussions have used different terminology. For example, the concept of social structural and cultural factors in career choice have much in common with related ideas of barriers to career development, as proposed by Crites (1976) and as applied especially to the understanding of women's career development by Farmer (1976), Harmon (1977), and later Betz and Fitzgerald (1987). Related to the notion of barriers is Gottfredson's (1986) concept of risk factors in career choice as especially useful in understanding problems faced by members of special groups, which include gender, racial/ethnic minorities, and handicapping conditions. Gottfredson presented a diagnostic framework that might be used for assessment and intervention in career counseling, and Osipow (1990) suggested that all career theories should be modified to include consideration of barriers to the implementation of desirable career choices. We believe that the framework of structural and cultural factors may be most useful because it doesn't assume that all differences are harmful (as do barriers and risk factors by definition), but rather that groups differ from the "white male model" in important ways that require consideration and validation from career theorists and counselors as well as in experiencing some forms of disadvantage, oppression, and unnecessary restriction.

In addition, it seems to us that a focus on structural and cultural factors as a focal point for both theoretical development and integration meshes well with integrative concepts suggested by others. For example, Lent and Hackett's (1992, this volume) emphasis on self-cognitions in general and self-efficacy expectations in particular fits well with an emphasis on gender, as it was the limiting effects of traditional gender-role socialization for women's career-related self-efficacy expectations that motivated Hackett and Betz (1981; Betz & Hackett, 1981) to first propose the utility of Bandura's self-efficacy concept to career development. Lent and Hackett (1992) also included outcome expectations in the theoretical framework they proposed, and these, too, may be negatively affected among groups experiencing prejudice or discrimination in a largely sexist, racist, and homophobic society.

SUMMARY

In summary, we believe that the concepts of structural and cultural factors can serve as an overarching focal point for theoretical and conceptual analyses and research aimed at making our career theories more relevant for all people in our society. Krumboltz has noted in this volume that theories by necessity avoid or ignore certain complexities. When "certain complexities" affect the majority of the work force, we suggest that the cost to science and practice of ignoring these complexities is simply too great to tolerate. Given the level of maturity attained by the major theories of career development, incorporation of the complexities of gender, race/ethnicity, and structural and cultural factors more generally, offers promise of enriching both individual theories and the entire conceptual basis of career psychology. As a final note, we emphasize that we consider our intellectual feet to be still firmly planted in the individual differences tradition and suggest that race, gender, ethnicity, and so on have always been core concepts in differential psycholgy (Betz & Fitzgerald, 1993). It is our position that taking such variables into account enriches rather than vitiates the individual differences tradition that each person be considered as an individual, in all of his or her richness and complexity.

REFERENCES

Beere, C. (1990). *Gender roles.* New York: Greenwood.

Betz, N. (1992, August). Theory and concepts in the study of women's career development. In W. Walsh (Chair), *Contemporary developments in career counseling for women.* Symposium conducted at the annual meeting of the American Psychological Association, Washington, DC.

Betz, N., & Fitzgerald, L. (1987). *The career psychology of women.* New York: Academic Press.

Betz, N., & Fitzgerald, L. (1993). Individuality and diversity: Theory and research in counseling psychology. *Annual Review of Psychology, 44,* 343–386.

Betz, N., & Hackett, G. (1981). A self-efficacy approach to the career development of women. *Journal of Counseling Psychology, 28,* 399–410.

Betz, N., Heesacker, R., & Shuttleworth, C. (1990). Moderators of the congruence and realism of major and occupational plans in college students. *Journal of Counseling Psychology, 37,* 269–276.

Bingham, R., & Ward, C. (1992, August). Career counseling with ethnic minority women. In W. Walsh (Chair), *Contemporary developments in career counseling for women.* Symposium conducted at the annual meeting of the American Psychological Association, Washington, DC.

Bowman, S. (1992, August). Career intervention strategies for ethnic minorities. In M. Savickas (Chair), *Multicultural career counseling.* Symposium conducted at the annual meeting of the American Psychological Association, Washington, DC.

Bozett, F. (1989). Gay fathers: A review of the literature. *Homosexuality, 18,* 137–162.

Coles, F. (1986). Forced to quit: Sexual harassment complaints and agency response. *Sex Roles, 14,* 81–95.

Crites, J. (1976). A comprehensive model of career development in early adulthood. *Journal of Vocational Behavior, 9,* 105–118.

Farmer, H. (1976). What inhibits achievement and career motivation in women? *The Counseling Psychologist, 6,* 12–14.

Fassinger, R. (1991). The hidden minority: Issues and challenges in working with lesbian women and gay men. *The Counseling Psychologist, 19,* 157–176.

Ferraro, G. (1984). Bridging the wage gap: Pay equity and job evaluations. *American Psychologist, 39,* 1166–1170.

Fitzgerald, L. (1993). *The last great open secret: Sexual harassment of women in the workplace and academia.* Washington, DC: Federation of Behavioral, Psychological and Cognitive Sciences.

Fitzgerald, L., & Rounds, J. (1993). Women and work: Theory encounters reality. In W. Walsh & S. Osipow (Eds.), *Career counseling for women* (pp. 327–354). Hillsdale, NJ: Erlbaum.

Fouad, N., & Dancer, L. (1992). Cross-cultural structure of interests: Mexico and the United States. *Journal of Vocational Behavior, 40,* 129–143.

Gottfredson, L. (1982). Vocational research priorities. *The Counseling Psychologist, 10,* 69–84.

Gottfredson, L. (1986). Special groups and the beneficial use of vocational interest inventories. In W. Walsh & S. Osipow (Eds.), *Advances in vocational psychology: The assessment of interests* (pp. 127–198). Hillsdale, NJ: Erlbaum.

Ghiselli, E., Campbell, J., & Zedeck, S. (1981). *Measurement theory for the behavioral sciences.* New York: Free Press.

Grant Foundation. (1988). *The forgotten half: Non-college bound youth in America.* Washington, DC: William T. Grant Foundation Commission on Work, Family, and Citizenship.

Greenlee, S., Damarin, F., & Walsh, W. (1988). Congruence and differentiation among black and white males in two non-college degree occupations. *Journal of Vocational Behavior, 32,* 298–306.

Hackett, G., & Lent, R. (1992). Theoretical advances and current inquiry in career psychology. In S. Brown & R. Lent (Eds.), *Handbook of counseling psychology* (2d ed., pp. 419–452). New York: Wiley.

Hackett, G., & Betz, N. (1981). A self-efficacy approach to the career development of women. *Journal of Vocational Behavior, 18,* 326–339.

Harmon, L. (1977). Career counseling for women. In E. Rawlings & D. Carter (Eds.), *Psychotherapy for women* (pp. 197–206). Springfield, IL: Thomas.

Helms, J. (1989). Considering some methodological issues in racial identity counseling research. *The Counseling Psychologist, 17*(2), 227–252.

Herr, E. (1992). *The school counselor and comprehensive programs for work-bound youth.* Alexandria, VA: American Counseling Association.

Hetherington, C., Hillerbrand, E., & Etringer, B. D. (1989). Career counseling with gay men: Issues and recommendations for research. *Journal of Counseling and Development, 67,* 452–454.

Holland, J., & Gottfredson, G. (1992). Studies of the hexagonal model: An evaluation (or, the perils of stacking the perfect hexagon). *Journal of Vocational Behavior, 40,* 158–170.

Hotchkiss, L., & Borrow, H. (1990). Sociological perspectives on work and career development. In D. Brown & L. Brooks (Eds.), *Career choice and development* (2d ed., pp. 262–307). San Francisco: Jossey-Bass.

Kerr, B., & Maresh, S. (1992, August). *Career counseling for gifted women.* In W. Walsh (Chair), *Contemporary developments in career counseling for women.* Symposium conducted at the annual meeting of the American Psychological Association, Washington, DC.

Lent, R., & Hackett, G. (1992, April). *Self-cognitions and personal agency in career development: Pantheoretical connections.* Paper presented at the Conference on Convergence in Theories of Career Choice and Development, East Lansing, MI.

Leong, F. (1985). Career development of Asian Americans. *Journal of College Student Personnel, 26,* 539–546.

Leong, F. (1992, August). The career counseling process with racial/ethnic minorities: Similarities and differences as illustrated by the case of Asian Americans. In M. Savickas (Chair), *Multicultural career counseling.* Symposium conducted at the annual meeting of the American Psychological Association, Washington, DC.

Leong, F. (Ed.). (in press). *Career development of racial and ethnic minorities.* Hillsdale, NJ: Erlbaum.

Morgan, K., & Brown, L. (1991). Lesbian career development, work behavior, and vocational counseling. *The Counseling Psychologist, 19,* 273–291.

Osipow, S. (1990). Convergence in theories of career choice and development: Review and prospect. *Journal of Vocational Behavior, 36,* 122–131.

Russo, N. (1976). The motherhood mandate. *Journal of Social Issues, 32,* 143–153.

Sheffey, M., Bingham, R., & Walsh, W. (1986). Concurrent validity of Holland's theory for college educated black men. *Journal of Multicultural Counseling and Development, 14,* 149–159.

Sidel, R. (1986). *Women and children last.* New York: Penguin.

Smith, E. (1983). Issues in racial minorities' career behavior. In W. Walsh & S. Osipow (Eds.), *Handbook of vocational psychology* (pp. 161–122). Hillsdale, NJ: Erlbaum.

Swanson, J. (1992). The structure of vocational interests for African-American college students. *Journal of Vocational Behavior, 40,* 144–157.

U.S. Merit Systems Protection Board. (1981). *Sexual harassment in the federal workplace: Is it a problem?* Washington, DC: U.S. Government Printing Office.

Walsh, W., Bingham, R., Horton, J., & Spokane, A. (1979). Holland's theory and college-degreed working black and white women. *Journal of Vocational Behavior, 15,* 217–223.

Walsh, W., & Osipow, S. (1994). *Advances in vocational psychology: Career counseling for women.* Hillsdale, NJ: Erlbaum.

Warnath, C. (1975). Vocational theories: Direction to nowhere. *Personnel and Guidance Journal, 53,* 422–428.

Wolfe, L., & Betz, N. (1981). Traditionality of choice and sex role identification as moderators of the congruence of occupational choice in college women. *Journal of Vocational Behavior, 19,* 61–77.

Zedeck, S. (1971). Problems with the use of "moderator" variables. *Psychological Bulletin, 76,* 295–310.

CHAPTER NINE

The Resolution of Incongruence and the Dynamics of Person-Environment Fit

Arnold R. Spokane
Lehigh University

He (sic) therefore that is about children; should well study their natures and aptitudes, and see, by often trials, what turn they easily take, and what becomes them; observe what their native stock is, how it may be improved, and what it is fit for. . . . In many cases, all that we can do, or should aim at, is to make the best of what nature has given; to prevent the vices and faults to which a constitution is most inclined, and give it all the advantages it is capable of. Every one's natural genius should be carried as far as it could; *but to attempt the putting another upon him, will be labour in vain; and what is so plaistered (sic) on, will at best sit untowardly, and have always hanging to it the ungracefulness of constraint and affection* [italics added].

—John Locke (1695)

THE PURPOSE OF this chapter is to discuss whether seemingly disparate models of career development converge with respect to the fundamental problem of how individuals select and fit themselves to various career possibilities. As Osipow (1990) noted, current career development theories may be more similar than is commonly believed: "As the major theories evolved, the influence of some diminished, while those remaining influential have come to resemble each other in important ways" (p. 122).

Osipow (1990) proposed several common themes among current career development theories: (a) biological factors in career development, (b) parental influences, (c) prediction of occupational fit, (d) use of personality variables, and (e) incorporation of life stages. Osipow cautioned (although nobody heard him) that in spite of any similarities, we should preserve the unique contributions and the applications deriving from each theoretical model until, and if, a unifying theory emerged.

Similar comments by Donald Super in part stimulated Mark Savickas and Bob Lent to organize the conference on cross-theoretical convergence on which this book is based. The remarkable conference at Michigan State University, which brought together proponents of five major theories—called foundational theorists—individuals actively doing research on integrative constructs, and eminent discussants was the result of this collaboration. Person-environment fit, or congruence, was one of five integrative ideas that served as a conceptual bridge among present foundational theories; the other four were identity development, environmental influences, self-efficacy, and decision making. As was apparent at the conference and is reflected in this volume, however, convergence was more easily proposed than achieved.

AN UNEASY TRUCE

There remains a fundamental difference in thinking between trait psychology and adult developmental or situational psychology that makes theoretical convergence difficult. Attempts at compromise among these positions during the 1970s and 1980s were satisfactory to neither party. Trait psychologists remain adamant about the stability of behavior and developmentalists seem convinced about the sequential, cumulative nature of change, as Costa, McRae, and Holland (1984) have noted: "Cross-sectional, longitudinal, and cross-sequential studies of a wide variety of personality variables have shown little or no consistent evidence of developmental increases or decreases over the course of adulthood" (p. 392).

Indeed, trait-oriented career psychologists, bruised from years of unfair and inaccurate criticism, are bolder than ever in defense of their assertion that measured interests, abilities, and personality are largely stable (Borgen, 1986; Rounds & Tracey, 1990). And as Rounds and Tracey (1990) have observed: "Reports of the death of trait-and-factor counseling have been greatly exaggerated, much of the current criticism is poorly thought out and weak in form" (p. 6).

It is unlikely that such individuals, at least as I know them, will accede to a compromise position on the subject of the stability and usefulness of traits. Convergence, then, may in reality be an agreement on terminology, which is not the same as convergence in philosophy or theory. Convergence may be illusory, for example, when we each refer to the term person-environment fit, but still mean very different things when we do. This may not represent real convergence. In spite of these caveats, the attempt at convergence is what was requested both at the conference and in this volume.

PERSON-ENVIRONMENT FIT: A REASONABLE
BUT FAR FROM UNIVERSAL CONSTRUCT

Congruence, sometimes called person-environment fit, and more recently referred to as person-environment interaction, has been a heuristic background principle for much of career development theory (Osipow, 1987), especially for adherents to an orthodox trait position. Zytowski and Borgen (1983), Borgen (1986), Betz, Fitzgerald, and Hill (1989), and Chartrand (1991) all maintained that a modern version of congruence was the fundamental underpinning for much vocational assessment and practice.

Most comprehensive vocational theorists begin with a model of individual personality and development and continue by describing, in a systematic manner, the structure and nature of the world of work. The interaction between the developing individual and the social and occupational environment impinging on that individual is, therefore, a natural topic for each theorist to address as he or she seeks to explain human behavior (Magnusson & Torestad, 1992).

John Holland (1992) has been the most ardent student of the interaction process in the career domain. The general statement of theory he provided (pp. 2–4) describes the congruence or fit position:

- In our culture, most people can be categorized as one of six types: realistic, investigative, artistic, social, enterprising, or conventional.
- There are six model environments: realistic, investigative, artistic, social, enterprising, and conventional.
- People search for environments that will let them exercise their skills and abilities, express their attitudes and values, and take on agreeable problems and roles.
- Behavior is determined by an interaction between personality and environment.

A generic version of the congruence hypothesis offered by Rounds and Tracey (1990, p. 10) stated the P-E fit position somewhat more differently:

- The well-adapted individuals within an occupation share certain psychological characteristics.
- There are measurable and practical significant differences in people and in occupations.
- Individual differences interact differentially with occupational differences. In other words, outcome is a function of person-environment fit.
- Person and job characteristics show sufficient temporal and situation consistency to justify prediction of outcome over the longer term.

As Osipow noted, however, it is not only the trait theorists who discuss fit and person-environment interaction. Donald Super (1990), for example, made the ubiquitous nature of congruence clear (if not also the difficulty of convergence in philosophy) when he compared his use of the term with that of John Holland:

> Self-concept theory. . . is both very similar to and very different from congruence theory, as Holland has used it. It is similar in that occupational choice is viewed as the choice by the individual of a role and of a setting in which he or she will fit comfortably and find satisfaction. It is different in that Holland's interest has been in a single choice. . . whereas mine has been in the nature, sequence, and determinants of the choices that constitute a career over a lifespan. (p. 219)

Convergence in Terminology Alone?

Table 1 is a rough estimate, at least from my perspective, of how each theorist treats the topic of person-environment fit, including the theory's classification, the name of the theory's congruence construct, and the mechanism that establishes congruence. The theories are classified, roughly, as differential, developmental, or situational, and theories that incorporate more than one classification are positioned between these classifications. Thus, I consider Gottfredson as differential and developmental; Vondracek as developmental and situational; and Holland as situational and differential. As is evident from table 1, there is some similarity in that all but the situational models include an explicit term referring to person-environment fit. This agreement in terminology, however, does not necessarily mean that the theories have converged.

I disagree with Osipow's (1990) assertion that all theorists use the term, since the qualities referred to by Krumboltz (e. g. , self-observations, task approach skills) are neither as stable nor as profound as traits. As far as I can tell, a classification of work environments is unnecessary to a social learning position, and the notion of fit need not be a central component of the social learning model.

Nevertheless, social learning theorists do not directly eschew the use of interest or ability inventories in practice and, thus, must accept to a certain degree that abilities and interests, even if learned dispositions, are useful in career intervention. This may be what Osipow (1990) was referring to when he suggested that self-observations lead to analysis of the environment and behavioral variability. The individual certainly interacts or, more appropriately, transacts with the environment in social learning theory, but fit does not seem necessary.

Some trait theorists suggest that social learning theory is not so much a theory of career choice as it is a specific instance of the general learning process common to all career theories. Thus, Holland's (this volume) suggestion that the social learning position be inserted into every theory implies that the social learning model may be more of a process model than a free-standing theory.

For the moment, at least, there is some agreement about the necessity of discussing how people interact and transact with their work environments, although not necessarily any consensus for including either a static or transitory "fitting" proposition as a part of the transactions studied. There is also widespread agreement about the coercive effects of the social environment on career choice

TABLE 1 Congruence Constructs in Developmental, Differential, and Situational Vocational Theories

	Theorist	Congruence Construct	Mechanism	Locus
	Holland	Congruence	Searching	Environment
Differential	Parsons	Fit	True Reasoning	None
	Williamson	Trait/Factor matching	?	None
	Lofquist & Dawis	Correspondence	Adjustment	None
	Roe	Need satisfaction	Orientation	None
	Gottfredson	Zone of acceptance	Circumscription	Individual
Developmental	Bordin	Impulse gratification	Sublimation	Individual
	Tiedeman	Decision making	Differentiation/Reintegration	Individual
	Super	Self-concept implementation	Synthesis	Individual
	Ginzberg	Fit	Optimization	Individual
	Vondracek	Goodness of fit	Contextual affordance	Mixed
Situational	Chance/Accident	?	Opportunity	Mixed
	Blau et al.	?	Compromise	Mixed
	Krumboltz	?	Task approach	Mixed
	Betz & Hackett	?		Individual
	Holland	Congruence	Searching	Environment

(Fitzgerald & Betz, this volume; Gottfredson, 1981), yet there is little agreement about what to do about those effects when they are detrimental.

INCONGRUENCE RESOLUTION: MECHANISMS AND PROCESSES

The similarity in the use of constructs in these theories is insufficient to reveal the processes involved in person-environment fit. Even among trait-driven models, opinions differ on the question of change. For example, Chartrand (1991) differentiated the person-environment perspective from the more static trait-and-factor models, noting that the fit model incorporates a certain amount of dynamic interplay between the person and the environment.

There are certainly, then, substantial differences in how these constructs are used by different vocational theorists. As Kendrick and Funder (1988) observed, the pure trait case has been erroneously caricatured as implying no change at all. This static straw-person model is frequently and unfairly used to criticize the robustness of the trait position (Rounds & Tracey, 1990). Rounds and Tracey (1990) noted that trait models of vocational behavior never assumed that individuals were incapable of change. Indeed, it was John Holland (1992) who coined the phrase "people change jobs, jobs change people." His theory is full of the dynamic interplay between the person and the environment:

- People find environments reinforcing and satisfying when environmental patterns resemble their personality patterns. This situation makes for stability of behavior because persons receive a good deal of selective reinforcement of their behavior.

- Incongruent interactions stimulate change in human behavior; conversely, congruent interactions encourage stability of behavior. Persons tend to change or become like the dominant persons in the environment. This tendency is greater, the greater the degree of congruence is between the person and the environment. Those persons who are most incongruent will be changed least.

- A person resolves incongruence by seeking a new and congruent environment, by remaking the present environment or by changing personal behavior and perceptions.

- The reciprocal interactions of person and successive jobs usually leads to a series of success and satisfaction cycles (pp. 53–54).

For unknown reasons, however, the complex nature of Holland's propositions and even of Williamson's earlier thinking is consistently oversimplified, distorted, or lost in communication (Rounds & Tracey, 1990). Chartrand's (1991) clarification of the "modern" position, then, is important so we can retire the static model and progress in our understanding of congruence processes.

A dynamic view of people in environments requires that we resolve the inherent contradiction between the stability of behavior on the one hand and the possibility of change on the other. The best way that I know to resolve the contradiction is to state the questions as clearly as possible. Stated simply, two questions must be addressed. First, does vocational choice require or involve any change in the person? And if so, what is the nature of that change? Second, is it necessary to postulate a cognitive process whereby the fit between an individual and a career choice or work environment occurs? These two questions must be resolved before any substantive progress toward a unified theory with implications for practice is possible.

Choice Versus Change

Is vocational choice a straightforward selection from among available alternatives, or does it involve a dynamic interaction, including changes in personality and the nature of the jobs undertaken? The answer to this question depends on how stable we believe the traits involved really are. For example, Borgen (1986) argued that

> career choice, does not necessarily involve a change process in the sense the term conveys. The person-job matching model implies that the person, if properly placed in a compatible environment will be better off.... There is nothing that says the individual must somehow change personal attributes...all that needs to change in the trait model is the individual's choice of environment in order to maximize outcomes. The individual's characteristics can be taken as a given. It is an allocation problem, rather than a change problem. It is not unlike dining in a restaurant with a diverse menu. The diner is not asked to change to have a satisfying meal—merely select the meal that will be satisfying. (p. 88)

Borgen's characterization of person-environment career theory implies that career choice and change involve an iterative series of selections, deselections, and reselections, but no change in the person or the work environment. My admiration for Borgen's work aside, I question this orthodox assertion on the basis of 15 years of clinical experience. Some change in the client is not only likely, but may be necessary for adequate career adjustment.

To illustrate, consider the case of Jeanette, whom I saw five years ago and again recently for vocational counseling. This 33-year-old woman had a bachelor's degree in business and, after completing a master's degree, had taken an entry-level position in the federal government. Jeanette complained that she had never felt comfortable in her job as a personnel administrator and that she hated the paperwork. Following counseling, she took a job as a corporate placement specialist and for five years had been quite successful. She returned because she was considering other options.

As her 1987 *Strong* profile report (figure 1) indicates, Jeanette displays a clear Enterprising-Artistic (EA) Holland type. If we examine her *Strong* profile closely, we can see a high level of agreement between her basic interest scales (e.g., a high score on Sales on the left side of profile) and her occupational scales (e.g., a high score on Florist on the right side of the profile), an indication that her *Strong* profile will be

STRONG-CAMPBELL INTEREST INVENTORY OF THE
STRONG VOCATIONAL INTEREST BLANK

PAGE 1   PROFILE REPORT FOR: DATE TESTED:

ID: DATE SCORED:
AGE: 33   SEX: FEMALE

SPECIAL SCALES: ACADEMIC COMFORT 15
INTROVERSION-EXTROVERSION 54

TOTAL RESPONSES: 325   INFREQUENT RESPONSES: 4

OCCUPATIONAL SCALES

STANDARD SCORES

				Occupational	F	M
REALISTIC						
GENERAL OCCUPATIONAL THEME - R LOW (36)						
BASIC INTEREST SCALES (STANDARD SCORE)						
AGRICULTURE VERY LOW (31)				Marine Corps enlisted personnel		5
NATURE MOD. LOW (43)				Navy enlisted personnel	17	18
ADVENTURE LOW (36)				Army officer	17	7
MILITARY ACTIVITIES VERY LOW (41)				Navy officer	21	6
MECHANICAL ACTIVITIES MOD. LOW (40)				Air Force officer	17	5
				Air Force enlisted personnel		13
				Police officer	8	1
				Bus driver	24	41
				Horticultural worker	30	34
				Farmer	23	22
				Vocational agriculture teacher	16	6
				Forester	-5	6
				Veterinarian		0
				Athletic trainer	-7	
				Emergency medical technician	-4	6
				Radiologic technologist	6	9
				Carpenter	5	3
				Electrician	13	13
				Architect	18	
				Engineer	9	3
INVESTIGATIVE						
GENERAL OCCUPATIONAL THEME - I LOW (36)				Computer programmer	17	10
BASIC INTEREST SCALES (STANDARD SCORE)				Systems analyst	18	11
SCIENCE VERY LOW (33)				Medical technologist	0	2
MATHEMATICS VERY LOW (32)				R & D manager	3	4
MEDICAL SCIENCE VERY LOW (30)				Geologist	0	2
MEDICAL SERVICE VERY LOW (34)				Biologist	-9	
				Chemist	-7	-9
				Physicist	-9	-9
				Veterinarian	-3	
				Science teacher	-9	-1
				Physical therapist	-7	-9
				Respiratory therapist	2	3
				Medical technician	11	1
				Pharmacist	10	15
				Dietitian	8	
				Nurse, RN		4
				Chiropractor	12	9
				Optometrist	16	4
				Dentist	6	3
				Physician	-4	-3
				Biologist		6
				Mathematician	-9	-3
				Geographer	12	12
				College professor	12	16
				Psychologist	18	28
				Sociologist	5	17
ARTISTIC						
GENERAL OCCUPATIONAL THEME - A AVERAGE (53)				Medical illustrator	4	24
BASIC INTEREST SCALES (STANDARD SCORE)				Art teacher	21	40
MUSIC/DRAMATICS AVERAGE (54)				Artist, fine	40	36
ART MOD. HIGH (61)				Artist, commercial	39	43
WRITING MOD. LOW (45)				Interior decorator	66	62
				Architect		30
				Photographer	44	41
				Musician	28	46
				Chef	34	
				Beautician		58
				Flight attendant	34	49
				Advertising executive	57	54
				Broadcaster	43	55
				Public relations director	44	48
				Lawyer	37	36
				Public administrator	39	36
				Reporter	28	29
				Librarian	24	38
				English teacher	26	31
				Foreign language teacher		30

CONSULTING PSYCHOLOGISTS PRESS

FIGURE 1   1987 *Strong Interest Inventory* Profile Report for Jeanette

FIGURE 1   1987 *Strong Interest Inventory* Profile Report for Jeanette (continued)

STRONG INTEREST INVENTORY OF THE
STRONG VOCATIONAL INTEREST BLANKS   PAGE 1

PROFILE REPORT FOR: DATE TESTED:

ID: DATE SCORED:
AGE: 37   SEX: F

SPECIAL SCALES: ACADEMIC COMFORT   18
INTROVERSION-EXTROVERSION   54

TOTAL RESPONSES: 325   INFREQUENT RESPONSES: 7

GOT	
R	Very Low
I	Low
A	Mod. High
S	Average
E	Mod. High
C	Mod. Low

OCCUPATIONAL SCALES

STANDARD SCORES

			F	M	VERY DISSIMILAR	MODERATELY DISSIMILAR	MID-RANGE	MODERATELY SIMILAR	SIMILAR	VERY SIMILAR

REALISTIC

GENERAL OCCUPATIONAL THEME - R   30 40 50 60 70
Very Low   32

BASIC INTEREST SCALES (STANDARD SCORE)
AGRICULTURE   Very Low   31
NATURE   Mod. Low   41
ADVENTURE   Low   36
MILITARY ACTIVITIES Very Low 40
MECHANICAL ACTIVITIES Mod. Low 38

code	code	Occupation	F	M
(CRS)	RC	Marine Corps enlisted personnel	(CRS)	7
RC	RC	Navy enlisted personnel	18	20
RC	RC	Army officer	11	5
RI	RC	Navy officer	20	8
R	R	Air Force officer	11	1
(C)	R	Air Force enlisted personnel	(C)	17
R	R	Police officer	9	5
R	R	Bus driver	23	39
R	R	Horticultural worker	37	42
RC	R	Farmer	24	26
R	RCS	Vocational agriculture teacher	23	10
RI	R	Forester	2	6
(IR)	R	Veterinarian	(IR)	6
RIS	(SR)	Athletic trainer	-6	(SR)
RS	R	Emergency medical technician	1	9
RI	RI	Radiologic technologist	20	13
RI	R	Carpenter	7	14
RI	R	Electrician	8	17
RIA	(ARI)	Architect	21	(ARI)
RI	RI	Engineer	9	5

INVESTIGATIVE

GENERAL OCCUPATIONAL THEME - I   30 40 50 60 70
Low   34

BASIC INTEREST SCALES (STANDARD SCORE)
SCIENCE   Very Low   32
MATHEMATICS   Very Low   32
MEDICAL SCIENCE Low   32
MEDICAL SERVICE Low   36

code	code	Occupation	F	M
IRC	IRC	Computer programmer	19	10
IRC	IRC	Systems analyst	16	4
IRC	IR	Medical technologist	5	8
IR	IR	R & D manager	5	0
IR	(I)	Geologist	0	13
IR	(I)	Biologist	-5	(I)
IR	IR	Chemist	-5	-6
IR	IR	Physicist	-15	-9
IR	(RI)	Veterinarian	4	(RI)
IRS	IR	Science teacher	-3	7
IRS	IRS	Physical therapist	7	0
IC	IR	Respiratory therapist	15	9
IC	IC	Medical technician	22	10
IC	IC	Pharmacist	23	17
ISR	(CSE)	Dietitian	11	(CSE)
(IR)	ISR	Nurse, RN	(SI)	13
IR	I	Chiropractor	19	11
IR	IR	Optometrist	19	10
IR	IR	Dentist	12	9
I	IA	Physician	2	9
(IR)	I	Biologist	(IR)	19
I	I	Mathematician	-7	1
IR	I	Geographer	15	14
I	I	College professor	19	22
IA	IA	Psychologist	11	27
IA	IA	Sociologist	-2	14

ARTISTIC

GENERAL OCCUPATIONAL THEME - A   30 40 50 60 70
Mod. High   59

BASIC INTEREST SCALES (STANDARD SCORE)
MUSIC/DRAMATICS Mod. High   61
ART   Very High   65
WRITING   Low   39

code	code	Occupation	F	M
AI	AI	Medical illustrator	21	36
A	A	Art teacher	38	52
A	A	Artist, fine	44	49
A	A	Artist, commercial	47	53
AE	A	Interior decorator	64	63
(RIA)	ARI	Architect	(RIA)	43
A	A	Photographer	45	44
A	A	Musician	43	53
AR	(EA)	Chef	44	(EA)
(E)	AE	Beautician	(E)	62
AE	A	Flight attendant	37	49
A	A	Advertising executive	49	51
A	A	Broadcaster	42	55
A	A	Public relations director	33	38
A	A	Lawyer	33	37
A	AS	Public administrator	28	31
A	A	Reporter	24	35
A	A	Librarian	24	41
AS	AS	English teacher	21	35
(SA)	AS	Foreign language teacher	(SA)	37

CONSULTING PSYCHOLOGISTS PRESS, INC.

4   1   0 P 3

FIGURE 2   1992 *Strong Interest Inventory* Profile Report for Jeanette

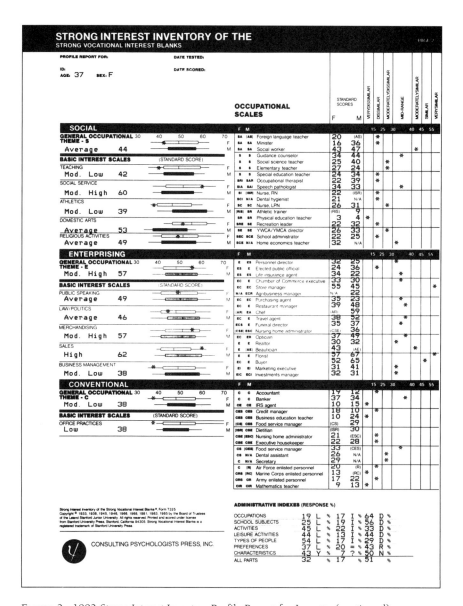

Figure 2 1992 *Strong Interest Inventory* Profile Report for Jeanette (continued)

highly predictive (as high as 70%) of her later career choices (Borgen & Seling, 1978). Was she typical? She was typical of my caseload. Has there been any change? Her 1992 *Strong* profile (figure 2) shows a somewhat different yet still clear EA configuration. In this case, the theme scales look like an Artistic-Enterprising (AE) type. There has been some reduction in the number of Enterprising scales and some modest shifts in Artistic type occupations. There were no major changes. The bulk of her personality will always be AE or EA, but a portion will adapt itself to her present circumstances.

Importantly, what was different for Jeanette in 1992 was an interest in having children. She worried that her demanding full-time job would not allow her to do so and was considering more flexible alternatives, most of them still of the EA code type. In Jeanette's case, the very difficult process of constructing a career role that integrated work and family had entered a critical and stressful phase. Yet even in this time of personal turmoil, most of the options Jeanette considered (pet care, personal shopper, and career counselor in industry) were congruent with her EA type. Although there was some clarification in her profile over five years, the profile remained essentially stable. There has been change, both in her interests and, most importantly, in her life circumstances, that brought about incongruence. Jeanette's case illustrates both the stability and change that occurs during a successful career adjustment.

Adapting to Resolve Incongruence

The resolution of incongruence occurs, in my view, in a two-phase process, during which time an individual initially aspires to and selects a congruent option, and if that initial attempt fails, engages in a secondary adjustment process, which resembles the fine-tuning knob on the old mechanical TV tuners. Osipow (1990) described a similar series of large and small changes—call it the earthquake model. An individual may be one of the fortunate successfuls (about one-third of people make initially congruent career choices), in which case over time the person shows the accentuation effects first described by Feldman and Newcomb (1969) and later documented by Walsh and Lacey (1969, 1970) and by Elton and Rose (1966, 1967, 1970). The remainder are the more common unsuccessfuls, or those who make incongruent choices, who must then engage in secondary adjustments. The potential for adjustment is limited, however, as was well stated by Kenneth Clark (1981), who argued that individuals do not generally "sort themselves into jobs" on the basis of their unique characteristics, and that even the best predictions by psychologists are only marginally accurate.

The two-phase position acknowledges the overall stability of personality, interests, and ability, and therefore the selection and reselection implied in Borgen's analysis. It also incorporates change as a necessary component in the career adjustment of some, if not most, individuals.

The secondary resolution process can be a relatively quick and painless adjustment, or a more lengthy and arduous one, depending on the degree of incongruence between the initial aspiration and any subsequent choice, and on the personality structure and overall mental health of the aspirant. It should be emphasized, however, that when the environment forces an incongruent choice or compromise, the result is a fragmentation of existing psychological structures concerning what career might be reasonable or obtainable. This fragmentation is distressing and motivational in nature, and must be resolved before a career choice can be successfully implemented. Some individuals will alter their interests to resolve the fragmentation (Malett, Spokane, & Vance, 1978), but more will change environments, sometimes repeatedly, but usually in a rational manner (Prestholdt, Lane, & Matthews, 1987), in order to restore the equilibrium between their aspirations and their actual careers.

I have been a student of the work on expressed and measured interests by Bob Slaney, Bob Dolliver, Fred Borgen, and others for many years, but have been unable until very recently to cast that work in a P-E framework. It is impossible, at least from a theoretical standpoint, to have expressed and measured interests that disagree, unless the social and environmental constraints operating on an individual force that person into an incongruent choice. It is difficult to imagine why any client would intentionally make an incongruent choice unless a congruent one was impossible because of social constraints. A discrepancy between expressed and measured interests, therefore, is an indicator of incongruence. The larger the discrepancy, the greater the fragmentation and, presumably, the level of distress. When expressed and measured interests disagree, the expressed interest is generally the better predictor of subsequent choices because expressed interests form the basis for action, whereas measured interests seem to reflect any adjustments after they are made—that is, a trailing rather than a leading indicator (Malett et al., 1978).

The distress induced by this fragmentation is one reason why career psychologists are so intensively pursuing the overlap between career development and mental health. Psychological fragmentation requires a painful reorganization—one reason why some professionals now conclude that career counseling is a subset of psychotherapy (Rounds & Tinsley, 1984; Rounds & Tracey, 1990). Whether this secondary process is development in the strict sense that Vondracek, Lerner, and Shulenberg (1986) meant, that is, progressive, or simply adaptation in the face of the fragmentation caused by environmental constraints, depends on whether the changes are cumulative and hierarchical or simply lateral.* The answer to our first

---

*I was surprised in 1985 (Spokane, 1985) when I found more than 20 studies of how congruence changed over time, and even more surprised when I reread Holland's (1992) book and realized that he had devoted considerable space to the change process involved in resolving incongruence. (He keeps telling me to read the theory.) I think that what needs clarifying is the extent of stability and change that is possible, and the locus of that change.

I am indebted to April Metzler and Alan Bain for feedback and suggestions for clarifying this secondary adjustment process.

question about whether vocational choice requires any change in the person, then, is that the person is largely stable and operates in a stable environment, but when forced into an incongruent position by environmental constraints must resolve the incongruence that results.

Cognition and Congruence

The second question we must address is the extent to which cognitive processes mediate between the individual and the environment (and the nature of these processes). It is only reasonable to postulate cognitive, behavioral, and emotional mediators between individual personality and the pressures and constraints of the social environment. This is the basis for the solid work by Betz and Hackett (1987), which follows from social learning theory that, simply stated, suggests that cognitions mediate behavior—in this case, self-efficacy cognitions. Self-efficacy involves a simple notion, that is, you think you can, and therefore you try. I believe that Vondracek et al.'s (1986) use of Gibson's "affordance" is also a simple but powerful principle—namely, you see an opening and you take it. Research suggests that there is a functional relationship between self-efficacy and congruence (Lent, Brown, & Larkin, 1987) and perceived group importance (Meir, Keinan, & Segal, 1986).

Although some cognitive process operates in career selection and adjustment and mediates between the character of the person and the characteristics of the environment, the nature of this cognitive process is still unknown. A problem-solving or information processing approach is both consistent with and crucial to a modern trait-and-factor theory (Rounds & Tracey, 1990). I do not agree with Rounds and Tracey's attempt to match clients to treatments, however, because I prefer to stimulate and enhance the natural exploratory process of each individual. Itamar Gati's work on computer tracking of the exploratory process (Gati & Tikotzki, 1989) may help inform future work on enhancing natural exploratory process.

There does seem to be a cognitive process whereby individuals systematically scan the work or social environment, making a determination about what fits, what one can do, or what might be open or possible. During this process, confirmatory information is accepted and bolsters options that are congruent with underlying structures or schemata, whereas information inconsistent with belief is poorly processed or discarded (Higgins & Bargh, 1987). Information rarely results in change itself, but as Grotevant, Cooper, and Kramer (1986) have shown, the greater the amount of exploratory behavior, the more likely it is that the individual will make a congruent choice. The exploratory process should also be more effective when a client is encouraged to consider disconfirming information. To me, the enhancement of natural exploratory process seems more realistic than matching a client to a treatment consistent with his or her current level of information processing and problem-solving skills.

RESEARCH STILL NEEDED ON CONGRUENCE

Research and scholarship on person-environment fit and career development is now in its third generation. First-generation studies examined differences between congruent and incongruent college students. Second-generation studies improved methodologies, broadened the range of variables and samples, and incorporated moderator variables and longitudinal changes. Third-generation studies are now emerging—longitudinal studies of the process involved in resolving incongruence. These third-generation studies more fully incorporate the complexity of the modern P-E fit models.

Important work on congruence over the past five years includes three-dimensional model building (Edwards, 1991), theory reviews (Betz, Fitzgerald, & Hill, 1989; Borgen, 1991; Gati, 1989; Meir, 1989; Walsh, Craik, & Price, 1992), meta-analyses (Assouline & Meir, 1987), empirical studies (Betz, Heesacker, & Shuttleworth, 1990; Elton & Smart, 1988; Gottfredson & Holland, 1990; Greenlee, Damarin, & Walsh, 1988; Grotevant et al., 1986; Lent et al., 1987; Meir & Navon, 1992; Meir & Yaari, 1988; Prestholdt, Lane, & Matthews, 1987), measurement advances (Camp & Chartrand, 1992; Holland & Gottfredson, 1992; Iachan, 1990; Matsui & Tsukamoto, 1991; Prediger & Vansickle, 1992), and cross-cultural studies (Fouad & Dancer, 1992; Khan, Alvi, Shaukat, Hussain, & Baig, 1990; Meir, Melamed, & Abu-Freha, 1990; Spokane, 1986; Tanaka & Ogawa, 1986). The literature accumulation since my last full review (Spokane, 1985) is now so large that even a partial review and reconsideration is well beyond the bounds of this brief chapter. Even a listing of the studies from 1985 to 1987 would require more space than is available. Further, this research and theory is rediscovering its roots in social psychology as a way to reinvigorate its premises—and it makes much more interesting reading for the clinician.

Two recent third-generation studies—Gottfredson and Holland (1990) and Meir and Navon (1992)—deserve special note. Both studies, coincidentally, examined bank tellers. Gottfredson and Holland tested 77 recently hired tellers during their orientation, and then followed up at four months after their hiring with measures of persistence, job satisfaction, stress, and counterproductive behavior. Congruence correlated .36 with overall satisfaction and .30 with job involvement, and was significantly related to competency utilization, but was not moderated by differentiation. Congruence was not significantly related to persistence, stress, or counterproductive behavior. Sixty-four percent of the tellers came from conventional jobs, and 61 percent of nonpersisters moved to conventional jobs after leaving the bank. Stability, then, was the norm in this sample.

Meir and Navon (1992) examined 95 bank tellers four to six months after screening, and found even stronger relationships between congruence and satisfaction (.40–.54), especially when the type of bank branch was considered. On retesting, 11 subjects had shifted from congruence to noncongruence, whereas 27 subjects had shifted from noncongruence to congruence.

Both of these excellent third-generation congruence studies have flaws, such as brief follow-up periods and early self-selection by subjects, but both represent the kind of complex methodology required to test the modern congruence model. Future studies must pinpoint why some individuals can tolerate incongruence better than others, and on the social-psychological process whereby incongruent individuals resolve their incongruent position, and on the cultural context in which this is done.

APPLYING THE CONVERGENT POSITION TO PRACTICE

If we can agree that some change in the individual is a natural and desirable component of career development, and we can agree that we need to study the cognitive process whereby the fitting occurs, the implications for practice are obvious:

- Some individuals will be naturally and fortunately congruent with their career choice and work environment. We should assist them by confirming the congruence and watching for situational changes that may induce incongruence and for which resolution may be needed.
- Clients who appear to be obviously incongruent must be assisted to understand any social constraints or situational influences (and their intractability) that might be producing the incongruence before any intervention occurs.
- Some assessment must be made of the degree of plasticity in the client's interests and personality as well as the type—that is, how much change can this client tolerate while resolving incongruence?
- The client's exploratory process should be guided by the leading edge of interests and personality, and the effects of any social constraints should be openly discussed (Spokane, 1991).

Convergence, in the true sense, must await a more complete understanding of the process by which incongruence arises and is resolved. The practical implications of this research will be far reaching.

REFERENCES

Assouline, M., & Meir, E. I. (1987). Meta-analysis of the relationship between congruence and well-being measures. *Journal of Vocational Behavior, 31,* 319–332.

Betz, N., Heesacker, R., & Shuttleworth, C. (1990). Moderators of the congruence and realism of major and occupational plans in college students: A replication and extension. *Journal of Counseling Psychology, 37,* 269–276.

Betz, N., Fitzgerald, L., & Hill, R. (1989). Trait-factor theories: Traditional cornerstone of career theory. In M. Arthur, D. Hall, & B. Lawrence (Eds.), *Handbook of career theory* (pp. 26–40). Cambridge, UK: Cambridge University Press.

Betz, N., & Hackett, G. (1987). Concept of agency in educational and career development. *Journal of Counseling Psychology, 34,* 299–308.

Borgen, F. (1986). New approaches to the assessment of interests. In W. Walsh & S. Osipow (Eds.), *Advances in vocational psychology: Vol. I. The assessment of interests* (pp. 83–126). Hillsdale, NJ: Erlbaum.

Borgen, F. (1991). Megatrends and milestones in vocational behavior: A 20-year counseling psychology retrospective. *Journal of Vocational Behavior, 9,* 263–290.

Borgen, F., & Seling, M. (1978). Expressed and inventoried interests revisited: Perspicacity in the person. *Journal of Counseling Psychology, 25,* 536–543.

Camp, C., & Chartrand, J. (1992). A comparison and evaluation of interest congruence indices. *Journal of Vocational Behavior, 41,* 162–182.

Chartrand, J. (1991). The evolution of trait-and-factor career counseling: A person x environment fit approach. *Journal of Counseling and Development, 69,* 518–524.

Clark, K. (1981, April). *Where have all the heroes gone?* Paper presented at the University of Rochester.

Costa, P. Jr., McRae, R., & Holland, J. (1984). Personality and interests in an adult sample. *Journal of Applied Psychology, 69,* 390–400.

Edwards, J. (1991). Person-job fit: A conceptual integration, literature review, and methodological critique. In C. Cooper & I. Robertson (Eds.), *International review of industrial and organizational psychology, 1991* (pp. 283–357). Chichester, UK: Wiley.

Elton, C., & Rose, H. (1966). Within university transfer: Its relation to personality characteristics. *Journal of Applied Psychology, 50,* 539–553.

Elton, C., & Rose, H. (1967). Personality characteristics of students who transfer out of engineering. *Personnel and Guidance Journal, 45,* 911–915.

Elton, C., & Rose, H. (1970). Male occupational constancy and change: Its prediction according to Holland's theory. *Journal of Counseling Psychology Monograph, 71* (Whole No. 6) 1–19.

Elton, C., & Smart, J. (1988). Extrinsic job satisfaction and person-environment congruence. *Journal of Vocational Behavior, 32,* 226–238.

Feldman, K., & Newcomb, T. (1969). *The impact of college on students.* San Francisco: Jossey-Bass.

Fouad, N., & Dancer, S. (1992). Cross-cultural interests: Mexico and the United States. *Journal of Vocational Behavior, 40,* 129–143.

Gati, I. (1989). Person-environment fit research: Problems and prospects. *Journal of Vocational Behavior, 35,* 181–193.

Gati, I., & Tikotzki, Y. (1989). Strategies for collection and processing of occupational information in making career decisions. *Journal of Counseling Psychology, 36,* 430–439.

Gottfredson, G., & Holland, J. (1990). A longitudinal test of the influence of congruence: Job satisfaction, competency utilization, and counterproductive behavior. *Journal of Counseling Psychology, 37,* 389–398.

Gottfredson, L. S. (1981). Circumscription and compromise: A developmental theory of occupational aspirations. *Journal of Counseling Psychology, 28,* 549–579.

Greenlee, S., Damarin, F., & Walsh, W. (1988). Congruence and differentiation among black and white males in two non-college-degreed occupations. *Journal of Vocational Behavior, 32,* 298–306.

Grotevant, H., Cooper, C., & Kramer, K. (1986). Exploration as a predictor of congruence in adolescent's career choices. *Journal of Vocational Behavior, 29,* 201–215.

Higgins, E., & Bargh, J. (1987). Social cognition and social perception. *Annual Review of Psychology, 38,* 369–425.

Holland, J. (1992). *Making vocational choices: A theory of vocational personalities and work environments.* Odessa, FL: Psychological Assessment Resources.

Holland, J., & Gottfredson, G. (1992). Studies of the hexagonal model: An evaluation (or, the perils of stalking the perfect hexagon). *Journal of Vocational Behavior, 40,* 158–170.

Iachan, R. (1990). Some extensions of the Iachan congruence index. *Journal of Vocational Behavior, 36,* 176–180.

Kendrick, D., & Funder, D. (1988). Profitting from controversy: Lessons from the person-situation debate. *American Psychologist, 43,* 23–34.

Khan, S., Alvi, A., Shaukat, N., Hussain, A., & Baig, T. (1990). A study of the validity of Holland's theory in a non-Western culture. *Journal of Vocational Behavior, 36,* 132–146.

Lent, R., Brown, S., & Larkin, K. (1987). Comparison of three theoretically derived variables in predicting career and academic behavior: Self-efficacy, interest congruence, and consequent thinking. *Journal of Counseling Psychology, 34,* 293–298.

Magnusson, D., & Torestad, B. (1992). The individual as an interactive agent in the environment. In W. Walsh, K. Craik, & R. Price (Eds.), *Person-environment psychology: Models and perspectives* (pp. 89–126). Hillsdale, NJ: Erlbaum.

Malett, S., Spokane, A., & Vance, F. (1978). Effects of vocationally relevant information on the expressed and measured interests of freshman males. *Journal of Counseling Psychology, 25,* 292–298.

Matsui, T., & Tsukamoto, S. I. (1991). Relation between career self-efficacy measures based on occupational titles and Holland codes and model environments: A methodological contribution. *Journal of Vocational Behavior, 38,* 78–91.

Meir, E. I. (1989). Integrative elaboration of the congruence theory. *Journal of Vocational Behavior, 35,* 219–230.

Meir, E., Keinan, G., & Segal, Z. (1986). Group importance as a mediator between personality-environment congruence and satisfaction. *Journal of Vocational Behavior, 28,* 60–69.

Meir, E., Melamed, S, & Abu-Freha, A. (1990). Vocational, avocational and skill utilization congruences and their relationship with well being in two cultures. *Journal of Vocational Behavior, 36,* 153–165.

Meir, E., & Navon, M. (1992). A longitudinal examination of congruence hypotheses. *Journal of Vocational Behavior, 41,* 35–47.

Meir, E., & Yaari, Y. (1988). The relationship between congruent specialty choice within occupations and satisfaction. *Journal of Vocational Behavior, 33,* 99–117.

Osipow, S. (1987). Applying person-environment theory to vocational behavior. *Journal of Vocational Behavior, 31,* 333–336.

Osipow, S. (1990). Convergence in theories of career choice and development: Review and prospect. *Journal of Vocational Behavior, 36,* 122–131.

Prediger, D., & Vansickle, T. (1992). Locating occupations on Holland's hexagon: Beyond RIASEC. *Journal of Vocational Behavior, 40,* 111–128.

Prestholdt, P., Lane, I., & Matthews, R. (1987). Nurse turnover as reasoned action: Development of a process model. *Journal of Applied Psychology, 72,* 221–227.

Rounds, J., & Tinsley, H. (1984). Diagnosis and treatment of vocational problems. In S. Brown & R. Lent (Eds.), *Handbook of counseling psychology* (pp. 137–177). New York: Wiley.

Rounds, J., & Tracey, T. (1990). From trait-and-factor to person-environment fit counseling: Theory and process. In W. Walsh & S. Osipow (Eds.), *Career counseling: Contemporary topics in vocational psychology* (pp. 1–44), Hillsdale, NJ: Erlbaum.

Spokane, A. (1985). A review of research on person-environment congruence in Holland's theory of careers. *Journal of Vocational Behavior, 26,* 306–343.

Spokane, A. (1986). Congruence in two cultures: Comments on professors Tanaka & Ogawa's paper. *Hiroshima Forum for Psychology, 11,* 83–86.

Spokane, A. (1991). *Career intervention.* Englewood Cliffs, NJ: Prentice-Hall.

Super, D. (1990). A life-span, life-space approach to career development. In D. Brown & L. Brooks (Eds.),*Career choice and development* (2d ed., pp. 197–261). San Francisco: Jossey-Bass.

Tanaka, K. , & Ogawa, K. (1986). Personality-environment congruence and attitudes among school teachers: A test of Holland's theory. *Hiroshima Forum for Psychology, 11,* 75–81.

Vondracek, F. W., Lerner, R. M.,& Schulenberg, J. E. (1986). *Career development: A life-span developmental approach.* Hillsdale, NJ: Erlbaum.

Walsh, W. B., Craik, K. H., & Price, R. H. (Eds.). (1992). *Person-environment psychology: Models and perspectives.* Hillsdale, NJ: Erlbaum.

Walsh, W. , & Lacey, D. (1969). Perceived change and Holland's theory. *Journal of Counseling Psychology, 16,* 348–352.

Walsh, W., & Lacey, D. (1970). Further exploration of perceived change and Holland's theory. *Journal of Counseling Psychology, 17,* 189–190.

Zytowski, D. , & Borgen, F. (1983). Assessment. In W. Walsh & S. Osipow (Eds.), *Handbook of vocational psychology, vol. 2. Applications* (pp. 5–40). Hillsdale, NJ: Erlbaum.

CHAPTER TEN

"Who Am I?"

The Question of Self and Identity in Career Development

David L. Blustein
University at Albany
State University of New York

U NDERSTANDING HOW INDIVIDUALS obtain and utilize the self-knowledge needed to develop satisfying careers has been a central concern for career development theory since Parsons (1909) first advanced his propositions in the early part of this century. Similarly, helping clients to learn more about themselves forms a major ingredient in most models of career counseling (e.g., Brown & Brooks, 1991; Spokane, 1991). In fact, each of the major theoretical models has attempted to explain the process by which individuals respond to the question, Who am I?, with such terms as self (Bordin, 1990), self-concept (Super, 1957, 1963, 1990), vocational identity (Holland, 1985), self-image (Lofquist & Dawis, 1991), and self-observation generalization (L. Mitchell & Krumboltz, 1990), which appear consistently across the major theoretical models.

In this chapter, I will address the question, Who am I?, from the vantage point of recent innovations in adolescent development and psychodynamic theories. Specifically, my intention is to describe how new developments in the study of identity, family relationship factors, and social and environmental factors in late adolescence provide a basis for the synthesis and elaboration of many important concepts in career development theory.

HISTORICAL FRAMEWORK

The notion that people benefit from accurate and accessible knowledge about themselves in order to progress in their career development represents an assumption that guides most, if not all, major career theories. Although there are some differences among the various constructs used to address issues of self and identity, important similarities exist. In effect, the various constructs used to define self-awareness or self-knowledge underscore the theoretical influences and assumptions of each particular theory.

In Super's life span development model, issues of self-knowledge fall under the rubric of self-concept theory (Super, 1963). Holland's (1985) person-environment (P-E) fit model employs the personality construct of identity. Bordin (1990) has drawn from traditional drive-oriented models and the newer relationally oriented psychoanalytic models in his inclusion of self (e.g., Kohut, 1977) and identity (e.g., Erikson, 1968) in his psychodynamic model. Krumboltz and his colleagues (e.g., Krumboltz, 1979; L. Mitchell, Jones, & Krumboltz, 1979; L. Mitchell & Krumboltz, 1990) have developed the construct of self-observation generalization, which is derived from social learning theory, to account for those intrapersonal factors that influence vocational behavior. Lofquist and Dawis (1991) use the self-image construct in their P-E correspondence model, which refers to subjective appraisals of one's personality attributes. In general, each of these constructs attempts to describe individuals' characteristic ways of constructing their identities and related personality attributes. The prevalence of constructs used to explore how individuals resolve the question, Who am I?, reflects the importance of intrapersonal or self experiences in career development theory.

Despite the similarities among these self-oriented constructs, important distinctions do exist. In effect, the constructs used to describe self-knowledge differ primarily with respect to their level of abstraction, with psychodynamic theory taking the most abstract theoretical perspective (Blustein & Palladino, 1991; Bordin, 1990). Super's (1963) notions also are relatively abstract in their reliance on a multidimensional definition of the self-concept, which is supplemented by a developmental sequence describing the growth and crystallization of the self-concept. The P-E fit constructs of identity (Holland, 1985) and self-image (Lofquist & Dawis, 1991) are less abstract and rely more on circumscribed definitions and theoretical influences. The self-observation generalization construct (L. Mitchell & Krumboltz, 1990) is presented in a relatively parsimonious fashion, utilizing an explicit social learning framework. A more elaborate comparison of these constructs, however, would likely conclude with a statement of the classic assets and liabilities of the major schools of thought in psychology. Rather than restate these distinctions, the remainder of this chapter deals with ways of advancing and integrating our conceptions of the question, Who am I?

EGO IDENTITY AS AN INTEGRATIVE CONSTRUCT

Because of the central position that psychology gives to issues pertaining to self and identity, considerable intellectual resources and insights may be derived from domains of inquiry outside of vocational psychology. In my research, I have found the work of Erikson (1968), as well as more recent adolescent development theorists such as Grotevant (1987, 1992) and Josselson (1987, 1988, 1992), to be quite helpful in understanding the antecedents and nature of how individuals acquire knowledge about themselves. In search of an informed theoretical framework to advance our knowledge in this area, I have concentrated primarily on the construct of ego identity.

According to Erikson (1968), a coherent ego identity refers to "a self-sameness and continuity...[in] the style of one's individuality" (p. 50). Reflecting the contemporary vigor of this line of work, recent theorists such as Grotevant (1987), Marcia (1988), and Waterman (1984) have expanded on Erikson's original ego-identity construct. Illustrating the sort of inclusive view that has been advanced in recent years, Josselson (1987) defined identity as "a dynamic fitting together of parts of the personality with the realities of the social world so that a person has a sense both of internal coherence and meaningful relatedness to the real world" (pp. 12–13).

Ego identity has been useful in understanding adolescent behavior in several important ways. First, research and theory on ego identity have utilized diverse empirical methodologies and paradigms that have yielded important insights into how adolescents experience their environments and construct their belief systems and self-perceptions (Adams, Gullotta, & Montemayor, 1992; Waterman, 1985). Second, although ego identity initially grew out of psychoanalytic theory in general and the ego psychology perspective in particular, it also has been examined from different theoretical vantage points. In effect, the work on ego identity has captured a broad interest among adolescent development researchers, which has encouraged a more theoretically convergent view of the construct. Third, the literature on ego identity has devoted explicit attention to the role of contextual factors in understanding the antecedents of identity formation (Markstrom-Adams, 1992; Vondracek, 1992).

One of the more common observations within the ego-identity perspective has to do with the central role that vocational issues play in one's identity development (Erikson, 1968; Grotevant, 1987, 1992). In recent years, a number of theorists (Bordin, 1990; Grotevant & Cooper, 1988; Raskin, 1985; Vondracek, 1992) and researchers (Blustein, Devenis, & Kidney, 1989; Munley, 1975; Savickas, 1985) have explored the relationships between career development and the development of an ego identity. For example, in a study conducted by my research group (Blustein et al., 1989), it was found that college students' exploratory activity in the vocational domain related to their exploration of various interpersonal and ideological domains. In another investigation (Blustein & Phillips, 1990), we observed that ego-identity statuses were predictably associated with differences in career decision-making styles in a sample of undergraduates.

Other studies (Fannin, 1979; Munley, 1975; Savickas, 1985) have identified similar relationships using different means of operationalizing both ego-identity and career constructs. However, it would not be entirely accurate to portray career development and identity formation as perfectly analogous processes. For example, when comparing two relatively similar studies on the contribution of family relationship factors in a career development context (Blustein, Walbridge, Friedlander, & Palladino, 1991) and an identity formation context (Palladino & Blustein, in press), the precise nature of the significant family predictors varied considerably, thereby suggesting the need for further research in this area.

From my perspective, the work of our colleagues in the identity formation domain provides important suggestions for theoretical innovation and potential for theoretical convergence, specifically with respect to the psychodynamic and life span developmental schools of thought. The focus on contextual factors, in particular, as a means of understanding developmental progress represents one of the more exciting trends in the identity development literature.

TOWARD THE CONTEXTUALIZATION OF IDENTITY

For the purposes of this chapter, context is defined as *that group of settings that influence developmental progress, encompassing contemporary and distal familial, social, and economic circumstances.* The attempt to broaden the scope of how we understand career development is clearly not new; for example, the importance of contextual factors is described in Super's (1957) classic work *The Psychology of Careers* and in the recent work of Vondracek and colleagues (Vondracek, 1992; Vondracek, Lerner, & Schulenberg, 1986). With these contributions serving as the foundation, the work on ego identity provides additional suggestions for how we might conceptualize the relationships between individuals and their context as they grapple with career development tasks.

Two levels of contextual factors have received considerable attention in the adolescent development literature. The first is the immediate familial and interpersonal context of the developing individual. The second is the more distal societal context represented by such factors as culture, economic opportunity, and environmental influences. The role of these two groups of contextual factors in identity formation is reviewed next with the objective of deriving meaningful inferences for the career development literature.

The Immediate Context: The Role of Relationships in Identity Development

One of the more intriguing findings from adolescent development and related lines of inquiry has been the important role that relationships play in human development. A group of theorists from such diverse areas as psychoanalysis (Fairbairn, 1952; Kohut, 1977; S. Mitchell, 1988, 1991; Winnicott, 1965), family systems (Bowen, 1986), feminist thought (Gilligan, 1982; Jordan, Kaplan, Miller, Stiver, & Surrey, 1991; Miller, 1986), and developmental theory (Bowlby, 1982; Grotevant,

1987; Josselson, 1992; Marcia, 1988) have underscored the fundamental significance of human connectedness or relatedness as an important antecedent to adaptive development. Falling under the rubric of relational models of human behavior, these diverse bodies of theories have attempted to redress the traditional lack of attention that psychology places on the importance of relationships.

Although these various theories differ in their explanatory objectives and their actual details, the relational models are based on a common set of assumptions about human behavior. For example, relational models emphasize the importance of early child-parent relationships in conjunction with current relationships as the critical explanatory factors in human development and behavior (Jordan et al., 1991; Josselson, 1992). In effect, the relational models have placed the need for connectedness at the forefront of human experience. As Josselson (1992) so aptly states in her recent book, "From many directions, the portents echo one another: relatedness is central—to physical health, to longevity, to meaningful social life, and to the growth and development of the self" (p. 3).

The central place of connectedness and attachment in relationships, which has been an outgrowth of the relational models, provides a significant point of contrast to those models of adolescent development that have emphasized the need for adolescents to separate and individuate from their families (Blos, 1979; Freud, 1958). In the identity formation realm, research has found that identity exploration and commitment are most likely to occur in a family system that encompasses some degree of parent-adolescent attachment in conjunction with an adaptive degree of adolescent individuation (Grotevant & Cooper, 1985).

With some notable exceptions in the career development domain (Luckey, 1974; Super, 1957), family influences historically have been explored in relation to explaining why individuals select specific vocational preferences (Bordin, Nachmann, & Segal, 1963; Holland, 1985; Roe, 1956). In contrast, much of the recent work in this area has concentrated on understanding how family relationships can facilitate career development (Spokane, 1991). For example, identifying the degree to which a family system facilitates or inhibits developmental progress in late adolescence has been a concern in my research program (Blustein & Palladino, 1991; Blustein et al., 1991; Palladino & Blustein, in press), as well as in the research of others in vocational psychology (Lopez, 1989; Palmer & Cochran, 1988). As in the ego-identity literature, various investigations have identified the role of both connectedness and autonomy as important ingredients in the career decision-making process (Blustein et al., 1991; Lopez, 1989; Palmer & Cochran, 1988; Penick & Jepsen, 1992).

In considering how relationships may be useful to individuals in their attempt to develop their identities in the career realm, one relevant concept is the secure base. The notion of the secure base, which was developed by theorists who have studied attachment relationships (Ainsworth, 1989; Bowlby, 1982), refers to one's experience of security and safety in relation to those individuals with whom one feels attached (Bowlby, 1982). In optimal development, individuals are thought to derive emotional support from family members and other close relationships as they venture out into the world, thereby allowing for more risk taking in their overall exploration of the environment.

One may argue that a similar process occurs in the career realm as individuals engage in exploration and decision making, which often involve some degree of risk and anxiety (Grotevant & Cooper, 1988). For example, the novel and complex activities of career exploration are likely to be more comfortable for a person if one is able to experience support, nurturance, and instrumental assistance from family members and friends (cf. Blustein et al., 1991; Hazan & Shaver, 1990; Palmer & Cochran, 1988). In contrast to a dependent approach to career decision making, individuals who provide the secure base for others do not necessarily resolve internal dilemmas or provide specific solutions. Rather, as the research on attachment and separation has suggested (Bowlby, 1982; Josselson, 1988, 1992), the secure base is thought to help individuals attain a state of independent and self-determined functioning via the provision of emotional support.

Another important aspect of family relationships is the notion of mirroring, which is an integral aspect of human connectedness. Mirroring refers to the experience of having one's needs to feel affirmed, recognized, accepted, and appreciated fulfilled—ideally in an interpersonal context that encourages the demonstration of one's talents and accomplishments (Kohut, 1977; Wolf, 1988). In the identity search process, mirroring would allow individuals to feel affirmed as they experiment with new ideas and value systems. Furthermore, being able to expose oneself honestly and to experiment with different aspects of oneself in a caring and empathic environment may foster the sort of self-discovery that is integral to the identity formation process. Mirroring in the vocational realm may be exemplified when parents encourage their children to demonstrate newly developed computer skills and when they respond with sincere interest in and admiration of their children's emerging talents. Adequate mirroring also would allow an individual to internalize self-esteem along with a sense of one's unique talents. In a relational context in which an individual receives sufficiently validating responses from others, one may be more likely to develop self-knowledge, which also may be relatively resistant to the vicissitudes of the career development process.

Given the importance of family relationships in the development of self-knowledge in both the ego-identity and career realms, it would seem useful to broaden our scope with respect to the role of relationships in career development. The relational factors that have been described here and in other contributions (Jordan et al., 1991; Josselson, 1992) may be useful in understanding some of the complex issues that are characteristic of the postimplementation stages of career development. For example, we know from research evidence that adults faced with involuntary job changes or unemployment cope better when they experience support from their families and social networks (DeFrank & Ivancevich, 1986; Kinicki & Latack, 1990). Another issue that may be examined fruitfully in light of relational theories is the role of mentors in career development, which may represent a different context for the supportive influence of others in our work lives (Kram, 1985; Noe, 1988).

The Broader Context: The Role of Social and Environmental Factors in Identity Development

One of the important lessons learned in recent decades, particularly in the study of the career psychology of women (Betz & Fitzgerald, 1987), is the profound significance of social and economic factors in career behavior. Although it would be incorrect to state that our core theoretical models have not addressed these issues (cf. Krumboltz, 1979; Super, 1957), it does seem that social, economic, and environmental factors have not been sufficiently investigated or conceptualized in our theoretical and research efforts. In contrast, Erikson's (1968) contributions on ego identity have incorporated explicit attention to the role of cultural and social factors, representing a trend that has continued in contemporary research (Grotevant, 1987; Kroger, 1989).

In the career realm, I propose that we need to pursue a more rigorous examination of relevant social and environmental factors. We need to understand more clearly the role of proximal factors such as family and close relationships, and we also need to examine more distal factors such as sexism, racism, lack of access to the opportunity structure, and other forms of social barriers. In this light, it is difficult to think of the formation of one's identity without first considering the extent to which one is able to view the social and economic world as accessible and attainable (Gottfredson, 1981; Grotevant, 1992).

In relation to the development of one's identity, a number of theorists have advanced notions that may be relevant to understanding how social and environmental factors are internalized into one's intrapsychic world. For example, Markus' construct of *possible selves* (Markus & Nurius, 1986) provides a means of conceptualizing an aspect of identity that is closely linked with the external world. Possible selves represent those aspects of self-knowledge that encompass one's hopes, dreams, fears, and beliefs and which guide behavior and provide a means of understanding current experiences.

Another relevant concept is the notion of the *embedded self,* which was articulated by Josselson (1988). In contrast to the social psychological perspective of possible selves, Josselson employs a different theoretical framework, using concepts from object relations, self psychology, feminist scholarship, existential philosophy, and recent findings in adolescent development. According to Josselson, the embedded self attempts to recast traditional views of the self into a more relational perspective. As opposed to views of the self that are based on separate and autonmous models of psychological health, Josselson's embedded self incorporates an inherently relational and environmental context. For Josselson, the embedded self rests on the assumption that we are inextricably related to others, even within our core self experiences. In Josselson's recent work (1992), the concept of embeddedness is defined further to encompass the broader social context that helps to constrain or enhance one's options, while providing many of the cultural elements of one's identity. Similar views regarding the importance of social, cultural, and economic influences have been detailed in recent identity research (for a review, see

Markstrom-Adams, 1992) and theory (Grotevant, 1987; Vondracek, 1992). Taken together, each of these theorists generally presents a picture of identity formation that builds on the psychosocial framework that guided Erikson's original thinking in this area.

In deriving relevant implications from these bodies of work, it seems that adolescents need to consider aspirations and dreams in order to feel energized to engage in the complex developmental tasks of self-definition and career implementation. Individuals who are constrained in their capacity to consider various means of identity expression may have difficulty initiating the challenging exploratory activities that are central to developmental progress. Similarly, the role of social and economic factors would seem to influence one's capacity to derive support from relationships. For example, families and friends who are overwhelmed with unending challenges to their own survival would likely find it difficult to provide adolescents with emotional and instrumental support to facilitate their identity exploration.

THE EMBEDDED IDENTITY
AS A CONVERGENT CONSTRUCT

As reflected in this chapter, I believe that an expanded research agenda for the study of identity in career development may facilitate important advances in our field. The work in the ego-identity realm has fostered a greater inclusion of relational factors, which I believe are very relevant to many aspects of career behavior. Furthermore, the relational models (Fairbairn, 1952; Jordan et al., 1991; Josselson, 1992; Kohut, 1977) in conjunction with the interpersonal and cultural schools of psychoanalysis (Sullivan, 1953)—all of which have incorporated a far greater emphasis on the environment—may allow for a theoretically meaningful synthesis of the psychodynamic and developmental schools. In this vein, the research on identity, which includes theoretical ideas and methodologies emerging from both the psychodynamic and developmental perspectives, may provide a framework for some degree of convergence in the career realm.

In a more general sense, I propose that the view of identity described herein may have broader utility in career theory. As a means of elaborating this point, I would like to extrapolate from Josselson's (1988) notion of the embedded self and from similar ideas about the relational and contextual components of identity (Forrest & Mikolaitis, 1986; Gilligan, 1982; Vondracek, 1992) in advancing the notion of an embedded identity for career theory. The embedded identity represents an extension of the aforementioned constructs and is offered as a means of providing a rubric for the integration of the various Who am I? constructs in career theory.

As in the original Erikson (1968) formulation of the ego-identity construct, an embedded identity attempts to capture the essense of one's internal experience of self-definition. However, in keeping with the trend toward providing a more integrative and comprehensive definition of identity (Grotevant, 1987; Josselson, 1987), the embedded identity is defined as encompassing the following four sets of characteristics:

- Actual *self-knowledge*—that is, one's core beliefs, values, and perceived attributes

- The *degree of commitment* that one experiences toward a cohesive and integrated set of goals and values—that is, the extent to which one has internalized the various content aspects of one's identity

- Contemporary and historical *familial factors* that influence how one develops an identity and become part of one's intrapsychic experiences, such as the opportunities for successful mirroring from one's parents, instrumental and emotional support from significant others, and one's internalized views of interpersonal relationships

- *Sociocultural factors* that influence how one develops an identity and become part of one's intrapsychic experiences, such as those aspects of culture that are inherent to identity, and the degree to which membership in a given culture and social group inhibits or facilitates opportunities for self-expression

In effect, the embedded identity places this construct into a theoretical framework that links intrapsychic experience with one's unique interpersonal history and current relational nexus, as well as the broader social network. In describing the complex network of internal and external forces that contribute to identity formation and expression, the embedded identity purports to incorporate the recent advances in relational models of human development (Kohut, 1977; S. Mitchell, 1988) and cultural variations that influence identity formation (Josselson, 1992). As such, the embedded identity is derived from and sustained by a complex array of sources, including historical and current relational influences, intrapsychic attributes, and one's social, economic, and cultural contexts. Adding the various social and historical factors inherent in the term *embedded* allows for a more explicit means of building a contextually informed set of ideas about how individuals respond to the question, Who am I? For example, the embedded identity would encourage theorists and practitioners to consider the complex developmental factors that contribute to the acquisition of self-knowledge and would similarly foster a greater understanding of the interpersonal, social, and cultural aspects of identity formation in the career realm.

A CASE ILLUSTRATION OF AN EMBEDDED IDENTITY

In order to demonstrate the embedded identity construct, a brief case vignette derived from fictional material is presented. To provide some structure to this case, a counselor will begin an initial consultation by asking a client to describe herself using the embedded identity as the organizing rubric. In order to operationalize the embedded identity, the counselor begins the consultation in the following way.

Counselor: As we begin our work, I am interested in learning more about you. Specifically, I would like you to tell me those characteristics that seem to define who you are, such as your values, beliefs, dreams, and goals. In other words, I would like to know about those aspects of yourself that form the basis of your inner sense of identity. In addition, I am curious about how you emerged with this particular sense of who you are; that is, help me understand how your family, peers, and community provided a way for you to understand yourself as you were growing up. I am particularly interested in understanding how your relationships and culture influenced your search for a meaningful identity, both personally and in the career realm. I am also wondering if you could tell me about your dreams for the future.

Let us assume that we have a very articulate client, who, upon hearing such an inviting opening, proceeds in the following way.

Client: You've really posed an interesting question, one that I think about a lot. I sometimes wonder how I got to be where I am now. It's almost as if I suddenly emerged here as a senior in college with a pretty clear sense of who I am, when in reality it took a lot of effort to get here.

I am the first born in an African-American family. I have two sisters, both in high school. My mother works as a computer programmer for a large state agency, and my father is a social worker. We come from a close family, although my grandparents and aunts and uncles live about three hours away. I'd say I have a close relationship with my mother, who has been really supportive. My father and I haven't always gotten along, although we've started to talk more openly in recent years. My mother was a great help because she let me have the chance to do all kinds of things. In high school, I thought that I wanted to be an actress and she didn't discourage me; in fact, she even helped me rehearse my parts for school plays. My father is very serious and always wanted me to do serious things, like my school work. But I think he was sometimes too critical of me during those years when I was really trying to figure out what I liked and what I was good at. My mother, however, would usually give me time to talk about what I was thinking about, and I could even show off a little in front of her without feeling uncomfortable.

Somewhere between the last few years of high school and my first two years at college, I began to get a clearer sense of what I liked and what my values were. I became really concerned with racism and the extremes of rich and poor in this country—all this is so apparent within my own community. And in my church, I developed important spiritual values and learned more about how much of a struggle African-Americans have had to deal with in this country. I also began to realize how racism has affected my parents, especially in their careers and how it exists in my life. At the same time, I began to think about myself in all sorts of different ways. I used to think that I would be a great politician or maybe even a singer, and even though I knew deep down that not all these dreams would come true, I found my mother and many of my friends willing to go along with me as I explored these different areas. No matter how wild my ideas or dreams were, my mother and sometimes even my father were there for me. They really supported me as I sorted through all of the different possibilities.

At this point, I see myself as a people-oriented person. I also feel strongly about getting involved in some sort of work in public affairs. I'm not certain if that means law school, but I'm thinking about it and would like to go over this idea in counseling. I'm also feeling clearer about who I am in terms of my relationships and friendships. I know the kind of people who I like to get involved with and I'm finding it easier to make good decisions about how I want to spend my time.

This case provides some important features of the embedded identity. The client's self-knowledge is apparent in her awareness of her interest in being with people, in her concern with social issues, and in her emerging clarity regarding the types of relationships she prefers. She seems committed to some aspects of her identity, such as her overall orientation to being with people; however, the specific career manifestation of her identity is not overly clarified. In fact, her use of counseling at this juncture may help to provide her with the needed exploratory and decision-making skills in conjunction with the support of the therapeutic alliance to foster further clarification of her career goals.

The more contextual elements of her identity were also apparent in this case vignette. The client's mother seemed to provide a secure base and was very instrumental in allowing the client to feel adequately mirrored. Specifically, when the client was encouraged to show off her emerging talents and interests, she was probably able to internalize a more robust sense of self-esteem while she also gained confidence to explore the world even further. The influence of the client's African-American culture is evident, and its impact on her identity is noteworthy. The client seems aware of the pernicious aspects of racism, but with the help of her family, community, and church, she has been able to develop a sense of hopefulness and personal competence, both of which seem well integrated into her identity.

As this example demonstrates, the embedded identity offers a way to conceptualize the question, Who am I?, in a manner that encourages an explicit integration of intrapsychic experience with the broader historical and social context.

THE EMBEDDED IDENTITY
AND THEORETICAL CONVERGENCE

In relation to the issue of convergence, the notion of an embedded identity may allow the different theoretical models to build upon a common core of assumptions in their investigation of intrapersonal experience. However, I acknowledge that some of the notions proposed here may not be entirely consistent with the wide array of theoretical assumptions that guide thinking about self and identity in vocational psychology. Yet I believe that the embedded identity may provide an understanding of the question, Who am I?, from a richer historical and social perspective. In explaining how individuals acquire knowledge about themselves, each of the major theories has sought to develop constructs that integrate aspects of individual personality and the environment.

By considering the embedded or contextual nature of one's identity, it may be possible to advance and perhaps integrate some of the Who am I? constructs in career theory. In the P-E fit theories, the embedded identity may provide a potentially useful historical and social perspective for both the Holland (1985) vocational identity and the Lofquist and Dawis (1991) self-image constructs. Specifically, the embedded identity would place these constructs into a clear social and relational perspective, thereby fostering greater inclusion of these important contextual influences into the "person" of the P-E fit theories. In the social learning model, the embedded identity may allow for a means of expanding upon the self-observation generalization construct in a manner that is potentially consistent with many of the core elements of the social learning theory. It is important to note that the embedded identity construct would not necessarily foster such an elaboration of these constructs. However, by attending to some of the important elements of the embedded identity, it may be possible to expand a given self-definition construct in a manner that fosters greater inclusion of historical and social factors. In each of these aforementioned theories, the embedded identity would involve an elaboration of the specific self-knowledge construct, which may not be entirely consistent with the parsimonious objectives of these theories. Yet a circumscribed utilizaton of the embedded identity construct may allow these theorists to focus primarily on the means by which important familial, social, and environmental influences are internalized into the individual.

The most obvious role for the embedded identity notion may be in facilitating an explicit application of the relational and contextual ideas discussed in this chapter to the psychodynamic and life span developmental theories of career behavior. As psychoanalytic theory has increasingly incorporated a relational, environmental, and life span focus (cf. Josselson, 1992; Kohut, 1977; S. Mitchell, 1988), it may become more relevant to the assumptions and theoretical propositions that presently guide the developmental school of thought. At the same time, recent life span developmental models (see Vondracek et al., 1986) have underscored the roles of familial, social, and environmental factors in fostering human development. By using the work on identity as a framework, it may be possible to fashion a psychoanalytically informed life span developmental model that encompasses the influence of past and current close relationships in tandem with pertinent social, cultural, and economic factors.

Although I am concluding on a relatively optimistic note about the potential scope and impact of identity in career theory, I should note that much research is needed in order to develop more fully the ideas presented in this chapter. One particularly fruitful area for investigation would be in examining the precise way in which self-knowledge is formed from the expanded theoretical perspective that has been identified in this chapter. Furthermore, attention to the social-cognitive and information processing literatures regarding the prevalence of biases and cognitive distortions in self-appraisal and the construction of self-knowledge would be very useful at this point and would help to explicate how an identity is formed and expressed (Berzonsky, 1988; Heppner & Frazier, 1992; Spokane, 1991).

In conclusion, as many of our leading theorists have done so successfully in the past, I propose that we can gain much in terms of ideas and research paradigms by continuing to review and consider the important contributions of our colleagues in developmental, social, and personality psychology.

I would like to acknowledge the useful input of the Phillips/Blustein research team during the spring 1992 semester to an earlier draft of this paper. I also acknowledge the very helpful comments of Debra Felsman, Hanoch Flum, Jay Hamer, Robert Lent, Donna E. Palladino, Susan D. Phillips, Michael Prezioso, Mark Savickas, and Victoria Shivy, who graciously reviewed previous drafts of this chapter.

REFERENCES

Adams, G., Gullotta, T., & Montemayor, R. (Eds.). (1992). *Adolescent identity formation.* Newbury Park, CA: Sage.

Ainsworth, M. (1989). Attachments beyond infancy. *American Psychologist, 44,* 709–716.

Berzonsky, M. (1988). Self-theorists, identity status, and social cognition. In D. Lapsley & F. Clark (Eds.), *Self, ego, and identity: Integrative approaches* (pp. 243–262). New York: Springer-Verlag.

Betz, N., & Fitzgerald, L. (1987). *The career psychology of women.* Orlando, FL: Academic Press.

Blos, P. (1979). *The adolescent passage: Developmental issues.* New York: International Universities Press.

Blustein, D., Devenis, L., & Kidney, B. (1989). Relationship between the identity formation process and career development. *Journal of Counseling Psychology, 36,* 196–202.

Blustein, D., & Palladino, D. (1991). Self and identity: A theoretical and empirical integration. *Journal of Adolescent Research, 6,* 437–453.

Blustein, D., & Phillips, S. (1990). Relation between ego identity statuses and decision-making styles. *Journal of Counseling Psychology, 37,* 160–168.

Blustein, D., Walbridge, M., Friedlander, M., & Palladino, D. (1991). Contributions of psychological separation and parental attachment to the career development process. *Journal of Counseling Psychology, 38,* 39–50.

Bordin, E. (1990). Psychodynamic models of career choice and satisfaction. In D. Brown & L. Brooks (Eds.), *Career choice and development: Applying contemporary theories to practice* (2d ed., pp. 102–144). San Francisco: Jossey-Bass.

Bordin, E., Nachmann, B., & Segal, S. (1963). An articulated framework for vocational development. *Journal of Counseling Psychology, 10,* 107–116.

Bowen, M. (1986). *Family therapy in clinical practice.* New York: Aronson.

Bowlby, J. (1982). *Attachment and loss: Volume 1. Attachment* (2d ed.). New York: Basic Books.

Brown, D., & Brooks, L. (1991). *Career counseling techniques.* Boston: Allyn & Bacon.

DeFrank, R., & Ivancevich, L. (1986). Job loss: An individual level review and model. *Journal of Vocational Behavior, 28,* 1–20.

Erikson, E. (1968). *Identity: Youth and crisis.* New York: Norton.

Fairbairn, W. (1952). *An object relations theory to the personality.* New York: Basic Books.

Fannin, P. (1979). The relation between ego identity status and sex-role attitude, work-role salience, atypicality of major, and self-esteem in college women. *Journal of Vocational Behavior, 14,* 12–22.

Forrest, L., & Mikolaitis, N. (1986). The relationship component of identity: An expansion of career development theory. *Career Development Quarterly, 35,* 76–88.

Freud, A. (1958). Adolescence. *Psychoanalytic Study of the Child, 16,* 225–278.

Gilligan, C. (1982). *In a different voice.* Cambridge, MA: Harvard University Press.

Gottfredson, L. (1981). Circumscription and compromise: A developmental theory of occupational aspirations. [Monograph]. *Journal of Counseling Psychology, 28,* 697–714.

Grotevant, H. (1987). Toward a process model of identity formation. *Journal of Adolescent Research, 2,* 203–222.

Grotevant, H. (1992). Assigned and chosen identity components: A process perspective on their integration. In G. Adams, T. Gullotta, & R. Montemayo (Eds.), *Adolescent identity formation* (pp. 73-90). Newbury Park, CA: Sage.

Grotevant, H., & Cooper, C. (1985). Patterns of interaction in family relationships and the development of identity exploration in adolescence. *Child Development, 56,* 415–428.

Grotevant, H., & Cooper, C. (1988). The role of family experience in career exploration: A life-span perspective. In P. Baltes, R. Lerner, & D. Featherman (Eds.), *Life-span development and behavior* (Vol. 8, pp. 231–258). Hillsdale, NJ: Erlbaum.

Hazan, C., & Shaver, P. (1990). Love and work: An attachment-theoretical perspective. *Journal of Personality and Social Psychology, 59,* 270–280.

Heppner, P., & Frazier, P. (1992). Social psychological processes in psychotherapy: Extrapolating basic research to counseling psychology. In S. Brown & R. Lent (Eds.), *Handbook of counseling psychology* (2d ed., pp. 141–175). New York: Wiley.

Holland, J. (1985). *Making vocational choices: A theory of vocational personalities and work environments* (2d ed.). Englewood Cliffs, NJ: Prentice-Hall.

Jordan, J., Kaplan, A., Miller, J., Stiver, I., & Surrey, J. (1991). *Women's growth in connection: Writings from the Stone Center.* New York: Guilford.

Josselson, R. (1987). *Finding herself: Pathways to identity development in women.* San Francisco: Jossey-Bass.

Josselson, R. (1988). The embedded self: I and thou revisted. In D. Lapsley & F. Clark (Eds.), *Self, ego, and identity: Integrative approaches* (pp. 91–106). New York: Springer-Verlag.

Josselson, R. (1992). *The space between us: Exploring the dimensions of human relationships.* San Francisco: Jossey-Bass.

Kinicki, A., & Latack, J. (1990). Explication of the construct of coping in the involuntary job loss. *Journal of Vocational Behavior, 36,* 339–360.

Kohut, H. (1977). *The restoration of the self.* New York: International Universities Press.

Kram, K. (1985). *Mentoring at work.* Glenview, IL: Scott-Foresman.

Kroger, J. (1989). *Identity in adolescence: The balance between self and other.* New York: Routledge.

Krumboltz, J. (1979). A social learning theory of career decision making. In A. Mitchell, G. Jones, & J. Krumboltz (Eds.), *Social learning and career decision making* (pp. 19–49). Cranston, RI: Carroll Press.

Lofquist, L., & Dawis, R. (1991). *Essentials of person-environment correspondence counseling.* Minneapolis: University of Minnesota Press.

Lopez, F. (1989). Current family dynamics, trait anxiety, and academic adjustment: Test of a family-based model of vocational identity. *Journal of Vocational Behavior, 35,* 76–87.

Luckey, E. (1974). The family: Perspectives on its role in development and choice. In E. Herr (Ed.), *Vocational guidance and human development* (pp. 203–231). Boston: Houghton Mifflin.

Marcia, J. (1988). Common processes underlying ego identity, cognitive/moral development, and individuation. In D. Lapsley & F. Power (Eds.), *Self, ego, and identity: Integrative approaches* (pp. 211–225). New York: Springer-Verlag.

Markstrom-Adams, C. (1992). A consideration of intervening factors in adolescent identity formation. In G. Adams, T. Gullotta, & R. Montemayor (Eds.), *Adolescent identity formation* (pp. 193–215). Newbury Park, CA: Sage.

Markus, H., & Nurius, P. (1986). Possible selves. *American Psychologist, 41,* 954–969.

Miller, J. B. (1986). *Toward a new psychology of women* (2d ed.). Boston: Beacon Press.

Mitchell, L., Jones, G., & Krumboltz, J. (1979). (Eds.), *Social learning and career decision making* (pp. 19–49). Cranston, RI: Carroll Press.

Mitchell, L., & Krumboltz, J. (1990). Social learning approach to career decision making: Krumboltz's theory. In D. Brown & L. Brooks (Eds.), *Career choice and development: Applying contemporary theories to practice* (2d ed., pp. 145–196). San Francisco: Jossey-Bass.

Mitchell, S. (1988). *Relational concepts in psychoanalysis.* Cambridge, MA: Harvard University Press.

Mitchell, S. (1991). Contemporary perspectives on self: Toward an integration. *Psychoanalytic Dialogues, 1,* 121–147.

Munley, P. (1975). Erikson's theory of psychosocial and vocational behavior. *Journal of Counseling Psychology, 23,* 314–319.

Noe, R. (1988). Women and mentoring: A review and research agenda. *Academy of Management Review, 13,* 65–78.

Palladino, D., & Blustein, D. (in press). Contributions of family relationship factors to the identity formation process. *Journal of Counseling and Development.*

Palmer, S., & Cochran, L. (1988). Parents as agents of career development. *Journal of Counseling Psychology, 35,* 71–76.

Parsons, F. (1909). *Choosing a vocation.* Boston: Houghton Mifflin.

Penick, N., & Jepsen, D. (1992). Family functioning and adolescent career development. *Career Development Quarterly, 40,* 208–222.

Raskin, P. (1985). Identity and vocational development. In A. Waterman (Ed.), *Identity in adolescence: Processes and concepts* (pp. 25–42). San Francisco: Jossey-Bass.

Roe, A. (1956). *The psychology of occupations.* New York: Wiley.

Savickas, M. (1985). Identity in vocational development. *Journal of Vocational Behavior, 27,* 329–337.

Spokane, A. (1991). *Career intervention.* Englewood Cliffs, NJ: Prentice-Hall.

Sullivan, H. (1953). *The interpersonal theory of psychiatry.* New York: Norton.

Super, D. (1957). *The psychology of careers.* New York: Harper & Row.

Super, D. (1963). Self concepts in vocational development. In D. Super, R. Starishevsky, N. Matlin, & J. Joordan (Eds.), *Career development: Self-concept theory* (pp. 1–16). New York: College Entrance Examination Board.

Super, D. (1990). A life-span, life-space approach to career development. In D. Brown & L. Brooks (Eds.), *Career choice and development: Applying contemporary theories to practice* (2d ed., pp. 197–261). San Francisco: Jossey-Bass.

Vondracek, F. (1992). The construct of identity and its use in career theory and research. *Career Development Quarterly, 41,* 130–144.

Vondracek, F., Lerner, R., & Schulenberg, J. (1986). *Career development: A life-span developmental model.* Hillsdale, NJ: Erlbaum.

Waterman, A. (1984). Identity formation: Discovery or creation? *Journal of Early Adolescence, 4,* 329–341.

Waterman, A. (1985). Identity in the context of adolescent psychology. In A. S. Waterman (Ed.), *Identity in adolescence: Processes and concepts* (pp. 5–24). San Francisco: Jossey-Bass.

Winnicott, D. (1965). *The maturational process and the facilitating environment.* New York: International Universities Press.

Wolf, E. (1988). *Treating the self: Elements of clinical self psychology.* New York: Guilford.

CHAPTER ELEVEN

Choice and Change

Convergence From the Decision-making Perspective

Susan D. Phillips
University at Albany,
State University of New York

I am a 17-year-old decider, the product of my disposition and my learning experiences. I have done my developmental preparation: I have a clear sense of who I am, my talents, my interests, my values, and my limitations; I am ready, in the best developmental sense, to decide. I am confronting a decision point. What advice do you have for me as I confront this task?

How do we, as theorists and researchers, answer this question? What can we offer by way of prescription or explanation? What do our theories suggest? What does our research support? Although we offer many answers for this 17-year-old, two of them will receive attention here: One concerns decision making, and the other concerns change.

DECISION MAKING

We first assert that this decider should thoroughly know herself and her options (Parsons, 1909). We warn her that by virtue of her own characteristics, she is differentially suited to the array of available alternatives (Holland, 1985; Super, 1953) and that, within limits, the various alternatives may be sufficiently elastic to permit the expression of her particular characteristics (Super, 1953). We encourage her to find the best "fit," to "implement her self-concept," and to "make a congruent match." We provide her with very well-validated and useable classification systems with which to think about herself and her options (Holland, 1985; Roe & Klos, 1969). And, we typically offer the not-very-specific suggestion that her search and choice should be conducted in a methodical, reasoned manner. We defer to the decision theorists to supply more detailed information on how to go about the tasks of search and choice.

The decision theorists, in turn, offer elaborate schemes that stem largely from the ideal of the "rational man," and that offer the additional embellishments of mathematical modeling, valence and utility assignment, and probability estimation (e.g., Gelatt, 1962; Kaldor & Zytowski, 1969; Katz, 1966; Pitz & Harren, 1980; see also Jepsen & Dilley, 1974, or Mitchell & Krumboltz, 1984, for reviews). Each encourages a comprehensive and objective process of weighting, evaluating, and eliminating alternatives to arrive at an optimal choice. They suggest, and we concur, that one must proceed in a methodical, rational manner in order to acquire, synthesize, weigh, evaluate, and cumulatively reduce the array of information and alternatives to the point of choice. If it is preceded by a suitably rational decision process, that point of choice is thought to reveal the best course of action.

Thus, from the perspective of decision making, our theories largely converge on the recommendation that decisions be made rationally. That is, with the possible exception of Bordin's (1990) work, our theories of career development, choice, and vocational behavior implicitly or explicitly endorse decision-making behavior that is logical, methodical, and objective, that is based on thorough consideration of knowable facts about oneself and one's alternatives, and that yields a best course of action.

And what of the evidence provided by observations and analysis of the process of judgment and choice? Does it support our convergence on decision-making rationality? Do people truly make decisions in this methodical, thorough, comprehensive, objective, and "rational" manner? If they do not, do they suffer negative outcomes? As summarized below, the evidence suggests "no, not necessarily" to these questions.

Are Decisions Really Made Rationally?

One need not look very far to find a good deal of controversy about this classical "rational" model. Those who attempt to describe—rather than prescribe—the decision-making process suggest that "rational man" is not much in evidence when real-life decisions are being made. The reasons for this suggestion vary in the particulars, but are nearly unanimous in the assertion that the rational model simply does not fit reality or human capacity. By way of illustration, consider the following challenges that have been advanced against the assumptions of the rational model.

Targeting questions of objectivity and predictability, Gelatt (1989) argued that the objectivity of individuals and the predictability of events can no longer be considered as givens. Once the hallmark of science and clearly the hallmark of the rational model of decision making, objectivity and predictability have been severely questioned as new perspectives emerge in the philosophy of science (e.g., Gergen, 1985; Howard, 1985). Indeed, evidence is readily available to illustrate the less-than-objective aspects of human functioning: Slovic, Fischhoff, and Lichtenstein (1977), for example, detailed a number of heuristics that bias the judgment process and highlight the limitations in an individual's capacity to absorb and use all available and relevant information.

Disparities have also been highlighted in the argument that the "rational" (classical) model does not rest on principles that represent the deciders' reality. Gati (1986), in particular, points out that the variability within alternatives, and the imprecision of individual preferences, are not well reflected in the classical assumptions of consistency and precision. This is a view also endorsed by March (1978), who characterized the rational model as requiring two accurate guesses: (a) what will happen and (b) how we will like it. He then suggests that prediction of the future is seldom accurate and that how we will evaluate a given outcome depends on individual tastes that are not necessarily precise, consistent, or stable.

Alternate descriptions of the decision-making process present a challenge to notions of thoroughness and the availability of a "best" choice: Arguing that sufficiency is a more "real" criterion than is optimalization, such writers as Simon (1955) and Hilton (1962) portray deciders as less than comprehensive in their search and deliberation, asserting that their choices reflect the "good enough" alternative, rather than that which is "optimally good." Other writers, such as Tversky (1972) and Gati (1986), describe a process in which the decider shortcuts the thorough evaluation of all alternatives. In this process, the decider sequentially eliminates from further consideration those alternatives that do not meet successively applied criteria, regardless of whether an alternative discarded earlier might meet criteria applied later.

In brief, it would seem that individuals do not proceed in an unbiased, comprehensive, systematic manner. Even within the vocational literature itself, it is evident that the search for information is not terribly thorough (Gati & Tikotzki, 1989; Krumboltz, Rude, Mitchell, Hamel, & Kinnier, 1982); that deciders will, of necessity, use shortcuts to manage the volume of cognitive data considered (Blustein & Strohmer, 1987; Gati & Tikotzki, 1989); that many will be unable to specify exactly how they reached their decision (Johnson, 1978); and that imprecision—"fuzziness"—may best describe how they evaluate any given alternative (Hesketh, Pryor, & Gleitzman, 1989).

Should Decisions Be Rational?

Despite these documented variations and deviations from the rational model, one might argue that there is value in maintaining a prescriptive ideal. After all, the argument continues, with perfect rationality as the desired goal, the damage done—or doable—by the presence of imperfection, emotion, and intuition may be minimized.

The counterpoints to this argument are many, ranging from the conciliatory to the oppositional. From those endorsing the rational model, it is suggested that its applicability might be limited in a dynamic situation (e.g., Pitz & Harren, 1980). Similarly, in a review of behavioral decision theory, Einhorn and Hogarth (1981) acknowledged the undeniable role of intuitive thought. Others assert that there is value in other-than-rational methods. Shanteau (1988) and Hammond, Hamm, Grassia, and Pearson (1987), for example, documented that the expertise of deciders includes intuitive, analytic, and consultative strategies. And, in a more dramatic position, Etzioni (1988) affirms the importance of affective elements of decision making, suggesting that such elements dictate the circumstances in which "logic" should and should not be used.

Counterpoints are also raised by the empirical evidence about career decision making. "Good" deciders are largely indistinguishable from "poor" deciders in terms of how they proceed (Krumboltz et al., 1982). Rational and intuitive strategies may yield similar developmental outcomes (Phillips, Pazienza, & Walsh, 1984; Phillips & Strohmer, 1982). If forced into a rational mold, those not so inclined may well suffer (Mau & Jepsen, 1992; Rubinton, 1980). There is even some evidence to support the use of consultation and "dependent" decision making in some situations (Phillips, Strohmer, Berthaume, & O'Leary, 1983).

So what are we really advocating in our convergence on prescribing a rational decision-making process? We advocate a strategy that corresponds poorly with a decider's reality and capacity. We advocate a strategy that does not necessarily yield "better" decisions. We advocate a strategy that might well put some deciders at a disadvantage. We treat emotion, intuition, affect, and consultation as nonrational phenomena that need to be controlled, rather than as "other-than-rational" resources that might serve as sources of creativity, imagination, and decisional assistance.

CHANGE

While we may pause to ponder our convergence on decision-making rationality and the dilemma that this convergence presents, we also issue another significant piece of advice to our decider: We warn her about change.

We are nearly unanimous in the admonition that she will not decide just once, but rather that she will be making a series of decisions over the course of her life (Myers, 1971; Osipow, 1990a, 1990b). We suggest that her decisions will be sequentially related—not only in that the consequences of one decision provide the groundwork of the next but also in that how she decides now will presage how she decides later (Phillips, 1982b). And, most significantly, we uniformly assure her that she *will* change over time. Some of her changes will be developmentally predictable (Super, 1957), some will be derived from chance (Bandura, 1982; Cabral & Salomone, 1990), some will be derived from evolving definitions of self

(Bordin, 1990), and some will be in response to her continuing interaction with the environment and the consequences of her prior decisions (Dawis & Lofquist, 1984; Holland, 1985; Krumboltz, 1976).

We say to her, in effect: "You may decide now, but you will change, and you will be deciding again many times later on." Faced with this prediction, she could, not unreasonably, respond by saying, "Can I, then, just be tentative for now? Can I refrain from wholehearted commitment, because you tell me that things are going to change?"

Our response to this is a fairly uniform "no." That is, if we respond from the developmentalist perspective (e.g., Super, 1957), to be tentative in one's commitments (i.e., to be "a little undecided") is fine, but only for a limited period of time. Eventually one must commit. Taken from the structuralist perspective (e.g., Holland, 1985), to be uncertain stems from an anomaly of one's personality pattern or, perhaps, from a lack of information about self or the available alternatives. And, taken from the perspective of our attempts to intervene, to remain undecided would suggest that the decider (or the intervention) has failed (see Phillips, 1992).

Here, then, is the second point of convergence from the perspective of decision making: While acknowledging that change will occur, our theories of career development, choice, and vocational behavior largely advise firm commitment and tolerate little tentativeness or indecision on the part of the decider.

And what of the evidence about commitment, tentativeness, and indecision? We are periodically reminded in the literature that indecision is a phenomenon with a variety of meanings (Slaney, 1988): One might be undecided—or lack the desired commitment—for a number of personal or situational reasons. Indeed, there is increasing evidence that the indecision of one individual is likely to mean something quite different from the indecision of another person (e.g., Larson, Heppner, Ham, & Dugan, 1988; Lucas & Epperson, 1990; Savickas & Jarjoura, 1991).

In addition, we are reminded that to be undecided is not always a negative event, and that tentativeness may be appropriate in early stages of development (Slaney, 1988), and even desirable in adulthood (Phillips, 1982a). There is even some reason to question the wisdom of not being tentative. The work of Blustein, Ellis, and Devenis (1989) suggests that some vocational commitments may represent an undesirable and premature foreclosure, while Tiedeman (1967) argued that one must be both committed and tentative in order to achieve the simultaneous necessities of thought and action.

These reminders from the literature shed a somewhat questionable light on our advice to arrive at a firm commitment. At a minimum, they suggest that we have much to learn about the nature of decidedness and indecision and that we are only beginning to ask questions about the possible adaptiveness of being undecided or the potential risks of being committed. Furthermore, despite our position on the inevitability of change, we have yet to consider seriously the possible necessity of maintaining a tentative posture toward one's choices.

CONVERGENCE AND CONTRADICTION
FROM THE DECISION-MAKING PERSPECTIVE

Returning to the initial query of our 17-year-old decider, what advice do we have to offer as she confronts a decision-making task? It has been suggested here that from the perspective of decision making, there are two important points of theoretical convergence and numerous points of contradictory evidence from which we might formulate a response. Taking convergence and contradiction together, our current response to her query would include, first, that she should proceed as if the present were comprehensively knowable and the future clear and unchangeable. However, we should probably also caution her that her capacity for obtaining and using comprehensive information is highly limited, and that we are quite sure that future change is inevitable. Second, we would advise that her decision is best made methodically, independently, and objectively. Every effort should be made to avoid emotion, intuition, and dependency. However, we may also acknowledge that objectivity is probably impossible, and we might hint that our prohibition of other-than-rational strategies may be a disservice to her. Third, we suggest to her that there is an optimal choice for her that awaits discovery through the rational decision-making process. However, we might also caution her that the process is not likely to be "rational" and that her choice may reflect only the alternative that is "good enough." Finally, we advise her that she must choose, and we encourage her to make a firm commitment to her choice. However, we may also acknowledge that some tentativeness in her commitment may be necessary and, perhaps, desirable.

In short, instead of responding with definitive advice, we pose quite a sizeable dilemma. A recent rendition of this dilemma, informed by advances in the philosophy of science and decision and management theory, is found in Gelatt's (1989) assertion that the time is past when one could truly advocate and expect rationality, precision, and certainty. Subjectivity and imagination must accompany attempts to cope with information overload; decision making should be oriented toward discovery rather than goals; and flexibility, adaptability, and provisional commitment are necessary in an uncertain world. "Changing one's mind," argued Gelatt, "will be an essential decision-making skill" (p. 252).

If we are to be able to offer some useable advice to our 17-year-old decider, then we need to address the questions raised by this dilemma:

- How can one be simultaneously planful, creative, thoughtful, and other-than-rational?

- How does one weigh what is known, what cannot be known, and what is yet to be known?

- How can commitment be accompanied by tentativeness?

- How does imprecision, uncertainty, and "changing one's mind" fit with existing predictive and explanatory schemes?

Clearly, we are left with some difficult questions, the answers to which are not easily discerned from the convergence and contradiction in our current theory, research, and practice. However, if we are to understand and assist an individual's career decision making, questions such as these represent our challenge and our future agenda.

My colleague, David Blustein, is owed a large measure of thanks for his encouragement, support, and critique. Thanks are no less due to the members of our joint research group, with particular appreciation of the contributions of Victoria Shivy and Deborah Belkin.

REFERENCES

Bandura, A. (1982). The psychology of chance encounters and life paths. *American Psychologist, 37,* 747–755.

Blustein, D., Ellis, M., & Devenis, L. (1989). The development and validation of a two-dimensional model of the commitment to career choices process [Monograph]. *Journal of Vocational Behavior, 35,* 342–378.

Blustein, D., & Strohmer, D. (1987). Vocational hypothesis testing in career decision making. *Journal of Vocational Behavior, 31,* 45–62.

Bordin, E. (1990). Psychodynamic model of career choice and satisfaction. In D. Brown & L. Brooks (Eds.), *Career choice and development: Applying contemporary theories to practice* (2d ed., pp. 102–144). San Francisco: Jossey-Bass.

Cabral, A., & Salomone, P. (1990). Chance and careers: Normative versus contextual development. *Career Development Quarterly, 39,* 5–17.

Dawis, R., & Lofquist, L. (1984). *A psychological theory of work adjustment.* Minneapolis: University of Minnesota Press.

Einhorn, H., & Hogarth, R. (1981). Behavioral decision theory: Processes of judgment and choice. *Annual Review of Psychology, 32,* 53–88.

Etzioni, A. (1988). Normative-affective factors: Toward a new decision-making model. *Journal of Economic Psychology, 9,* 125–150.

Gati, I. (1986). Making career decisions—A sequential elimination approach. *Journal of Counseling Psychology, 33,* 408 ff.

Gati, I., & Tikotzki, Y. (1989). Strategies for collection and processing of occupational information in making career decisions. *Journal of Counseling Psychology, 36,* 430–439.

Gelatt, H. (1962). Decision making: A conceptual frame of reference for counseling. *Journal of Counseling Psychology, 9,* 240–245.

Gelatt, H. (1989). Positive uncertainty: A new decision-making framework for counseling. *Journal of Counseling Psychology, 36,* 252–256.

Gergen, K. (1985). The social constructionist movement in modern psychology. *American Psychologist, 40,* 266–275.

Hammond, K., Hamm, R., Grassia, J., & Pearson, T. (1987). Direct comparison of the efficacy of intuitive and analytic cognition in expert judgment. *IEEE Transactions on Systems, Man, and Cybernetics, 17,* 753–770.

Hesketh, B., Pryor, R., & Gleitzman, M. (1989). Fuzzy logic: Toward measuring Gottfredson's concept of occupational social space. *Journal of Counseling Psychology, 36*, 103–109.

Hilton, T. (1962). Career decision making. *Journal of Counseling Psychology, 9*, 291–298.

Holland, J. (1985). *Making vocational choices: A theory of vocational personalities and work environments* (2d ed.). Englewood Cliffs, NJ: Prentice-Hall.

Howard, G. (1985). The role of values in the science of psychology. *American Psychologist, 40*, 255–265.

Jepsen, D., & Dilley, J. (1974). Vocational decision making models: A review and comparative analysis. *Review of Educational Research, 44*, 331–349.

Johnson, R. (1978). Individual styles of decision making: A theoretical model for counseling. *Personnel and Guidance Journal, 56*, 530–536.

Kaldor, D., & Zytowski, D. (1969). A maximizing model of occupational decision making. *Personnel and Guidance Journal, 47*, 781–788.

Katz, M. (1966). A model of guidance for career decision-making. *Vocational Guidance Quarterly, 15*, 2–10.

Krumboltz, J. (1976). A social learning theory of career selection. *The Counseling Psychologist, 6*, 71–80.

Krumboltz, J., Rude, S., Mitchell, L., Hamel, D., & Kinnier, R. (1982). Behaviors associated with "good" and "poor" outcomes in a simulated career decision. *Journal of Vocational Behavior, 21*, 349–358.

Larson, L., Heppner, P., Ham, T., & Dugan, K. (1988). Investigating multiple subtypes of career indecision through cluster analysis. *Journal of Counseling Psychology, 35*, 439–446.

Lucas, M., & Epperson, D. (1990). Types of vocational undecidedness: A replication and refinement. *Journal of Counseling Psychology, 37*, 382–388.

March, J. (1978). Bounded rationality, ambiguity, and the engineering of choice. *Bell Journal of Economics, 9*, 587–608.

Mau, W., & Jepsen, D. (1992). Effects of computer-assisted instruction in using formal decision-making strategies to choose a college major. *Journal of Counseling Psychology, 39*, 185–192.

Mitchell, L., & Krumboltz, J. (1984). Research on human decision making: Implications for career decision making and counseling. In S. Brown & R. Lent (Eds.), *Handbook of counseling psychology* (pp. 238–280). New York: Wiley.

Myers, R. (1971). Research on educational and vocational counseling. In A. Bergin & S. Garfield (Eds.), *Handbook of psychotherapy and behavior change: An empirical analysis* (pp. 863–891). New York: Wiley.

Osipow, S. (1990a). Careers: Research and personal. *The Counseling Psychologist, 18*(2), 338–347.

Osipow, S. (1990b). Convergence in theories of career choice and development: Review and prospect. *Journal of Vocational Behavior, 36*, 122–131.

Parsons, F. (1909). *Choosing a vocation.* Boston: Houghton Mifflin.

Phillips, S. (1982a). Career exploration in adulthood. *Journal of Vocational Behavior, 20*, 129–140.

Phillips, S. (1982b). The development of career choices: The relationship between patterns of commitment and career outcomes in adulthood. *Journal of Vocational Behavior, 20*, 141–152.

Phillips, S. (1992). Career counseling: Choice and implementation. In S. Brown & R. Lent (Eds.), *Handbook of counseling psychology* (2d ed., pp. 513-548). New York: Wiley.

Phillips, S., Pazienza, N., & Walsh, D. (1984). Decision making styles and progress in occupational decision making. *Journal of Vocational Behavior, 25,* 96–105.

Phillips, S., & Strohmer, D. (1982). Decision making style and vocational maturity. *Journal of Vocational Behavior, 20,* 215–222.

Phillips, S., Strohmer, D., Berthaume, B., & O'Leary, J. (1983). Career development of special populations: A framework for research. *Journal of Vocational Behavior, 22,* 12–29.

Pitz, G., & Harren, V. (1980). An analysis of career decision making from the point of view of information processing and decision theory. *Journal of Vocational Behavior, 16,* 320–346.

Roe, A., & Klos, D. (1969). Occupational classification. *The Counseling Psychologist, 1,* 84–92.

Rubinton, N. (1980). Instruction in career decision making and decision-making styles. *Journal of Counseling Psychology, 27,* 581–588.

Savickas, M., & Jarjoura, D. (1991). The Career Decision Scale as a type indicator. *Journal of Counseling Psychology, 38,* 85–90.

Shanteau, J. (1988). Psychological characteristics and strategies of expert decision makers. *Acta Psychologica, 68,* 203–215.

Simon, H. (1955). A behavioral model of rational choice. *Quarterly Journal of Economics, 69,* 99–118.

Slaney, R. (1988). The assessment of career decision making. In W. Walsh & S. Osipow (Eds.), *Career decision making* (pp. 33–76). Hillsdale, NJ: Erlbaum.

Slovic, P., Fischhoff, B., & Lichtenstein, S. (1977). Behavioral decision theory. *Annual Review of Psychology, 28,* 1–39.

Super, D. (1953). A theory of vocational development. *American Psychologist, 8,* 185–190.

Super, D. E. (1957). *The psychology of careers.* New York: Harper & Row.

Tiedeman, D. (1967). Predicament, problem, and psychology: The case for paradox in life and counseling psychology. *Journal of Counseling Psychology, 14,* 1–8.

Tversky, A. (1972). Elimination by aspects: A theory of choice. *Psychological Review, 79,* 281–299.

PART THREE

PROBLEMS AND POSSIBILITIES IN THEORY CONVERGENCE

IN PART 3, the focus expands to include additional perspectives on theory convergence—those of practitioners, educators, and scholars who use the career theories in their work. Participants at the conference that gave rise to this book were divided into five work groups that correspond to the five theories presented in part 1. These work groups were facilitated by teams of distinguished career scientist-practitioners. In addition to reacting to the main conference presentations, the work groups were invited to generate novel perspectives on theory convergence and renovation. In preparing their chapters for this work, the facilitators were asked to summarize their work groups' views and reactions, including perceptions of the relevance of theory convergence to practice. The facilitators were also encouraged to share their own perspectives.

In chapter 12, the social learning theory (SLT) work group, led by Subich and Taylor, sees Krumboltz's model as useful in explaining the learning processes that undergird other career theories' core constructs. Expanding on Krumboltz's map metaphor, Subich and Taylor endorse the value of having diverse guides to understanding career behavior. They argue that such theoretical variety is necessary for assisting diverse people who live in diverse environments. However, a *meta-map*, or guide for systematically selecting particular theories for specific purposes, may prove useful. The SLT group also considered the need for stronger ties between career theory and counseling.

In chapter 13, Rounds and Hesketh, leaders of the work group on work adjustment theory, suggest two unifying principles for career development theory: person-environment transaction and human agency, the latter referring to people's capacity to actively shape their work environments. They also propose that a unifying framework for the theories could stem from efforts to clarify the latent structure of career-relevant predictor and criterion variables, along with the various moderators of their relationships. Finally, they suggest how interactionist models such as the theory of work adjustment can be used to explore the influence of cultural diversity and discrimination on career development.

Representing another person-environment (P-E) fit perspective in chapter 14—that of Holland's theory—Walsh and Chartrand's work group cautions that there may not be a sufficient fund of knowledge from which to fashion stable bridges among the career theories. However, they offer hope that metatheories—containing higher order constructs and anchored, perhaps, in cognitive psychology—might be developed to provide conceptual umbrellas for organizing knowledge of career behavior. Walsh and Chartrand cite several "transtheoretical concepts" and assumptions that may suggest a starting point for theory convergence, such as the view of persons as active agents in their own career development, and the centrality of abilities, intrinsic motivations, and P-E congruence.

The work group on psychodynamic and personological approaches, facilitated by Brown and Watkins, suggests a number of topics that deserve greater attention by career scientists and counselors in chapter 15, for example, the impact of psychodynamic factors on career development across the life span. Newer trends in psychodynamic thought, such as object relations and ego psychology theories, are seen as offering potential applications to the career domain. Finally, Brown and Watkins discuss recent research on the structure of normal personality, conducted apart from the psychodynamic tradition, that may inform career theories and efforts to bridge them.

Vondracek and Fouad, who facilitated the group aligned with the developmental position, highlight three primary discussion themes in chapter 16: (a) concerns about the value and viability of career theory convergence, (b) the need for better understanding of, and interventions for, the vocational development of diverse cultural groups, and (c) the need to translate career theory into practice. Vondracek and Fouad note several advantages to adopting a developmental-contextual approach to career behavior across the life span.

CHAPTER TWELVE

Emerging Directions of Social Learning Theory

Linda Mezydlo Subich
University of Akron

Karen M. Taylor
Ohio State University

THE STATED GOAL for the convergence project's social learning theory work group was to discuss the convergence of social learning theory (SLT) with other theories of vocational behavior and career development. We observed that this might best be accomplished by thinking of SLT as the glue that holds together the other theoretical approaches. Specifically, SLT may provide an accounting of the mechanisms that underlie aspects of other theories. That is, SLT may explain how needs and motives that drive vocational behavior originate, how personal and career development occur, how interests form, how family members affect a person's career development, and how an individual adapts to a specific work situation. The learning principles that form the foundation of SLT may be fundamental to processes imbedded within other career development theories.

Indeed, one may readily delineate how elements of SLT explicate specific variables and mechanisms included in other theories. For example, the needs and motives important to the theories of Bordin and of Lofquist and Dawis may be a function of the environmental influences described by Krumboltz. Super's process of self-concept development and implementation may be influenced and shaped by an individual's self-observation generalizations, worldview generalizations, and task approach skills. The interests, values, and abilities addressed by Holland, Super, and others may be acquired through instrumental and associative learning experiences. Parental impact on children's vocational behavior, as described by Bordin, may be a result of the status of parents as role models. Finally, Lofquist and

Dawis' occupational adaptation process clearly operates in accordance with basic learning principles (e.g., principles of reinforcement). The aforementioned examples support the position that a reasonable place for SLT convergence is at the level of the processes intrinsic to the operation of those theories.

This manner of convergence garnered further support from the observation that cognitive constructs are central to many of our career development theories and that cognitive processes are essential to SLT. The importance to career development of such constructs as interests, values, motives, and career maturity is widely recognized, and SLT offers a perspective from which to understand how these constructs evolve and explicitly influence career development. For example, interests may be learned as a function of modeling and reinforcement, and they may influence occupational choice in part by contributing to one's self-observation generalizations. Additionally, certain cognitive constructs derived from SLT are acknowledged to be important in understanding behavior from other theoretical perspectives as well. Although firmly rooted in the SLT framework, self-efficacy and other cognitive constructs relevant to career development, such as beliefs, attributions, and expectations, may operate across theoretical boundaries. Self-efficacy is a prime exemplar of such action, as research already has demonstrated its relevance to diverse aspects of career behavior.

A CHANGE IN FOCUS

The previously described focus on the role of SLT in theory convergence, however, was overshadowed by disagreement among group members regarding whether theory convergence in itself is a useful objective. Group members held divergent views; some participants endorsed the value of exploring convergence of *vocational behavior* and career development theories, while others expressed interest in dealing with convergence of career counseling theories. It became clear that we needed to sort out these issues and address both in our discussions.

The first topic seemed indicative of a desire to develop a comprehensive understanding of how and why people follow particular vocational paths, an understanding that is not dependent on adherence to a specific theoretical view. Some suggested that this would eliminate duplication of research efforts and perhaps result in a unified, more parsimonious theory of vocational behavior and career development that would ultimately be more useful than the plethora of theories we now use. Other people, however, indicated that it is not the duplication of efforts or excess verbiage that limits the efforts of vocational theorists, but instead their inattention to the pragmatic application of theory to practice. These group members argued for the need to develop a unified view of what interventions help which people engaged in particular aspects of the career development process. As is often the case when considering the interface of research and practice, we returned to Paul's (1967) classic observation about treatment specificity guiding inquiry.

This disagreement altered the course of our discussion. We moved from a focus on the specific role of SLT in theory convergence to consideration of whether energy should be invested in attempting to converge our theories of career development or our knowledge about career counseling. The remainder of this chapter, therefore, is divided into consideration of these latter two issues and their relationship to one another.

THE QUESTION OF THEORY CONVERGENCE

In speaking about theory convergence and SLT, John Krumboltz used a map metaphor to describe each separate theory: Maps of the same physical area may differ in their purpose, scale, accuracy, and distortion, and vocational theories may similarly differ. We suggest that rather than viewing each theory as a separate map created from the theorist's unique perspective of the terrain we call *vocational behavior*, one might view the individual theories as different routes on a map of this terrain. And rather than attempting to collapse the various vocational theories into one another, perhaps we should consider the value of having alternate routes available to aid our understanding of diverse people in idiosyncratic life situations.

This revision of Krumboltz's metaphor offers a way to organize some of our observations about the value, or futility, of attempting theory convergence. In so doing, we take the perspective that our vocational theories may converge at certain destination points, but that they often also represent diverse routes to those destinations—all of which may have some utility. This might be termed an integrative *meta-map*. Rather than aiming for a single unified theory of vocational behavior and career development, perhaps we should aim for a coherent framework from which to view all of our theories.

The realm, or map, of vocational behavior, then, may be conceptualized as including many destinations (e.g., exploration, choice, development, adaptation, and retirement) and many routes to these destinations (e.g., those charted by Krumboltz, Bordin, Super, Holland, Dawis, and others), although not every route may reach every destination. It is also likely that certain routes may share the same roadway or at times follow parallel roads while on the way to a particular destination (e.g., the concepts of congruence and correspondence as ways to understand vocational fit). A theorist's choice of route may be conceptualized as dependent upon what scenery the person wants to see along the way (e.g., a life span view, person-environment fit, the impact of learning experiences, play) and what aspects of the terrain he or she prefers to examine most closely (e.g., the most efficient route to matching a person to an occupation).

The availability of routes to a particular destination may be a function of where one begins the trip (e.g., the gender, race, sexual orientation, age, or socioeconomic status of the person in question) and what resources are available to make the trip (i.e., will one drive a Yugo or a Rolls Royce?). It is also crucial to note that detours, roadblocks, and dead ends (e.g., taking time out for family responsibilities, age discrimination, reaching a glass ceiling) are all potentially present along a chosen route at a given time, and these factors may determine the route's ability to guide a person's vocational behavior. Often an individual's point of origin may predict whether such obstacles are likely to be encountered. Finally, it is also true that different routes may be differentially suited for particular purposes (e.g., Super's theory offers a four-lane route to understanding the development of a person's career over the life span, but offers a less well-developed, two-lane route to understanding a person's specific vocational choices).

It also seems important to recognize that new routes to destinations may be developed at any time and may offer improved, or simply different, ways of reaching a destination. One way to develop such routes may be to identify the paths to vocational destinations taken by other related areas of social science (e.g., sociology, organizational psychology, clinical psychology, feminist scholarship) and then work to pave them as vocational behavior and career development routes. Another way may be to observe those informal paths that people take to a destination but which theorists have thus far overlooked; these may then be developed into new routes as well. Further, old routes may require periodic expansion and extension, and such reconstruction should be a priority; many of these routes were developed decades ago from a Caucasian, middle class, male point of origin, and they may need to be updated, extended, or expanded to function more effectively from other points of origin over changed social and economic terrain.

Consider the case of two people who want to choose a career direction, both sharing the same intended destination. To understand the vocational behavior of the first individual, a Caucasian middle class man, we may have our pick of routes. One could focus on the fit of his Holland coded interests to the options offered by the world of work, or one might consider how his needs and abilities correspond to an organizational setting. One could also explore how his background, learning history, and experiences have prepared him to make particular choices. One could target planning for an orderly and upwardly mobile career across the life span, or one might contemplate how to integrate play into this man's vocational choice. There may be few environmental constraints (perhaps only the economic conditions present), and our choice of a route to understand this man's career development may thus depend on his ways of perceiving the world, on our theoretical orientation, or on how much energy and time is to be invested in developing an understanding of him. Any of the available routes may adequately meet our need to conceptualize his vocational choice behavior.

The second individual is a middle-aged Hispanic woman of poor economic circumstances, which may therefore limit the choice of routes available to us in comprehending her vocational choice behavior. Matching her interests and abilities to the work world or to a particular organization, or attending to how she might incorporate intrinsic satisfaction into her vocational plans, may not be routes that lead us to a complete or accurate view of her future vocational choice and satisfaction. These routes may ultimately be dead ends, given her point of departure. The fit of her interests and abilities with occupations or organizations may be overridden by conflicting familial roles and responsibilities, and for her the importance of intrinsic satisfaction may be secondary to the importance of meeting basic survival needs. Similarly, developmental stages may not help us grasp her vocational behavior if her life does not fit our available patterns. This woman's destination may be better reached through use of a route that explicitly attends to gender, class, and cultural influences, perhaps through the application of constructs like instrumental and associative learning or worldview generalizations. And somehow we also need to factor in explicitly how elements of the environment, such as social prejudice and limited resources, affect her vocational choice. Many of our standard theories either do not service this woman's point of origin or appear to do so inadequately.

These examples are admittedly simplistic and utilize global stereotypes, but they help to highlight how people may be differentially understood within the context of our various theories. Different routes may be necessary to apprehend different people's vocational behavior and the obstacles they may encounter. These different routes may also provide us with alternate paths to understand and facilitate individuals' vocational behavior and career development. Discovery of one "truth" may not be necessary or even desirable. Thus, the idea of convergence in career theory may be most meaningful if it focuses on how to coordinate the diversity of the available theoretical approaches. What we may need to develop is a systematic guide that informs us about what routes are available from particular points of origin to various destinations and what the advantages and disadvantages are of each. Osipow's (1990) analysis of current theories of career choice and development— one of the stimuli for the theory convergence project—may provide the basis for such a guide, serving as a foundation upon which to elaborate so as to extend the theory-mapping process we suggest.

Given the diversity we know to exist in humans, the availability of diverse theoretical stances from which to understand human behavior seems a solid advantage. Rather than viewing this diversity as untidy or unparsimonious, perhaps we should learn from other domains of psychology that emphasize the advantages of having multiple behavioral alternatives or choices (e.g., Bem's [1975] concept of androgyny). It may be that we need to reframe our outlook and become more comfortable with the idea that each of our theories has its place in a complex system of vocational behavior that does not lend itself to a single generic theory.

PRACTICE CONVERGENCE

Although an integrative meta-map may help us understand the interplay of current theories of vocational behavior and career development, it does not necessarily address the other issue that emerged in the group discussion—the potential for convergence of career counseling theory. Group members did not argue for the independence of career counseling from theories of vocational choice and career development, but the extent to which the two are directly connected was hotly debated. It was suggested that current theories of career development often do not help practitioners who seek to facilitate this process, and, therefore, attempts to converge current theories may lack relevance.

Consequently, it was argued that convergence might be more practical and worthwhile in the area of career counseling than in the area of career development theory. The strategies and methods used by counselors of diverse theoretical perspectives were noted often to bear a striking resemblance to one another, such as in counselors' common attention to client interests, needs, preferences, and values, yet there seems no coherent conceptual model integrating these methods and strategies.

The observation of commonalities in career counseling practice within the theory convergence discussion brings to mind Goldfried's (1980) examination of the potential for integrating diverse approaches to psychotherapy. In his book, *Converging Themes in Psychotherapy,* Goldfried (1982) and others explored further the idea of convergence of theories of psychotherapy. Goldfried suggested viewing theories as having various levels of abstraction; philosophical stance and theoretical framework represent the highest level of abstraction, while therapeutic techniques and clinical procedures represent the lowest level of abstraction. Goldfried suggested that a middle level of abstraction between theory and technique, which he labeled *clinical strategies* or *principles of change,* may provide the most fruitful ground for useful convergence. Although coming from a different perspective, his conceptualization may be helpful in the quest for reaching career counseling convergence. We may want to examine the fundamental aspects or principles of career counseling that are essential, regardless of theoretical orientation. One possibility for this middle-level convergence could be a focus on the examination of self variables to assist in answering some part of the Who am I? question.

Alternatively, a return to the map analogy may provide another perspective from which to view the issue of practice convergence, and with it the implicit assumption that theory and practice are related but slightly different issues. Our focus now is not on the characteristics of the meta-map, but rather on how a counselor uses the map. The counselor is analogous to a travel agent who consults a map to help clients reach their destinations as happily, pragmatically, or efficiently as possible.

An effective travel agent is a professional familiar with the available routes and the practical application of those routes; this requires an extensive data base, prior experience, and perhaps personal travel on those routes. Such an agent knows that although the numerous routes from New York to California may share certain characteristics, such as a general westward direction, they are differentially suited for clients' needs. It is the agent's job to identify which routes are most convenient from the client's point of origin, while also best circumventing obstacles, and providing the type of travel the client desires.

It is also true that travel agents sometimes have, and act on, preferences for one route over another. And they may find working with some clients easier than others who face more restrictions on their planning. Further, planning trips to some destinations may be more difficult due to barriers such as lack of prior itineraries, the agent's prior experience, and a lack of salient information on the map.

Given our conceptual framework, it seems unlikely, and perhaps undesirable, to search for a single travel plan applicable to every individual; it also seems unrealistic to attempt to identify a finite set of customer profiles for which certain travel packages would then be consistently recommended. One person's idea of the ideal route to a tropical vacation is likely to be at least marginally different from another's. Client needs must be analyzed individually and, as such, the agent's charge is to approach each new customer with a fresh notepad on which to collect critical data.

Likewise, vocational counselors often are approached by clients who seek help in changing occupational directions due to dissatisfaction with a current situation. One client may enter into the counseling relationship with varied skills, considerable personal insight, and resources that allow an optimal choice to be made. This person's situation may be effectively approached from multiple directions or routes. An examination of interests or needs and their fit to the work world may lead the client to a new choice. Similarly, an examination of how life roles and past experiences have resulted in the current situation may be useful in helping the client to take new action. With such a client, the counselor may be able to facilitate change through use of any number of career counseling techniques. This may be the "ideal" or "standard" person on whom so many early career theories were based.

Another client, however, may enter counseling with more limited resources and share that he or she must contend with certain restrictions in planning a career change. After considering these limits, along with other client information and the available routes to career change, the counselor may deduce that the client's goal would best be reached through attention to social and environmental conditions that impinge on career change. Maximizing potential for intrinsic satisfaction may be seen as secondary for the present. Such limits, personal and environmental, may narrow the range of the counselor's choice of applicable career interventions. As there are fewer degrees of freedom available, intervention strategies may become constrained, just as travel plans become constrained when timetables are tight and connections must be made.

Although this metaphor of the career counselor as travel agent provides an integrative conceptualization of how one might use current career development theories in career counseling, it still does not address the issue of the practicality, or lack thereof, of those theories. What the travel agent—especially the newer agent or the agent confronted with a new problem—needs is a map that magnifies the details of the actual route. The line that represents the route must be translated into the reality of such factors as road conditions, detours, tolls, and rest stops. Similarly, the variables and mechanisms that comprise our career development theories must be defined clearly and pragmatically to enable the counselor to apply theory to his or her actual cases. Currently, some theories are much closer to this goal than others. Although theorists may be most interested in creating and refining formal symbolic maps that fit some set of data about the terrain, counselors need maps that are more realistic and concrete to guide their planning.

Numerous examples of specific areas in need of translation, development, and elaboration emerged from our discussion of the practice of career counseling. Given the original focus on SLT, it was not surprising that a predominant theme concerned the role of cognitions in career counseling. For instance, we need to know such things as how self-efficacy mediates specific career behaviors, the impact of overly high and low self-efficacy, and how and when to modify self-efficacy. We need to better define "choice" in a way that recognizes the fact that not everyone has a true choice, at least in the sense of many of the traditional theories of vocational behavior. Further, we must determine what assumptions our theories make about the meaning of work in a person's life. We must also have more explicit frameworks with which to account for the influence on vocational behavior of variables such as race, ethnicity, gender, and sexual orientation. The broad, nonspecific statements that are typically included by theorists about these variables are all too easily ignored in favor of more specific and well-defined constructs like ability and interest. Clearly, an enormous research and theory development agenda awaits us, and it is one that would be best approached with theorists, researchers, and practitioners working in concert to identify and operationalize the elements of the routes on our map.

SUMMARY

After initial consideration of the role of SLT in theory convergence, the SLT work group moved into a more general discussion of the value of theory convergence. Using the ideas generated in that discussion, we have made a case in this chapter for the value of theoretical, and perhaps practical, diversity and presented a metaphorical framework from which to understand it, our meta-map. This metaphor assumes an intimate connection between theory and practice in career counseling and recognizes that the complexity of the human experience leaves the career counselor with a difficult task—a great deal of data collection and analysis that must be done in order to select the best route to the client's destination.

The metaphor, however, may be greeted coolly by practitioners similar to some in our group who were skeptical of the practical value of current vocational research and theory. They questioned whether current theories and research are able to inform practice and whether practice is ever allowed to inform theory; consequently, their investment in the discussion of convergence of current theories and the relevance of such convergence to practice was limited.

Nevertheless, we propose with our metaphor, not a convergence of disparate theoretical notions, but rather an integration of the salient and relevant features of each theory. This integration would preserve the individual contributions of each theory to understanding career choice and development. Such an integration could potentially lead to a more thoughtful consideration of the central question that Paul (1967) asked—"*What* treatment, by *whom*, is most effective for *this* individual with *that* specific problem, and under *which* set of circumstances?" (p. 111).

REFERENCES

Bem, S. (1975). Sex role adaptability: One consequence of psychological androgyny. *Journal of Personality and Social Psychology, 31,* 634–643.

Goldfried, M. (1980). Toward the delineation of therapeutic change principles. *American Psychologist, 35,* 991–999.

Goldfried, M. (Ed.). (1982). *Converging themes in psychotherapy.* New York: Springer.

Osipow, S. (1990). Convergence in theories of career choice and development: Review and prospect. *Journal of Vocational Behavior, 36,* 122–130.

Paul, G. (1967). Strategy in outcome research in psychotherapy. *Journal of Consulting Psychology, 31,* 109–118.

CHAPTER THIRTEEN

The Theory of Work Adjustment
Unifying Principles and Concepts

James Rounds
University of Illinois at Urbana-Champaign

Beryl Hesketh
University of New South Wales, Australia

THE THEORY OF work adjustment (TWA), introduced in 1964 (Dawis, England, & Lofquist), and revised in 1969 (Lofquist & Dawis) and 1984 (Dawis & Lofquist), bridges the two traditional vocational perspectives of counseling psychology and industrial and organizational psychology. The strength of TWA's core concepts, with its emphasis on the vocational choice process, adult career development, and rehabilitation, makes it applicable to the counseling psychology tradition. It is equally useful in many areas of the industrial and organizational tradition, such as in selection, training, work motivation, and ergonomic design (Hesketh & Dawis, 1991). Because TWA is not centered in either tradition, it has a unique role in attempts to create a unifying theoretical framework.

The purpose of this chapter is to report ideas discussed in the study group on the work adjustment perspective and, when necessary, to elaborate on certain of these ideas. Our study group focused on the advantages of using TWA as a framework for examining a number of important vocational and organizational behavior issues, the elements of TWA that lend themselves to the development of a unified theory, and issues of diversity as they intersect with a TWA perspective.

We focus the chapter on principles and concepts from TWA that could be used to develop an outline for a unified theory. Following Staats' (1991) idea of a framework theory, we used a methodology suggested by Campbell (1992) to locate elements of TWA that lend themselves to such a project. Campbell argues that convergence within the field of industrial and organizational psychology is best achieved by clarifying the latent structure of predictor and criterion variables and the various moderators of these relationships. In the course of the discussion, we highlight several research questions that may advance knowledge about the adjustment process and inform future theoretical developments. We leave the task of developing a unified career development theory to others; our purpose here is to present ideas that are important to consider in any attempt to build a unifying career theory.

UNIFYING PRINCIPLES

We contend that a unifying principle for career development theory is person-environment transaction, grounded in interactional psychology (e.g., Magnusson, 1988). We maintain that vocational behavior is expressed through the constant, dynamic, reciprocal interaction between an individual and that individual's environment. The basic principle of person-environment transaction imbues most current vocational behavior theory (Spokane, 1987). Although each career development theory has origins in different psychological traditions (Dawis, this volume), each theory, to quote Osipow (1990), has "adopted a more or less implicit or an explicit person-environment or trait-oriented approach to career choice and implementation" (p. 128). The central assumptions of a P-E model of vocational behavior can be found in Rounds and Tracey (1990).

An important advantage of a P-E model, especially as is evident in TWA, is its systems or control theory orientation (Dawis & Lofquist, 1978) and its capacity to deal with adjustment and change over time (Rounds & Tracey, 1990). The 1984 revision of TWA introduced adjustment modes on both sides of the P-E equation, allowing for a reciprocal determinism. The TWA active and reactive modes of adjustment return the person-situation interaction to a desired state. Thus, from the perspective of TWA, the individual functions as an intentional agent and, because "people make the place" (Schneider, 1987), an organization can also function as an intentional agent. We contend that a second unifying principle for career development theory is human agency, considered from the perspective of the person actively shaping the work environment as well as the perspective of the work environment actively shaping the person (see Borgen, 1991, for a more complete discussion of agency in vocational behavior).

CONCEPTUAL ANALYSIS OF THE P-E MODEL

Campbell (1992) has proposed that clarifying the latent structure of both predictor and criterion variables and the various moderators of these relationships could provide a framework to unify different conceptions and theories of vocational behavior within the industrial and organizational domain. Although the focus here is on the P-E model as it is broadly defined, we use the TWA as a protypical paradigm

TABLE 1   An Illustrative Analysis of Components of an Interactional Model
of Vocational Behavior

Unit of Analysis

Person	Environment	Interaction or Fit (P x E)

Matching Variables for Person and Environment

Personality traits	Sex-type
Values and needs	Prestige
Interests	EEO climate
Self-concept	Type of contract
Abilities and skills	Type of career path

Criterion (outcome) Variables by P-E Component

Person	Environment	Interaction
Satisfaction	Performance	Turnover
Mental health	Productivity	Tenure
Well-being	Safe behavior	Withdrawal behaviors
Stress		
Self-esteem		
Self-efficacy		

P-E Process Variables

Activeness	Problem-focused coping
Reactiveness	Emotional-focused coping
Perseverance	Action-focused thinking
Flexibility	Self-focused thinking

Time (repeated measures or longitudinal data)

to guide the analysis. Five levels of analysis are apparent when extending Campbell's method to a P-E model of vocational behavior: (a) unit of analysis, (b) types of matching variables, (c) types of criterion variables, (d) types of process variables, and (e) time framework. By way of illustration, table 1 provides a tentative five-level analysis of the components of an interactional model of vocational behavior. These levels can be crossed, although obviously no study can include all matching variables, outcome variables, or process variables, and most do not include repeated measures.

Unit of Analysis

The first level in the analysis of the P-E model is the unit of analysis, namely, whether the focus of assessment is on the person, the environment, or the person-environment interaction component. On the one hand, conceptual clarity demands that these components be kept separate in order to understand their respective and interacting contributions to outcome (dependent) measures (Edwards, 1991; Hesketh, in press) and how each is affected by change. On the other hand, several theorists (e.g.,

Endler, 1983) have argued that it is difficult, if not impossible, to study the process of reciprocal causation when interaction between separate P-E components is studied, especially if change over time is taken into account. Therefore, before any one form of a P-E model is adopted, it seems important to actively pursue the following research questions: What forms have P-E models and theories taken in psychology (not just vocational psychology)? What are the relative advantages of adopting one form of a P-E model over another?

A brief example using Holland's theory, Gustafson and Magnusson's (1991) pattern approach (cf. Endler & Parker, 1991), and TWA may help to clarify the research problem. These three models differ in how the person and environment are conceptualized. In Holland's theory, the person is the environment. In Gustafson and Magnusson's approach, the individual in the environment is the analytic unit, where the person is defined using patterns of P and E variables. In TWA, the individual and environment are viewed as discrete entities, allowing separate and possible independent assessments of the person and the environment. Such different conceptualizations of the P-E model have certain advantages and disadvantages in studying various research problems.

Matching Constructs

The second level of analysis relates to the various common attributes that can be used to assess the person and the environment. The matching constructs of TWA are work values and abilities on the person side of the P-E equation and reinforcer factors and ability requirements on the environment side. Following Hesketh and Dawis' (1991) recent formulations, however, we take a much broader view of these matching constructs of TWA. We use the variables of reinforcer requirements (what the individual needs) and behavior supplies (what the individual offers) on the person side of the P-E equation, and reinforcer supplies (what the work environment offers) and behavior requirements (what the work environment requires) on the environment side. French, Rodgers, and Cobb (1974) have suggested similar matching constructs.

As is shown in table 1, the traditional variables (e.g., values, interests, and abilities) can easily be extended to include personality, Gottfredson's (1981) concepts of sex-type and prestige, equal employment opportunity climate, the nature of the psychological contracts that are sought and offered (Rousseau & Parks, 1993), and, perhaps more importantly in light of current changes occurring in the work context, the typical career paths or trajectories that are sought and supplied (i.e., linear, steady state, spiral, and transitory; Driver & Brousseau, 1988). To capture the discorrespondence in career trajectories or contracts, the matching variables used within a P-E framework require a much wider lens than has been used typically, yet these broader-based matching variables are quite compatible with the latent or conceptual base of TWA or a P-E model (Hesketh & Gardner, 1993; Hesketh, Gardner, & Lissner, 1992).

A major research task ahead is to clarify the latent structure underlying the relationship among these matching variables. Surprisingly little is known about the relationships among abilities, interests, values, and personality traits. For example, since the 1950s, the relationship between abilities and interests has rarely been investigated (Randahl, 1991). Similarly, in the last 20 years, with the exception of some occasional research on Holland's types, research on personality traits and vocational behavior had almost disappeared from the literature. However, since the convergence of personality research on what has been called the Big Five (John, 1990)—extroversion, agreeableness, conscientiousness, neuroticism, and open-ness—there seems to be a renewed interest in personality traits and vocational behavior (Borgen, 1986; Costa, McCrae, & Holland, 1984).

Are work values, vocational interests, or Holland's types better understood as parts of a larger system of personality, such as Costa and McCrae's proposed conceptual classification of personality traits into five broad domains (Big Five) or Wiggins' interpersonal circumplex model? We are not suggesting another round of zero-order correlational studies. We do advocate approaching the issue from (a) the perspective of latent structure; for example, Holland's RIASEC model (see Rounds, Tracey, & Hubert, 1992, for a discussion of different forms of Holland's model) and Lofquist and Dawis' three-dimensional model of work values; and (b) a longitudinal perspective, charting the course of how these central constructs develop and unfold.

We simply need to determine whether interests or values are the cause or the effect of personality traits, or whether they influence each other and, if so, how (see Dawis, 1991, for a different perspective). The same holds true for work values and vocational interests. We may arrive at some answers to these old questions by combining the structural and longitudinal perspectives.

Outcome Variables

Campbell (1992) stressed the importance of a careful analysis of the latent structure underlying outcome or criterion variables. In TWA, these include such factors as satisfaction, satisfactory performance, and tenure (turnover, commitment, and other indicators of withdrawal behavior). As shown in table 1, these can be broadened to include affect, mood, and stress. Similarly, Lofquist and Dawis (1991) view self-esteem, self-efficacy, and self-concept as outcomes of the ongoing, person-environment encounter. From a developmental perspective (e.g., Vondracek, Lerner, & Schulenburg, 1986), vocational maturity and related concepts develop from the continuous act-reaction-act-reaction between the person and contextual demands (i.e., vocational tasks).

Process Variables

The next level of analysis, which has considerable practical relevance, relates to the methods used by people to resolve discorrespondence or incongruence: possible moderators or mediators of the matching and criterion relations. Dawis and Lofquist

(1984) proposed a process component of work adjustment, called *adjustment styles,* to account for how an individual and an environment maintain ongoing correspondence and cope with discorrespondence (mismatches) before an employee leaves the environment or the organization tells an employee to do so. Adjustment styles are applied to both sides of the P-E equation: They are preferred or typical modes of responding or characteristics of work environments (e.g., occupations differ in the flexibility with which they tolerate discorrespondence). As is shown in table 1, four adjustment styles were proposed: flexibility, activeness, reactiveness, and perseverance. Other theorists have proposed concepts similar to the activeness and reactiveness styles: problem- and emotional-focused coping (Lazarus & Folkman, 1984) and action- and self-focused thinking (Carver & Scheier, 1981).

Time

The final level of analysis outlined in table 1 is time, which involves repeated measurements of the person and the environment on one or more matching and criterion factors. This level is essential to understanding the dynamic or process (self-regulatory) aspect of person-environment transactions. Because of the dearth of longitudinal studies, we have yet to develop an understanding of what time frames best capture the ongoing and reciprocal process of P-E encounters.

PERSON-ENVIRONMENT TRANSACTIONS AND CULTURAL DIVERSITY

Group Differences

Dawis (this volume) argued that issues of cultural diversity, such as ethnicity, sexual orientation, age, religion, and gender, can be accommodated by TWA's individual differences approach. We agree with Dawis that such group membership variables are "inaccurate and unreliable bases" for estimating matching factors and process variables in TWA and that an individual's reinforcement history, which includes culture, shapes an individual's vocational behavior. However, we also maintain that even if group or cultural effects are mediated through reinforcement history, there are advantages to retaining group factors in our research designs to help make explicit the implicit influences of diversity on work adjustment.

Studies of group differences, however, are often fraught with method problems and are in themselves not very informative. We suggest that researchers study how culture or ethnic/racial status influence the development of key vocational concepts and work adjustment by using within-group longitudinal designs. For example, Gustafson and Magnusson's (1991) research, a prototypic within-group longitudinal study, examined the vocational development of women from early adolescence through early adulthood. Rather than studying sex differences, their research focused on differential processes among women.

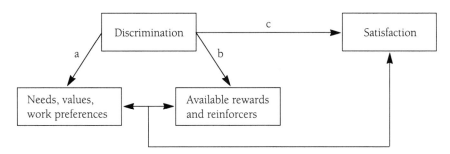

FIGURE 1   Two Hypotheses of How Discrimination Influences
the Central Concepts of TWA's Proposition III

Discrimination

An important issue with considerable practical relevance is the influence of group status discrimination (e.g., bias based on gender, ethnicity, or race) on the prediction and process of work adjustment. The question is not whether discriminatory practices in the workplace influence work adjustment but how the influence can be explained. Figure 1 illustrates two alternative hypotheses of how discrimination influences the central concepts in TWA's proposition III—that is, that correspondence between work values and occupational rewards predicts job satisfaction. In the figure, paths a and b illustrate the indirect effects of discrimination on job satisfaction that are mediated by values (path a) and reinforcers (path b). Path c depicts the direct effects of discrimination on satisfaction.

If TWA's proposition III can accommodate discrimination in explaining work adjustment, discrimination would be found to influence the individual's work values or perceptions of the work reinforcers, but not to have a direct effect on job satisfaction (indirect effect hypothesis). As is shown in figure 1, path a or path b would be significant and path c would be nonsignificant. Hence, discrimination would be mediated through work value-reinforcer correspondence. If discrimination has a direct or an additive effect on job satisfaction (direct effect hypothesis), path c would be significant, indicating, contrary to current conceptions of work adjustment, that the concept of discrimination would be a justifiable addition to the TWA framework. One path missing from figure 1 may also be important to examine: a path that moderates the relationship of value-reward correspondence to satisfaction (moderator effects hypothesis). In a discussion of sexual harassment and TWA, Fitzgerald and Rounds (1993) argue that when sexual harassment is present, it may attenuate the relationship between correspondence and job satisfaction. Likewise, the model shown in figure 1 could be extended to study the effects of discrimination on the links among ability-requirement correspondence, satisfactoriness, and tenure—an area that has been studied extensively in the context of selection.

When discussing the prediction model of TWA, it is important to remember that the contents of the model (e.g., the *Minnesota Importance Questionnaire* to assess needs and values and the *Occupational Reinforcer Patterns* to describe reinforcers) are only one approach to measuring TWA's central constructs; the theory allows multiple approaches. Hence, when evaluating the model depicted in figure 1, the types of work values and job perceptions should be broadened to include preferences and perceptions that address fairness issues (e.g., "supervisors create an environment of mutual respect," "my supervisor and co-workers treat me fairly," "promotions are based on merit"), or they should address discrimination (e.g., "company policies concerning discriminatory practices are enforced").

CONCLUSION

We draw three conclusions from the comments made in the work adjustment study group and our elaboration of these ideas. First, a unifying principle for career development theory is person-environment transaction, grounded in interactional psychology with both the person and environment conceived as intentional agents. Second, convergence of career development theories is best achieved by clarifying from an interactional perspective the latent structure of predictor and criterion variables and the various moderators of these relationships. Third, the influence of cultural diversity and discrimination on career development, issues with considerable practical relevance, can be best studied from an interactionist perspective using within-group longitudinal designs.

REFERENCES

Borgen, F. (1986). New approaches to the assessment of interests. In W. Walsh & S. Osipow (Eds.), *Advances in vocational psychology: Vol. 1. The assessment of interest* (pp. 31–54). Hillsdale, NJ: Erlbaum.

Borgen, F. (1991). Megatrends and milestones in vocational behavior: A 20-year counseling psychology retrospective. *Journal of Vocational Behavior, 39,* 263–290.

Campbell, J. (1992). *The latent structure underlying science and practice.* Distinguished Scientific Contribution Award presentation at the annual meeting of the Society for Industrial and Organizational Psychology, Montreal.

Carver, C., & Scheier, M. (1981). *Attention and self regulation: A control theory approach to human behavior.* New York: Springer-Verlag.

Costa, P., Jr., McCrae, R., & Holland, J. (1984). Personality and vocational interests in an adult sample. *Journal of Applied Psychology, 69,* 390–400.

Dawis, R. (1991). Vocational interests, values, and preferences. In M. D. Dunnette & L. Hough (Eds.), *Handbook of industrial and organizational psychology* (2d ed., vol. 2, pp. 833–872). Palo Alto, CA: Consulting Psychologists Press.

Dawis, R., England, G., & Lofquist, L. (1964). A theory of work adjustment (a revision). *Minnesota Studies in Vocational Rehabilitation. 15.*

Dawis, R., & Lofquist, L. (1978). A note on the dynamics of work adjustment. *Journal of Vocational Behavior, 12,* 76–79.

Dawis, R., & Lofquist, L. (1984). *A psychological theory of work adjustment.* Minneapolis: University of Minnesota Press.

Driver, M., & Brousseau, K. (1988). *Four career concepts.* Santa Monica, CA: Decision Dynamics Corporation.

Edwards, J. (1991). Person-job fit: A conceptual integration, literature review, and methodological critique. In C. Cooper & I. Robertson, *International review of industrial and organizational psychology, 1991* (pp. 283–357). Chichester, UK: Wiley.

Endler, N. (1983). Interactionism: A personality model, but not yet a theory. In M. Page (Ed.), *Nebraska Symposium on Motivation 1982: Personality-current theory and research* (pp. 155–200). Lincoln: University of Nebraska Press.

Endler, N., & Parker, J. (1991). Personality research: Theories, issues, and methods. In M. Hersen, A. Kazdin, & A. Bellack (Eds.), *The clinical psychology handbook* (2d ed., pp. 258–278). New York: Pergamon.

Fitzgerald, L., & Rounds, J. (1993). Women and work: Theory encounters reality. In W. Walsh & S. Osipow (Eds.), *Career counseling for women* (pp. 327–354). Hillsdale, NJ: Erlbaum.

French, J., Jr., Rodgers, W., & Cobb, S. (1974). Adjustment as person-environment fit. In G. V. Coelho, D. A. Hamberg, & J. E. Adams (Eds.), *Coping and adaption.* New York: Basic Books.

Gottfredson, L. (1981). Circumscription and compromise: A developmental theory of occupational aspirations. *Journal of Counseling Psychology* [Monograph], *28,* 545–579.

Gustafson, S., & Magnusson, D. (1991). *Female life careers: A pattern approach* (Vol. 3). Hillsdale, NJ: Erlbaum.

Hesketh, B. (in press). Measurement issues in industrial and organizational psychology. In C. Cooper & I. Robertson (Eds.), *International review of industrial and organizational psychology, 1993.* Chichester, UK: Wiley.

Hesketh, B., & Dawis, R. (1991). The Minnesota Theory of Work Adjustment: A conceptual framework. In B. Hesketh & A. Adams (Eds.), *Psychological perspectives on occupational health and rehabilitation* (pp. 1–16). Sydney: Harcourt Brace Jovanovich.

Hesketh, B., & Gardner, D. (1993). Person-environment fit models: A reconceptualization and empirical test. *Journal of Vocational Behavior, 42,* 315–332.

Hesketh, B., Gardner, D., & Lissner, D. (1992). Technical and managerial career paths: An unresolved dilemma. *International Journal of Career Management, 4,* 9–16.

John, O. (1990). The "Big Five" factor taxonomy: Dimensions of personality in the natural language and in questionnaires. In L. A. Pervin (Ed.), *Handbook of personality theory and research* (pp. 66–100). New York: Guilford Press.

Lazarus, R., & Folkman, S. (1984). *Stress, appraisal, and coping.* New York: Springer.

Lofquist, L., & Dawis, R. (1969). *Adjustment to work.* New York: Prentice-Hall.

Lofquist, L., & Dawis, R. (1991). *Essentials of person-environment correspondence counseling.* Minneapolis: University of Minnesota Press.

Magnusson, D. (1988). *Individual development from an interactional perspective: A longitudinal study* (Vol. 1). Hillsdale, NJ: Erlbaum.

Osipow, S. (1990). Convergence in theories of career choice and development: Review and prospect. *Journal of Vocational Behavior, 36,* 122–131.

Randahl, G. (1991). A topological analysis of the relations between measured vocational interests and abilities. *Journal of Vocational Behavior, 38,* 333–350.

Rounds, J., & Tracey, T. (1990). From trait-and-factor to person-environment fit counseling: Theory and process. In W. Walsh & S. Osipow (Eds.), *Career counseling: Contemporary topics in vocational psychology* (pp. 1–44). Hillsdale, NJ: Erlbaum.

Rounds, J., Tracey, T., & Hubert, L. (1992). Methods for evaluating vocational interest structural hypotheses. *Journal of Vocational Behavior, 40,* 239–259.

Rousseau, D., & Parks, J. (1993). The contracts of individuals and organizations. In L. Cummings & B. Staw, *Research in Organizational Behavior, 15.* Greenwich,CT: JAI Press.

Schneider, B. (1987). The people make the place. *Personnel Psychology, 40,* 437–454.

Spokane, A. (Ed.). (1987). Conceptual and methodological issues in person-environment fit research [Special issue]. *Journal of Vocational Behavior, 31,* 217–221.

Staats, A. (1991). Unified positivism and unification of psychology. *American Psychologist, 46,* 899–912.

Vondracek, F., Lerner, R., & Schulenberg, J. (1986). *Career development: A life-span development approach.* Hillsdale, NJ: Erlbaum.

CHAPTER FOURTEEN

Emerging Directions of Person-Environment Fit

W. Bruce Walsh
Ohio State University

Judy M. Chartrand
Virginia Commonwealth University

Scientific progress is often characterized by a shift from disunity, where rival scholars advocate different theories, to unity, where investigators collaborate to identify common underlying principles (Staats, 1991). A shift toward unity is evident in this work on convergence in career theories, and it is a sign of a maturing field. Because there is enough confidence in our current career theories, the goal of unity can now be broached. The salient questions become: How do we define convergence? How far do we push convergence? And where will convergence take theories of career choice and development? In this chapter, we examine these questions and theories of action from the perspective of person-environment fit psychology. More specifically, we discuss the advantages of theory convergence, specific points of convergence, and convergence in research. We next look to the future of convergence in career theories by focusing on theories of action and convergence in person-environment research models, convergence in personality factors, an evolutionary perspective on person-environment interaction, and a contemporary view on the concept of congruence.

IS CONVERGENCE BENEFICIAL?

Our work group was cautiously optimistic about the prospect of convergence among career theories. The primary concern was that there is not yet sufficient knowledge to find stable points of convergence across theories. Participants questioned whether the practice of replication and building on a base of overlapping knowledge would be neglected if researchers forge ahead too quickly. This concern is related to a second issue, namely, that convergence to a higher order theory of career choice and development might reify parts of theories that are of questionable validity. An integrated theory that contains ambiguous constructs drawn from different theories is likely to lead to confusion rather than clarity.

In light of these concerns, our group recommended strategies that included analysis at a microlevel. Constructive piecemeal theory building was deemed more efficient than efforts to integrate current theories. There was strong sentiment toward conducting more intervention and application-focused research using primary constructs, such as congruence from Holland's theory. This approach can simultaneously bolster understanding of how major theoretical constructs operate, and reduce the disparity between science and practice activities.

Another option that accommodates the dual desire for unity and prudent scientific practice is the development of an interlevel theoretical framework. Theories of career choice and development differ in purpose, and the constructs across these theories are not isomorphic. However, each theory contains elements that can be translated into common higher order constructs and relations. It is possible to take theories organized around separate constructs and translate them into a basic theoretical language that can then be related to more basic theories of psychology. As Staats (1991) has observed, the "ability to see commonality, in principle, through thickets of superficial difference is at the heart of creating a unified science" (p. 905). If unity is a goal, then interlevel theorizing is a necessary process.

The difficulty with convergence arises when theories of career choice and development are viewed from a horizontal perspective. A vertical perspective is needed to bypass entrenched theoretical demarcations (each supported by extensive research efforts) and to trace common elements. A debate for the future may become which metatheory should serve as the conceptual umbrella for organizing knowledge of career choice and development. If vocational psychologists follow the field, the choice is likely to be cognitive theory. This trend has already occurred with the emergence of self-efficacy theory (Hackett, Lent, & Greenhaus, 1991), and is presaged by the acknowledgment at the convergence conference that social learning theory can be the cement that bonds the structural components of Holland's and Super's theories.

POINTS OF CONVERGENCE

A starting point for convergence is the basic assumption, shared by each theory, that people are active agents who move toward career choice, development, and adjustment (cf. Borgen, 1991). Each theory deals with intrinsic motivation, albeit in a slightly different way. The theory of work adjustment (TWA; Dawis & Lofquist,

1984) uses needs and values. Super's theory uses values and emphasizes implementation of the self-concept. Social learning theory (Krumboltz & Nichols, 1990) articulates the role of goals in guiding behavior. The psychodynamic approach presented by Bordin (1990) uses intrinsic motives, which are conceptually similar to Holland's (1985) personality types. For example, the description of the nurturance motive bears a striking resemblance to Holland's Social type, and the aesthetic expression motive is similar to Holland's Artistic type. Beyond articulated differences, there are many similarities in the motivational constructs of theories of career choice, development, and adjustment.

The importance of abilities or aptitudes in the selection of realistic career choices is also explicitly acknowledged in each of the major theories, with the exception of psychodynamic theory as it is presented by Bordin (1990). Watkins and Savickas' (1990) psychodynamic interpretation, which is more eclectic, does include abilities as an important construct. Inclusion of ability constructs in each theory underscores the importance of predicting, understanding, and explaining abilities and their influence on career choice and development. The assessment of ability and aptitude has a long and profound history that has shaped the practice of vocational guidance and counseling (Dawis, 1992). More than any other construct, abilities link counseling and organizational career theories and the differential tradition in psychology. The ability construct can be clearly defined, has applied significance, and should have a prominent place in an interlevel vocational theory.

Another transtheoretical concept is congruence, the fit between individual characteristics and environmental presses. Not only is this concept common to theories of career choice and development (Osipow, 1990), but it derives its heritage from what has become a basic axiom of psychology: Behavior is a joint function of the person and the environment (Lewin, 1935).

The challenge for vocational theorists is to delimit the definition of congruence so that it is not a catchall construct. Theorists need to clarify conceptual definitions, and researchers need to improve their measures of this construct. For example, is it conceptually equivalent to define the environment by (a) objective requirements in the workplace (TWA) and (b) common person characteristics, such as the personality orientation of workers in the environment (Holland, 1985)? Is it accurate to assume that the relationship between congruence and work adjustment is linear? Is it useful to aggregate the results of congruence studies in which different person constructs (e.g., self-reported abilities, interests) were used?

Similarly, there are numerous methods for measuring congruence, most of which do not yield equivalent results, even when the same sample and person and environment codes are used (e.g., Camp & Chartrand, 1992). As researchers move from item to scale to construct to theory, verisimilitude is often lost. This conceptual slippage is costly because conclusions are typically aimed at theoretical propositions rather than scale items. Often hypotheses are not adequately tested. Care in scale development and consistency in usage of constructs has long been advocated, but is still not realized. Better communication about the meaning and measurement of congruence is needed.

RESEARCH IN ACTION:
A STUDY OF TEENAGE LIFE

Often reviews include suggestions for where the field needs to go or what type of research should be pursued. Rarely is there an opportunity to present illustrative research examples. Fortunately, a study that was recently conducted by Csikszentmihalyi and colleagues (Whalen, personal communication, July 23, 1992) offers a glimpse at integrative research that may be a prototype for the future.

The project sample consisted of middle and high school students drawn from rural, suburban, and urban areas in or surrounding Chicago. An experience sampling technique was used in which students were asked to complete a questionnaire at eight randomly sampled points in a day for seven consecutive days. A preprogrammed computerized watch would beep as a signal for students to respond to the questionnaire. The experience sampling form asked students to respond by describing what was happening at the moment the signal occurred.

Data were collected on both the person and the environmental context. The environmental context was assessed by asking students where they were, what they were doing, and who they were with when the signal occurred. Students were also asked what they had been doing since the last time they were signaled. The students were assessed by evaluation of their emotional tone and by their evaluation of the salience of the activity they were engaged in, their motivation and interest in the activity, their self-esteem, and the challenge of the activity. These behavioral pieces, which are acknowledged in social learning theory, are likely sources for the more global dispositions emphasized in several career theories, such as Holland's six personality orientations.

After the seven-day collection phase, a follow-up interview was conducted with students. The topics included time spent with friends and family, goals, and work. The students' most evocative experience sampling forms were covered in more depth by selecting those with career activities that were rated as important in relation to goals.

With respect to work and goals, a series of questions was covered. Some questions simply elicited more information, such as asking more about what was happening at the moment they were signaled or what other ideas they had about work. Several other questions can be framed within the theoretical language of current career theories. Motivation, an important psychodynamic construct, was explored by asking students why they wanted to pursue a particular goal or job. A question about how goals are connected to future career aspirations epitomizes the role of goals as articulated by Krumboltz and Nichols (1990). Asking about relevant role models is also important from the perspective of social learning theory, and asking about perceived constraints acknowledges the roles of the sociocultural environment in career development. The significance of this latter point is clearly stated in the chapter by Fitzgerald and Betz in this volume.

Several questions addressed developmental career concepts. For example, students were asked about their level of job information and their knowledge about gathering information and implementing plans, both of which reflect career maturity. Similarly, students were asked what they would do if they had the opportunity to pursue any career they wanted. This question offers insight into the level of realism of their career aspirations.

An effort was made to move this investigation beyond self-report data. For example, evaluators rated the interviews in terms of occupational clarity and access to role models. Similarly, principals and guidance counselors were interviewed to learn more about the students' environment.

This investigation, which was not driven by any single career theory, contains the basic elements of several major theories. The person-in-environment focus was captured and progressively integrated to form a picture of motivational and behavioral repertoires for this sample of adolescents. This type of research is particularly exciting because it considers the development of cognitive and affective career-focused schemas by studying the person in his or her environmental context. The next section looks to the future on person-environment research models from an action-oriented perspective.

THEORIES OF ACTION

It seems possible to classify the various theories of career choice and development into four more general theories of action. A theory of action is defined in this chapter as *a way of identifying the prime mover or the locus of action in a model or theory.* First, there is a set of traditions that focuses primarily on the person. These theories, which are oriented to individual, purposive, and rational action, concentrate largely on individual motivation, need/satisfaction, or the pursuit of some goal. The operative environment for these theories becomes the task environment in which individual goals or aspirations are pursued. All the models presented at the convergence conference tend to be consistent, to some extent, with this theory of action. Their focus is primarily on the person rather than the environment. All the theories tend to adopt a more or less implicit or explicit trait-oriented approach to career choice and implementation, such as Holland's personality types, Super's self-concept implementation in work, TWA's work personality, social learning theory's self-observation generalizations, and Bordin's psychoanalytic motives and drives.

A second general theory of action is one in which the individual is primarily responding to demands or contingencies in the external environment. The emphasis is primarily on the stimulus environment as a controlling context of behavior. Krumboltz's social learning model, which suggests that vocational behavior is a function of antecedent conditions and past experiences, tends to fit here. The most essential concept in this theory is the concept of learning. Different reinforcement histories, interacting with differences in biology and environment, produce certain sets of response skills and attitudes in individuals.

A third theoretical tradition emphasizes the match or fit between the individual and the environment as a primary mechanism or dynamic. Often it is not clear how this matching takes place (either by shaping or selection), but fit and congruence nevertheless become a major explanatory story line in this theoretical frame. As noted by Osipow (1990), all the theories try to predict occupational fit, and in that sense they are all person-environment oriented. However, as noted above, the focus tends to be primarily on the person and not the environment. We need research on the measurement of environments within the context of all of the theoretical perspectives. Practical ways to assess environments in terms of the various theoretical perspectives would be valuable. Unfortunately, research along these lines is rarely performed.

In sum, the theories of career choice and development, consistent with traditional positivist assumptions, are primarily concerned with prediction. Research designs and measures are determined prior to the researcher's exposure to a life domain, and prediction is a very important outcome. There is no question that the positivist worldview has been a dominant and productive force in career choice and development research over the years. Prediction and control have resulted in a very solid data base.

However, a fourth theoretical tradition (Walsh, Craik, & Price, 1992) is emerging that may be described as interpretative and social constructionist in orientation. This tradition focuses primarily on the way in which actors in the social environment interpret their current circumstances and past circumstances or actions. This perspective is perhaps the most skeptical about the possibility of prediction and departs most from our traditional positivist assumptions. A primary aim of this model is to gain an in-depth understanding of people using idiographic methods and to communicate that understanding. Prediction and control are less likely outcomes of this research. Research designs and measures are not determined prior to the researcher's exposure to a given life domain. Instead, they are formulated as the researcher encounters the events to be understood. In this paradigm, conceptual and theoretical development is regarded as a continual evolving process, and qualitative research methods are frequently used because of their flexibility and sensitivity.

This may be a fresh perspective for pursuing person-environment fit that career theory and research needs to consider. People and environments are not logically independent of one another in the real world (Campbell, 1986). However, in many respects, in career theory and research we tend to investigate the person and the environment as independent variables. As noted by Altman and Rogoff (1987), person and context coexist and jointly define one another and contribute to the meaning and nature of a holistic event. In addition, from an applied perspective, the idiographic/holistic person-environment approach may assist us in learning more about the career counseling process and desired outcomes.

THE BIG FIVE

In the personality field, a consensus seems to be developing among trait theorists that there are five overarching factors, termed the Big Five (John, 1990). The five factors are extroversion, agreeableness, conscientiousness (will to achieve), emotional stability, and intellect (openness). Whether the five-factor model of personality is universal is a question that is still to be answered. However, the research reviewed by Buss (1991) demonstrated the robustness of the five-factor model across time, contexts, cultures, and data sources. Buss (1991) argued that personality traits such as extroversion, agreeableness, and conscientiousness are very important psychological dimensions of our social adaptive landscape. They provide information for answering important life questions and would seem to help individuals actively shape their careers through the processes of evoking, cognitively restructuring, and manipulating features of their environments. Examples of adaptation-relevant life career questions include: Who is high or low in the social hierarchy? Who is likely to rise in the future? Who will make a good member of my coalition? Who possesses the resources that I need? Who will be a good cooperator and reciprocator? Who might do me harm? Who can I trust? Who will betray my trust? Few of the major approaches to career behavior draw upon the five-factor model of personality. One exception is Holland's framework, where research has demonstrated some meaningful relationships between the Big Five personality factors and the Holland personality types. The obvious question here is whether the theoretical models should be paying more attention to these adaptive dimensions of human action.

AN EVOLUTIONARY PERSPECTIVE ON INTERACTIONISM

As noted above, recent work has centered on the role of people in selecting, evoking, cognitively restructuring, and manipulating features of their environments (Buss, 1991). These active and reactive person-generated processes create links between features of people and the features of their environments. Aggressive children, for example, apparently expect others to be hostile, thereby eliciting hostility from others and creating an environment populated with more belligerent acts than an environment created by children who are less aggressive. People selectively attend to and elicit behaviors from others that confirm their prior self-concepts. Adults select as mates individuals who have similar personality dispositions, attitudes, and interests, thus creating an enduring environment that they may inhabit for decades. Selection, evocation, and manipulation describe interactional processes that link features of people with features of their environments, creating person-environment correspondences. The theories of career choice and development tend to say a great deal about selection or occupational fit, but very little about evoking, cognitively restructuring, and manipulating processes.

ON THE CONCEPT OF CONGRUENCE

Spokane in this volume refers to Gibson's (1979) concept of affordances. Gibson (1979) defined affordances as functional utilities or action possibilities offered by the physical or social environment. According to Spokane, within the context of congruence, this may be interpreted to mean that if you see an opportunity, take advantage of it. Recently, Pervin (1992) suggested that we generalize Gibson's concept of affordances one step further. Pervin (1992) suggested that individual-environment transactions involve the interplay among multiple goals and multiple paths for goal enactment. On the individual side, we have goals and routes, or plans, through which these goals can be achieved. On the environment side, we have affordances or functional utilities or action possibilities offered by the physical or social environment. These action possibilities may or may not be congruent with the individual's goals and plans. It is important to note that multiple goals may be involved with multiple affordances, and the environment may provide for action possibilities congruent with some plans but not with others. In sum, Pervin seems to be suggesting that we need to think about congruence in a more multivariate context.

SUMMARY

The purpose of the convergence project was to facilitate theory integration, stimulate theory unification research, and prompt more explicit use of theory in guiding vocational research. To accomplish these goals, the convergence conference and this book have examined prospects for building clearer connections among the major career choice and development theories, discussed important distinctions, and considered future research on theory integration and unification. We believe the next step is to consider a second conference that would focus on translating career theory into practice. Stated differently, how can the science of career theory enrich the practice of career counseling? This conference could potentially focus on the applied implications of career theory models for diagnosis and assessment, the process of intervention, and the outcomes of career counseling. Methods translate the career theory models into operational terms. Methods include the interview techniques used by the counselor, the test and test interpretation procedures that the counselor and client engage in, and the use of occupational information. The applied implications of career theories (diagnosis, process, and outcomes) and their methods (tests and inventories, interview techniques, test interpretation, and occupational information) would serve as a good basis for an integrated science/practice conference. We think such a conference would serve well to link career theory with the practice of career counseling.

REFERENCES

Altman, I., & Rogoff, B. (1987). World views in psychology: Trait, interactional, organismic, and transactional perspectives. In D. Stokols & I. Altman (Eds.), *Handbook of environmental psychology, 1,* 1–40. New York: Wiley.

Bordin, E. (1990). Psychodynamic model of career choice and satisfaction. In D. Brown & L. Brooks (Eds.), *Career choice and development: Applying contemporary theories to practice* (2d ed., pp. 102–144). San Francisco: Jossey-Bass.

Borgen, F. (1991). Megatrends and milestones in vocational behavior: A 20-year counseling psychology retrospective. *Journal of Vocational Behavior, 39,* 263–290.

Buss, D. M. (1991). Evolutionary personality psychology. In M. Rosenweig & L. Porter (Eds.), *The annual review of psychology* (Vol. 49, pp. 459–493). Palo Alto, CA: Annual Reviews and Company.

Camp, C., & Chartrand, J. (1992). A comparison and evaluation of interest congruence indices. *Journal of Vocational Behavior, 41,* 162–182.

Campbell, A. (1986). The streets and violence. In A. Campbell & J. Gibbs (Eds.), *Violent transactions: The limits of personality* (pp. 115–131). New York: Basil Blackwell.

Dawis, R. (1992). The individual differences tradition in counseling psychology. *Journal of Counseling Psychology, 39,* 7–19.

Dawis, R., & Lofquist, L. (1984). *A psychological theory of work adjustment: An individual differences model and its application.* Minneapolis: University of Minnesota Press.

Gibson, J. (1979). *The ecological approach to visual perception.* Boston: Houghton Mifflin.

Hackett, G., Lent, R., & Greenhaus, J. (1991). Advances in vocational theory and research: A 20-year retrospective. *Journal of Vocational Behavior, 38,* 3–38.

Holland, J. (1985). *Making vocational choices: A theory of vocational personalities and work environments* (2d ed.). Englewood Cliffs, NJ: Prentice-Hall.

John, O. (1990). The big-five factor taxonomy: Dimension of personality in the natural language and in questionnaires. In L. Pervin (Ed.), *Handbook of personality theory and research* (pp. 66–97). New York: Guilford.

Krumboltz, J., & Nichols, C. (1990). Integrating the social learning theory of career decision making. In W. Walsh & S. Osipow (Eds.), *Career counseling* (pp. 159–192). Hillsdale, NJ: Erlbaum.

Lewin, K. (1935). *A dynamic theory of personality: Selected papers.* New York: McGraw-Hill.

Osipow, S. (1990). Convergence in theories of career choice and development: Review and prospect. *Journal of Vocational Behavior, 36,* 122–131.

Pervin, L. (1992). Transversing the individual environment landscape: A personal odyssey. In W. Walsh, K. Craik, & R. Price (Eds.), *Person-environment psychology: Models and perspectives* (pp. 71–88). Hillsdale, NJ: Erlbaum.

Staats, A. (1991). Unified positivism and unification psychology: Fad or new field? *American Psychologist, 46,* 899–912.

Walsh, W., Craik, K., & Price, R. (1992). Person-environment psychology: A summary and commentary. In W. Walsh, K. Craik, & R. Price (Eds.), *Person-environment psychology: Models and perspective* (pp. 243–269). Hillsdale, NJ: Erlbaum.

Watkins, C., Jr., & Savickas, M. (1990). Psychodynamic career counseling. In W. Walsh & S. Osipow (Eds.), *Career counseling* (pp. 79–116). Hillsdale, NJ: Erlbaum.

CHAPTER FIFTEEN

Psychodynamic and Personological Perspectives on Vocational Behavior

Steven D. Brown
Loyola University Chicago

C. Edward Watkins, Jr.
University of North Texas

PSYCHODYNAMIC AND PERSONOLOGICAL perspectives may provide important insights on theory conversion in career psychology. Our work group focused largely on the role of psychodynamic viewpoints in career psychology theory integration and resulted in what we think are some thought-provoking and informative recommendations for future theoretical and empirical work. The first section of this chapter summarizes our discussion and presents our group's recommendations.

In this chapter, we would also like to take a broader perspective by considering how theory and research on normal personality, along with psychodynamic theory, might inform career development theories. Thus, we include in this chapter a second section that presents some basic personality research from outside the psychodynamic tradition that we believe has much to offer career theories and their possible integration. In the end, we hope to show how several rich literatures that have developed apart from mainstream vocational psychology can enrich our understanding of the vocational aspirations, choices, and adjustments that people make throughout their lives.

SOME PSYCHODYNAMIC CONSIDERATIONS

Seven primary issues emerged from our discussion. Three of these could best be characterized as needs, or areas currently in need of focus in career theory, research, and practice. Two seemed to center on points of convergence, or concepts or constructs that might serve to connect psychodynamic theory with other career theories. Finally, the last two issues, which could not be neatly categorized, are termed "other" for purposes of discussion. In the remainder of this section, we will present these seven issues and elaborate briefly on each.

Issues Concerning Needs

The Role of Affect in Career Development.   We need to understand better the role of affect in career development. This issue seemed to generate much interest in the work group. The consensus was that the role of affect in career development has not been adequately addressed in either theory or research. Many, and perhaps all, group members, therefore, suggested that career theory and practice may be advanced by concerted efforts to understand how affect may influence, and be influenced by, career development and counseling processes. It was also suggested in our work group that the rich literature on affect and emotion in psychotherapy could facilitate such efforts. We discuss research that might inform future research on this important topic in the next section of this chapter.

The Role of the Family in Shaping Career Identity and Development.   We need to better understand the role that the family system plays in shaping vocational identity and development. How does the family system affect the formation and maintenance of a work identity? What effect does the family system have on the development and implementation of vocational behavior? Many believed that the role of the family system in the career development process has not been well explicated in the career literature. However, some excellent ground-breaking work has begun to appear over the last several years (e.g., Blustein, Walbridge, Friedlander, & Palladino, 1991; Lopez, 1989; Lopez & Andrews, 1987; see also Lopez, 1992, for a review) that could provide the necessary underpinnings for future theoretical and research endeavors. Many felt that this work could inform attempts to understand not only the role of the family in the process of normal career development, but also its role in impeding, delaying, or disturbing normal identity formation and career development. Thus, a consensus emerged that continued theoretical and empirical work derived from family systems perspectives could do much to advance our understanding of both normal and abnormal vocational development.

Psychodynamic Factors Across the Life Span.   We need to better understand how psychodynamic factors across the life span affect the career lives of individuals. What implications, if any, do the infant or toddler period have for the later career lives of individuals? For that matter, what implications do all preidentity, preadolescent periods of development have for later career life? What psychodynamic factors may critically affect the career development process of the adult, particularly the postcollege-age adult, and how might these be different from the factors affecting someone younger?

Most group members agreed with emerging opinion (see Harmon and Osipow's chapters in this volume) that much of our career literature deals too exclusively with adolescents and young adults, with very little attention given to other age groups. It appears, then, that a much broader, more informed perspective about career development as it exists across the full life span is needed. The group also believed that psychodynamic theory, with its inherent developmental focus, could—if creatively stretched—do much to advance our understanding of career development in its totality.

Issues Concerning Points of Convergence

Embedded Identity as a Convergent Construct.   Embedded identity can serve as a convergent construct between psychodynamic theory and other career development theories. The group accepted the embedded identity construct of Blustein (this volume) and embraced it as a possible point of convergence between psychodynamic theory and one or more of the other theories represented in this book. As Blustein has conveyed, embedded identity has cross-theoretical applicability and could be a unifying construct to guide future career theory, research, and practice efforts.

The Impact of Relationships on the Career Development Process.   Human relationships and their impact on the career development process can also serve as a point of convergence between psychodynamic and some other career theories. Contemporary thought in psychodynamic theory, especially that which is emerging from the object relations and ego psychology schools, has emphasized the critical importance of interpersonal relationships in fostering psychological development (e.g., Greenberg & Mitchell, 1983). By extension, object relational and ego psychology models suggest that relationships are of critical importance in fostering career development as well. Relationships, in some shape or form, also seem to have a place in most, if not all, of the major career perspectives (e.g., Krumboltz, this volume; Mitchell & Krumboltz, 1990; Super, 1990, this volume) Thus, it seems time to give serious attention to understanding how relationships affect the career development process and can perhaps serve as a bridge to theory integration.

Other Issues

Psychodynamic Theory Is Not Freud Circa 1909.   Object relations and ego psychology theories have advanced rapidly and significantly in the last half century and have certainly had an impact on career theorizing (see Bordin, 1990, this volume). We see this reflected, for instance, in recent career theory and research that has been stimulated by the seminal thinking of Erikson (e.g., Blustein, Devenis, & Kidney, 1989; Blustein & Phillips, 1990), Adler (e.g., Watkins, 1984, 1992; Watkins & Savickas, 1990), and Kohut (Robbins, 1989; Robbins & Patton, 1985; Robbins & Tucker, 1986). Although these are but a few examples, they nicely illustrate how psychodynamic theory has expanded and can now be meaningfully applied to the career domain.

The Complementarity of Psychodynamic Methodology.   Psychodynamic theory provides different methodologies for knowing, and these methodologies can be used to complement other methods that we now use in career psychology research. Qualitative research methods, which are used by some psychodynamic researchers, have much to offer research in career psychology. Such alternative methodologies, in conjunction with more traditional and widely used methods, may generally allow us to gain a more complete perspective on career development. More specifically, many in our group thought that these methods might do a better job than traditional methods of enabling us to get a fuller appreciation of the person as an agent of his or her own career development.

From our perspective, these seven points represent our essential recommendations for future thinking and research on career topics. With these points identified, we next turn our attention to a consideration of how recent research in personality psychology may fine-tune recommendations derived from psychodynamic viewpoints (e.g., on the role of affect in career development) and inform the primary career theories represented in this book.

THE STRUCTURE OF NORMAL PERSONALITY

Theory and Research

Recent research in personality psychology has converged on a five-factor model of normal personality. Factor analytic investigations of natural language trait terms and personality questionnaires have consistently identified five robust orthogonal factors (neuroticism, extroversion, openness to experience, agreeableness, and conscientiousness) that seem to be invariant across factor extraction and rotation methods, instruments and trait terms, respondents (e.g., self, spouse, or peer), and cultures (see Digman, 1990, and Wiggins & Pincus, 1992, for reviews).

Recent research has also suggested that these personality dimensions may be related to career interests and other important dimensions of vocational choice and adjustment. For example, extroversion, defined interpersonally by sociability and dominance and temperamentally by cheerfulness and other positive affects, has been shown to relate to social and enterprising interests (Costa, McCrae, & Holland, 1984). Further, agreeableness—being altruistic, sympathetic, and cooperative versus being egocentric, skeptical, and competitive—may differentiate the vocational preferences of extroverts: "Agreeable" extroverts appear to prefer social occupations, while "disagreeable" extroverts prefer enterprising occupations (Costa & McCrae, 1985).

The degree to which an individual is imaginative, intellectually curious, aesthetically sensitive, and open minded (i.e., openness to experience) seems to be related to preferences for artistic and investigative occupations and to the breadth of vocational and avocational interests (Costa et al., 1984). Open individuals are also more likely than are closed individuals to experience vocational indecision and to change careers at midlife (McCrae & Costa, 1985).

Neuroticism and conscientiousness, while not relating to vocational interests and preferences, appear to be implicated in work adjustment outcomes. Neuroticism is characterized by a propensity to experience a variety of aversive emotional states, such as anger, frustration, sadness, or guilt, and a ruminative, introspective perceptual/cognitive style that accentuates the negative aspects of self, situation (e.g., job, choice barriers), and worldview. A growing body of research has found that neuroticism relates negatively, though sometimes modestly, to various indices of job satisfaction (e.g., Brief, Burke, George, Robinson, & Webster, 1988; Brown, Brennan, DeGraaf-Kaser, Gore, & Heath, 1993; Schaubroeck, Ganster, & Fox, 1992), and may moderate the relationship of person-environment congruence (Holland, 1985) to career choice satisfaction and certainty (Brown, 1993). In relation to the potential moderator effects of neuroticism, Brown (1993) hypothesized that congruence may be unrelated to certainty and satisfaction among people high in neuroticism, presumably because of their tendencies to report reduced satisfaction regardless of other conditions, and to perceive more barriers to career choices than do people low in neuroticism.

Conscientiousness, characterized primarily by dependability (i.e., being thorough, responsible, and planful) and achievement orientation (i.e., being hardworking and persevering), has been shown consistently to relate to vocational performance (e.g., Barrick & Mount, 1991). In fact, in a review of research on job performance, Schmidt and Hunter (1992) concluded that "conscientiousness may eventually come to be viewed as the most important trait motivation variable in the work domain" (p. 91). Finally, Brown (1993) suggested that conscientiousness may function as an important moderator of the relationship between ability-ability requirement correspondence and work performance ratings posited by the Minnesota theory of work adjustment (Dawis & Lofquist, 1984) and other congruence theories (e.g., Holland's, 1985, performance hypothesis). According to Brown's argument, performance will not be as predictable from person-environment congruence among people who are high in conscientiousness because of their tendencies to perform better (or at least to be rated as better performers) across ability levels.

Implications

We suggest that research on the structure of normal personality has several important implications for career theories and practice. First, three of the dimensions—extroversion, agreeableness, and openness to experience—may provide added precision in promoting optimal choices from interests and values, and openness to experience may inform research on occupational change at midlife.

Second, incorporating research on neuroticism and conscientiousness into person-environment congruence theories (Dawis, this volume; Dawis & Lofquist, 1984; Holland, 1985, this volume) may facilitate the abilities of such theories to predict occupational satisfaction and success. A consideration of neuroticism and conscientiousness may also have implications for counseling from a person-environment congruence perspective. Specifically, we suggest that people high in neuroticism may benefit little in terms of satisfaction and choice certainty from congruence-oriented counseling without a concomitant focus on their tendencies to experience dissatisfaction across jobs and time, and to overestimate barriers to career choice and implementation. We also suggest that efforts to match a person's abilities with job requirements will be more important for people low in conscientiousness than it will be for those high in that quality, and that counseling efforts to increase individuals' levels of conscientiousness will provide them with more flexibility in occupational choices.

Third, as the second suggestion implies, we believe that cross-theoretical research on personality trait modification may serve career theory and practice well. There is ample evidence that all five basic dimensions of personality become quite stable by the time people reach their mid-twenties (i.e., people do not change much in relative levels of neuroticism, extroversion, openness to experience, agreeableness, and conscientiousness in the normal course of adult life; Costa & McCrae, 1988). However, we are not aware of any research that has addressed whether and how these traits may be modified therapeutically, although a symposium at a recent meeting of the American Psychological Association was devoted in part (Kazdin, 1992) to discussing some possibilities. This seems to be an important direction for future research in career counseling, especially if we are correct in our speculations about the influences of neuroticism and conscientiousness on career choice and adjustment.

Fourth, developmental theories of careers (e.g., Super, 1990, this volume) seem to be perfectly positioned to address questions about normal personality development and the influence of personality at different stages in the career development process. Fifth, we suggest that social learning theory (Krumboltz, this volume; Mitchell & Krumboltz, 1990) would also benefit from a consideration of individual differences in normal personality. For example, might neuroticism moderate the degree to which individuals benefit from self-efficacy–enhancing experiences and might conscientiousness somehow interact with self-efficacy in promoting occupational performance and persistence (see Lent, Brown, & Hackett, in press)?

Sixth, the definitions of neuroticism and extroversion that we provided earlier in this chapter indicated that each has strong affective components and there is ample research to support this view of them. For example, research on the structure of affective experiences (see Watson & Tellegen, 1985) has revealed two broad orthogonal factors when affective terms are factored: negative affect and positive affect. Recent research (e.g., Meyer & Shack, 1989) has also demonstrated quite clearly that these two affective dimensions converge remarkably with neuroticism and extroversion personality dimensions when personality and affective measures are factored together—that is, measures of negative affect load on neuroticism and measures of positive affect load on extroversion. We have already cited some research showing that neuroticism tends to relate in predictable ways to affective dimensions of work adjustment (e.g., job satisfaction). We therefore finally suggest that a fuller consideration of research on the structure of human affect and the affective components of neuroticism and extroversion may facilitate efforts to address our work group's recommendation of more fully explicating the role of affect in the career development process.

CONCLUSION

In conclusion, we have suggested how psychodynamic and structural personality theories might inform career theory and practice. Although we have also attempted to suggest how these theoretical perspectives may serve theory integration functions, our thoughts in this regard are far from complete. Whether personality perspectives may ultimately serve as bridges to theory integration is uncertain, but we leave that possibility open for future investigation.

REFERENCES

Barrick, M., & Mount, M. (1991). The Big Five personality dimensions and job performance: A meta-analysis. *Personnel Psychology, 44,* 1–26.

Blustein, D., Devenis, L., & Kidney, B. (1989). Relationship between identity formation process and career development. *Journal of Counseling Psychology, 36,* 196–202.

Blustein, D., & Phillips, S. (1990). Relation between ego identity statuses and decision making styles. *Journal of Counseling Psychology, 37,* 160–168.

Blustein, D., Walbridge, M., Friedlander, M., & Palladino, D. (1991). Contributions of psychological separation and parental attachment to the career development process. *Journal of Counseling Psychology, 38,* 39–50.

Bordin, E. (1990). Psychodynamic models of career choice and satisfaction. In D. Brown & L. Brooks (Eds.), *Career choice and development: Applying contemporary theories to practice* (2d ed., pp. 102–144). San Francisco: Jossey-Bass.

Brief, A., Burke, M., George, J., Robinson, B., & Webster, J. (1988). Should negative affectivity remain an unmeasured variable in the study of job stress. *Journal of Applied Psychology, 73,* 193–198.

Brown, S. (1993). Contemporary psychological science and the theory of work adjustment: A proposal for integration and a favor returned. *Journal of Vocational Behavior, 43,* 58–60.

Brown, S. D., Brennan, M., DeGraaf-Kaser, R., Gore, P. A., Jr., & Heath, L. (1993, August). *Interest congruence and career choice: Moderating role of negative affectivity.* Paper presented at the annual meeting of the American Psychological Association, Toronto.

Costa, P., Jr., & McCrae, R. (1985). *Manual for the NEO Personality Inventory.* Odessa, FL: Psychological Assessment Resources.

Costa, P., Jr., & McCrae, R. (1988). Personality in adulthood: A six-year longitudinal study of self-reports and spouse ratings on the NEO Personality Inventory. *Journal of Social and Clinical Psychology, 54,* 853–863.

Costa, P., Jr., McCrae, R., & Holland, J. (1984). Personality and vocational interests in an adult sample. *Journal of Applied Psychology, 69,* 390–400.

Dawis, R., & Lofquist, L. (1984). *A psychological theory of work adjustment.* Minneapolis: University of Minnesota Press.

Digman, J. (1990). Personality structure: Emergence of the five-factor model. *Annual Review of Psychology, 41,* 417–440.

Greenberg, J., & Mitchell, S. (1983). *Object relations in psychodynamic theory.* Cambridge, MA: Harvard University Press.

Holland, J. (1985). *Making vocational choices: A theory of vocational personalities and work environments* (2d ed.). Englewood Cliffs, NJ: Prentice-Hall.

Kazdin, A. (1992, August). Does psychotherapy change personality? In L. Pervin (Chair), *Can personality change? Basic issues in stability and change.* Symposium conducted at the annual meeting of the American Psychological Association, Washington, DC.

Lent, R., Brown, S., & Hackett, G. (in press). Toward a unified social cognitive theory of career/academic interest, choice, and performance. *Journal of Vocational Behavior.*

Lopez, F. (1989). Current family dynamics, trait anxiety, and academic adjustment: Test of a family-based model of vocational identity. *Journal of Vocational Behavior, 35,* 76–87.

Lopez, F. (1992). Family dynamics and late adolescent identity development. In S. Brown & R. Lent (Eds.), *Handbook of counseling psychology* (2d ed., pp. 251–284). New York: Wiley.

Lopez, F., & Andrews, S. (1987). Career indecision: A family systems perspective. *Journal of Counseling and Development, 65,* 304–307.

McCrae, R., & Costa, P., Jr. (1985). Openness to experience. In R. Hogan & W. Jones (Eds.), *Perspectives in personality: Theory, measurement, and interpersonal dynamics* (Vol. 1, pp. 145–172). Greenwich, CT: JAI Press.

Meyer, G., & Shack, J. (1989). Structural convergence of mood and personality: Evidence for old and new directions. *Journal of Personality and Social Psychology, 57,* 691–706.

Mitchell, L., & Krumboltz, J. (1990). Social learning approach to career decision making: Krumboltz's theory. In D. Brown & L. Brooks (Eds.), *Career choice and development: Applying contemporary theories to practice* (2d ed., pp. 145–196). San Francisco: Jossey-Bass.

Robbins, S. (1989). Role of contemporary psychoanalysis in counseling psychology. *Journal of Counseling Psychology, 36,* 267–278.

Robbins, S., & Patton, M. (1985). Self-psychology and career development: Construction of the superiority and goal instability scales. *Journal of Counseling Psychology, 32,* 221–231.

Robbins, S., & Tucker, K., Jr. (1986). Relation of goal instability to self-directed and interactional career workshops. *Journal of Counseling Psychology, 33,* 418–424.

Schaubroeck, J., Ganster, D., & Fox, M. (1992). Dispositional affect and work-related stress. *Journal of Applied Psychology, 77,* 322–335.

Schmidt, F., & Hunter, J. (1992). Development of a causal model of processes in determining job performance. *Current Directions in Psychologial Science, 1,* 88–92.

Super, D. (1990). A life-span, life-space approach to career development. In D. Brown & L. Brooks (Eds.), *Career choice and development: Applying contemporary theories to practice* (2d ed., pp. 197–261). San Francisco: Jossey-Bass.

Watkins, C., Jr. (1984). The individual psychology of Alfred Adler: Toward an Adlerian vocational theory. *Journal of Vocational Behavior, 24,* 27–48.

Watkins, C., Jr. (1992). Adlerian-oriented early memory research: What does it tell us? *Journal of Personality Assessment, 59,* 248–263.

Watkins, C., Jr., & Savickas, M. (1990). Psychodynamic career counseling. In W. Walsh & S. Osipow (Eds.), *Career counseling: Contemporary topics in vocational psychology* (pp. 79–116). Hillsdale, NJ: Erlbaum.

Watson, D., & Tellegen, A. (1985). Toward a consensual structure of mood. *Psychological Bulletin, 98,* 219–235.

Wiggins, J., & Pincus, A. (1992). Personality: Structure and assessment. *Annual Review of Psychology, 43,* 473–504.

CHAPTER SIXTEEN

Developmental Contextualism

An Integrative Framework for Theory and Practice

Fred W. Vondracek
Pennsylvania State University

Nadya A. Fouad
University of Wisconsin, Milwaukee

Concern with the problem of theoretical convergence, cross-cultural applications, and considerations for practice are important issues relevant to the convergence project that is at the heart of this book. Participants in the project's work group designated to explore these perspectives all expressed interest in the developmental focus, as well as concern with how advances in career theory can be translated into practical work with clients. In this chapter, we will focus on the three areas mentioned above and expand our discussion of translating theory into practice within the cultural context by reference to developmental contextualism.

THEORETICAL CONVERGENCE

The idea of converging career theories was not met with uniform acceptance by our work group for a variety of reasons: in trying to make sense of the variety of variables in career behavior, developmental theories were viewed as being too complex and as likely to ultimately reduce our capability to explain individual behavior; the merger of different theories was seen as potentially taking away the counselor's creativity to construct his or her own theory of behavior; it was observed that not enough is known to converge theories—convergence is premature when there is still so much to be learned about vocational behavior; and, finally, it was noted that developmental theories could in fact be viewed as umbrella theories that actually represent the convergence of all other theories. There was agreement that it was most important to acknowledge the contributions of various theories and to recognize areas in which they were complementary, while still recognizing that much work remained to be done to better explain vocational behavior and more effectively help clients.

In the course of the conference, interesting presentations were made by established career theorists Bordin, Dawis, Holland, Krumboltz, and Super, who argued eloquently that their approach may or may not be a candidate or vehicle for convergence. Implicit in these presentations was the assumption that, if convergence were to be realized, it would be convergence among the theories that have dominated the past. Although there is every reason to assume that these major theories will continue to significantly contribute to our understanding of career behavior and development, a new approach may offer a more powerful means of convergence and integration.

That approach, introduced as a life span developmental or *developmental-contextual approach* (Vondracek, Lerner, & Schulenberg, 1986), has been associated with "a distinguishable shift in thinking among career developmental theorists toward adopting more of the transactional world view and its assumptions" (Jepsen, 1990, pp. 146–147). It offers the possibility of integrating developmental perspectives with other perspectives that view various features of the context as critical in the determination of career behaviors and development. Moreover, it was introduced as a conceptual model that might serve as a useful guide to theory development and assist in the selection of individual and ecological variables deemed important in career development.

At the conference, Krumboltz made the point that trait-and-factor theory omits important variables, assumes a static or at least stable person, and may be too simple, while developmental theory tries to deal with too many variables, assumes that everything is constantly changing, and may be too complex. Super proposed that he has solved this latter problem with his "segmentalist" approach, which he felt demonstrated "complex simplicity." It seems to us that the current issue in career theory is not whether it should be simple or complex, but whether it serves its intended purpose and whether it can be improved by convergence or by some other means. If a theory is primarily designed to be of immediate and tangible assistance to practitioners and clients—a claim Holland makes for his theory—then it serves a limited purpose and may quite appropriately limit the range and diversity of behaviors it explains or predicts. In contrast, if a theory is designed to be a general theory of career development, then it must be far more inclusive.

CULTURAL CONTEXT

There was an expressed concern about the need to arrive at a better understanding of special groups of clients and to design intervention strategies that could address their particular needs. For example, we recognized the need for better intervention programs for junior high school-age and younger children to sensitize them to career issues and provide them with career information so that they can arrive at initial career decisions better prepared than the majority of contemporary high school seniors. Also, we recognized the need for new techniques for dealing with adult career issues, including those surrounding retirement.

Much frustration was expressed about the fact that, as Fitzgerald and Betz note in this volume, career theory and practice have dealt mostly with relatively privileged groups. Although developmental interventions may be particularly appropriate for such groups, much more needs to be done in this area—not just in the development of appropriate theory and methods but in producing macro level interventions in the areas of policy and public education (see the discussion that follows).

The cultural context in which an individual makes a career choice cannot be overemphasized. Career counselors who are raised in the majority culture and trained in counselor education programs reflecting majority cultural values and norms almost inevitably assume that all clients will adopt those values. And yet some clients will not place their own individual achievement above that of the group; they will accept—and expect—their parents' choice of career for them, or they will adopt culturally appropriate behaviors that make some careers unacceptable to them. By the same token, counselors have an obligation to help clients consider a wide range of vocational options and to act as advocates on behalf of clients who are victims of racism or other forms of discrimination.

Career counselors must meet the competency standards for culturally skilled counselors (Sue, Arredondo, & McDavis, 1992). These apply to general counseling, as well as to career counseling, and incorporate a 3 x 3 matrix of competencies. The first set of three describes counselor characteristics: (a) self-awareness of their own biases and assumptions about behavior and career choice, (b) awareness of the worldviews of their clients, and (c) ability to develop appropriate strategies and interventions. The second set of three competencies in the matrix involves the dimensions of (a) attitudes, (b) knowledge, and (c) skills. This matrix yields nine areas of competency (e.g., attitudes, knowledge, and skills in awareness of one's own biases and assumptions).

To illustrate how this matrix can operate, assume you have a young Hispanic woman, Consuelo, who seeks career counseling. The counselor, Gwen, gives her the standard battery of instruments to assess abilities and interests. Gwen finds that Consuelo has extremely high abilities in math and science and has interests that are very similar to engineers, physicians, and systems analysts. Consuelo feels pressure from her family to go to a local community college because they do not want her to live away from home and are not supportive of her education.

To effectively counsel Consuelo, Gwen needs to become aware of her own attitude that people should use their highest potential and that women, in particular, should find employment in nontraditional jobs. She should be aware that Hispanic culture tends to prescribe traditional roles for women (Baruth & Manning,

1991) and that Consuelo's culture does not place the same value on individual achievement as does the majority culture. In counseling Consuelo, Gwen should have a repertoire of skills that would help Consuelo incorporate her test results into her cultural framework. If Consuelo chooses to pursue a career as an engineer or a doctor, Gwen might need to act as advocate with her family and help Consuelo realize the potential cultural consequences of her career choice.

What the foregoing suggests is that career counselors should have a thorough knowledge of the cross-cultural use of vocational assessment (Fouad, 1993), career interventions (Bowman, 1993), and career counseling processes (Leong, 1993). Quite clearly, this implies an expanded framework for counselor education and the application of more complex theoretical models that explicitly view behaviors as emerging from the interaction of the developing individual and the multiple contexts within which he or she lives.

PRACTITIONER FOCUS

Our strongest concern surrounded the need to translate theory into practice. We felt it extremely important to have a holistic approach and to view clients over a series of age spans. To practitioners, adopting a developmental framework means not viewing clients from a static perspective. It also gives clients a sense of future and continuity, which is extremely helpful when working with clients who lack hope, such as dislocated workers, retirees, and other groups.

Practitioners expressed disappointment in the lack of adequate instrumentation within this theoretical framework. This problem appears to be based on the observation that "the technology necessary for confident application seems to have lagged far behind the understanding" [of development] (Jepsen, 1990, p. 146). Indeed, this lag stands in stark contrast to most other approaches, which favor much more direct transformation of theory into practice. Without question, this is one of the great advantages of trait-and-factor approaches, such as Holland's (1985).

There are signs of progress, however, in the developmental area. The developmental-contextual model of life span career development (Vondracek et al., 1986) has been receiving increasing attention. Super's (1980) inclusion of the concept of multiple life roles that have differential salience during different stages of career development also represents a major advance in developmental career theory. In his review of developmental career counseling, Jepsen (1990) acknowledged that developmental counseling approaches have become more complex as a consequence of these theoretical advances. At this point, however, further advances are needed in developmental career counseling to match the advances in career theory and to provide practitioners with effective tools and techniques to help clients cope with complex developmental and contextual circumstances, including the fulfillment of multiple life roles and life and career transitions.

DEVELOPMENTAL CONTEXTUALISM

The developmental-contextual approach to life span career development is not a theory. It is a general conceptual model, a way of thinking about human development in general, and career development in particular, that is intended to help guide theory development (Vondracek et al., 1986). It has several characteristics that make its application to the field of career development particularly appropriate and that may suggest directions for future theorizing and research in this area.

First, the use of this framework places career development squarely within the domain of human development. In 1983, Osipow, frequently an accurate predictor of the direction of our field, stated that "the fruitful career development theory will take shape within the larger context of human development" (p. 324). Moreover, because human development is a multidisciplinary field, the study of career development from a human development perspective will facilitate the increased use of multidisciplinary perspectives in career development, something that has been viewed as desirable and necessary by an increasing number of researchers (e.g., Arthur, Hall, & Lawrence, 1989), and which may promote integration and convergence.

Second, the contextual focus of the developmental-contextual framework highlights the fact that stage models of career development (all current developmental theories in the field) cannot account for the ever-changing socioeconomic and cultural influences on career development, something that the developmental-contextual model can do quite well. Use of this model would eliminate the need to have different theories for different groups and, in Fouad's (1988) words, facilitate the conduct of much needed research on "the pattern and development of vocational tasks in other cultures" (p. 51). Perhaps most importantly, it is an approach that facilitates the study of diverse people in the real world. It could also serve to integrate research on the impact of different contexts on career development, such as the family (e.g., Grotevant & Cooper, 1988; Penick & Jepsen, 1992), the organization (e.g., Hall, 1990), and part-time work (e.g., Mortimer, 1990). Needless to say, these areas of research are for the most part conducted by different disciplines and not integrated into the mainstream of career development research.

Third, the application of the developmental contextual model would necessitate the use of change-sensitive longitudinal methods, such as cohort-sequential designs, that could, contrary to Harmon's (1991) claim, account for environmental fluctuations and historical change (Vondracek, 1990; Vondracek et al., 1986). Such methods would also permit a more sophisticated analysis of the processes involved in the "dynamic interaction" (Lerner, 1984) of individual and environment, or a shift in research emphasis from "who and what" to "why and how" (Osipow, 1991).

The most obvious benefit of using the developmental-contextual approach to career development is its life span orientation. For many years, vocational psychology was preoccupied with the process of initial career choice. Today there is increasing concern about midlife career changes (e.g., Levinson, Darrow, Klein, Levinson, & McKee, 1978) and the career implications of a rapidly aging population (e.g., London & Greller, 1991). Retirement issues and the health consequences of alternate career development trajectories will also be of increasing interest, as will be the developmental antecedents of various career development constructs (Vondracek et al., 1986). In sum, if career theory is to deal with the full range of career development issues in the real world, it must take a life span approach.

The concept of *embeddedness,* which is a key concept of the developmental-contextual approach, offers an exciting perspective for the conduct of career interventions. The basic idea of embeddedness is that the key phenomena of human life exist at multiple levels of analysis (e.g., biological, individual-psychological, dyadic, organizational, social, societal, cultural, physical-ecological, historical). At any time, variables and processes from any and all of these multiple levels may contribute to human functioning (Vondracek et al., 1986). Importantly, these levels do not act independently; rather, each level reciprocally interacts with the others, resulting in *dynamic interaction.*

One implication of dynamic interaction is that it is inappropriate to consider one level of analysis as the prime mover or the primary determinant of change. Because changes on one level are reciprocally related to changes at other levels, it is possible, in principle, to alter the status of a given career variable or process by intervening at one or several levels of analysis. It is thus clear that this conceptual model can incorporate intervention strategies aimed at any level, thereby breaking down the artificial distinction between individual, group, organizational, and policy interventions.

Another implication of the developmental-contextual approach is that intervention is possible not just at different levels of analysis but also across the entire life span. It needs to be stressed, however, that although change through intervention is possible across the entire life span, there are always constraints on change, and they are likely to increase as a person ages (cf. Baltes & Baltes, 1980). Thus, it may be more efficient and effective to intervene early in life rather than later. Young people are simply more capable of considering more career options than are their older counterparts, who usually have more internal and external constraints. If early intervention is not possible or is unsuccessful, all is not lost, since there may be ways, albeit more difficult or costly, to intervene later in life and still produce desired outcomes.

CONCLUSION

Clearly, neither the developmental-contextual approach, nor any other, is a panacea for all that ails career development theory and practice. However, it does constitute a potentially powerful conceptual framework, and specific theoretical formulations about various aspects of career development can be derived from it. This has yet to be accomplished to any great extent. The framework also makes it possible to identify specific, particularly promising variables for research and to hypothesize how they dynamically interact with the contexts in which they operate. Some studies of this sort are now being reported (e.g., Grotevant & Cooper, 1988). Finally, specific interventions need to be developed that follow from theoretical formulations and empirical findings derived from this framework. As Jepsen (1990) has noted, such endeavors are costly and time consuming, and making significant progress is hampered by a professional community that seems to share the contemporary societal value on efficient, quick, and simple solutions to both social and personal problems.

REFERENCES

Arthur, M., Hall, D., & Lawrence, B. (1989). Generating new directions in career theory: The case for a transdisciplinary approach. In M. Arthur, D. Hall, & B. Lawrence (Eds.), *Handbook of career theory* (pp. 7–25). Cambridge, UK: Cambridge University Press.

Baltes, P., & Baltes, M. (1980). Plasticity and variablity in psychological aging: Methodological and theoretical issues. In G. Gurski (Ed.), *Determining the effects of aging on the central nervous system* (pp. 41–66). Berlin: Schering.

Baruth, L., & Manning, M. (1991). *Multicultural counseling and psychotherapy: A lifespan perspective.* New York: Merrill.

Bowman, S. (1993). Career intervention strategies with ethnic minorities. *Career Development Quarterly, 42,* 14–25.

Fouad, N. (1988). The construct of career maturity in the United States and Israel. *Journal of Vocational Behavior, 32,* 49–59.

Fouad, N. (1993). Cross-cultural vocational assessment. *Career Development Quarterly, 42,* 4–10.

Grotevant, H., & Cooper, C. (1988). The role of family experience in career exploration: A life-span perspective. In P. B. Baltes, D. L. Featherman, & R. M. Lerner (Eds.), *Life-span development and behavior* (pp. 231–258). Hillsdale, NJ: Erlbaum.

Hall, D. (1990). Career development theory in organization. In D. Brown & L. Brooks (Eds.), *Career choice and development: Applying contemporary theories to practice* (2d ed., pp. 422–454). San Francisco: Jossey-Bass.

Harmon, L. (1991). Twenty years of the Journal of Vocational Behavior. *Journal of Vocational Behavior, 39,* 297–304.

Holland, J. (1985). *Making vocational choices: A theory of vocational personalities and work environments* (2d ed.). Englewood Cliffs, NJ: Prentice-Hall.

Jepsen, D. (1990). Developmental career counseling. In W. Walsh & S. Osipow (Eds.), *Career counseling: Contemporary topics in vocational psychology* (pp. 117–157). Hillsdale, NJ: Erlbaum.

Leong, F. (1993). The career counseling process with racial/ethnic minorities: Asian-Americans' similarities and differences as illustrated by the case. *Career Development Quarterly, 42,* 26–40.

Lerner, R. (1984). *On the nature of human plasticity.* New York: Cambridge University Press.

Levinson, D., Darrow, C., Klein, E., Levinson, M., & McKee, B. (1978). *The seasons of a man's life.* New York: Knopf.

London, M., & Greller, M. (1991). Demographic trends and vocational behavior: A twenty-year retrospective and agenda for the 1990's. *Journal of Vocational Behavior, 38,* 237–287.

Mortimer, J. (1990). Introduction. *Youth and Society, 22,* 131–138.

Osipow, S. (1983). *Theories of career development* (3d ed.). Englewood Cliffs, NJ: Prentice-Hall.

Osipow, S. (1991). Observations about career psychology. *Journal of Vocational Behavior, 39,* 291–296.

Penick, N., & Jepsen, D. (1992). Family functioning and adolescent career development. *Career Development Quarterly, 40,* 208–222.

Sue, D., Arredondo, P., & McDavis, R. (1992). Multicultural counseling competencies and standards: A call to the profession. *Journal of Multicultural Counseling and Development, 20,* 64–88.

Super, D. (1980). A life-span, life-space approach to career development. *Journal of Vocational Behavior, 16,* 282–298.

Vondracek, F. (1990). A developmental-contextual approach to career development research. In R. Young & W. Borgen (Eds.), *Methodological approaches to the study of careers* (pp. 37–56). New York: Praeger.

Vondracek, F., Lerner, R., & Schulenberg, J. (1986). *Career development: A life-span developmental approach.* Hillsdale, NJ: Erlbaum.

PART FOUR

OVERVIEW AND FUTURE DIRECTIONS

I~N PART~ 4, three discussants each reflect on the contributions and limitations of the career theory convergence project. The discussants, representing the vantage points of theory, research, and practice, also share their own views on the problems and possibilities for integration of career choice and development theories.

In chapter 17, Osipow suggests that the major career theories have already converged in important respects, though key differences remain. He sees convergence as part of a natural process of theory renewal. Eventually, as the theories evolve further, or are succeeded by newer conceptual schemes, the links among them may become more pronounced. He cautions, however, that committee-type efforts aimed specifically at unifying the theories are premature and, perhaps, unwise in that they risk impeding the creativity of individual career theorists. In essence, Osipow recommends supporting theoretical diversity, while allowing convergence to take its natural course. He also cites several areas in which the extant theories might be improved, and argues that career development theories are not sufficient to direct career interventions. Separate, unique career counseling theories may be needed for this purpose.

Reflecting on her experience as a professor and researcher, Harmon laments the absence of a satisfactory overarching conceptual scheme for organizing knowledge about career choice, development, and adjustment in chapter 18. She also views the current theories as limited in their capacity to inspire innovative, socially meaningful research, and questions their practical relevance for the majority of potential career clients. Harmon considers several directions for improving career inquiry and its social impact. For example, she notes that advances in computer technology may enable more complex, multidimensional study of career phenomena. She urges career scientists to study problems of relevance to policy and practice, and to consider more fully the systemic and economic forces that affect people's career lives.

In chapter 19, Savickas contends that efforts devoted to career theory convergence can facilitate renovation of existing theories, advance research, and contribute to practice. In addition to highlighting topics that the career theories tend to neglect or underemphasize, he considers factors that may have disrupted the intimate, reciprocal relationship between career theory and practice. Focusing on common problems presented by career clients, such as vocational indecision, Savickas illustrates how researchers may profitably explore the connections among particular theories, leading to advances in both understanding and intervention. Finally, considering convergence at the level of practice, Savickas presents a conceptual model describing how different career services relate to particular career theories.

CHAPTER SEVENTEEN

Moving Career Theory Into the Twenty-first Century

Samuel H. Osipow
Ohio State University

THE ANNOUNCEMENTS FOR the conference that formed the basis for this book credited me with providing the driving force for the meeting with my recent paper on convergence in career choice and development theory (Osipow, 1990b). It is a rare pleasure to observe directly the influence of one's writing on other people. At the same time, many conference participants agreed with me that all the major speakers, and many of the respondents, viewed the idea of theory convergence with disfavor. Furthermore, the eloquence of the presenters generally seemed to persuade the conference participants that career theory convergence was a premature idea whose time might never come. My own view is that convergence is part of the natural evolution of career development theory.

John Holland is the most adamantly opposed to theory convergence efforts. His view, loosely translated by me, is that a theory designed at a conference or by a group will produce a product reminiscent of the old joke that a camel is a horse designed by a committee: unwieldy and clumsy. However, using that analogy loses sight of the functional usefulness of the beast in its proper environment. At the other end of the spectrum is Donald Super, who, while more enthusiastic about the usefulness of career theory convergence, appears to hold the hope that looking for ways that our theories relate to each other will advance our research and practice approaches.

This chapter has three major objectives. The first is to review briefly the motivation and basis of the original career theory convergence paper (Osipow, 1990b). The second is to briefly review the major ideas posed by the presenters and discussants at the conference. And, finally, the third is to reassess career theory convergence.

WHY CAREER CONVERGENCE?

My motivation in writing the original career theory convergence paper was simple and evolved over a period of years. In teaching my annual course entitled "The Psychology of Career Development," I routinely present material that describes the basic concepts for each of the major career theories, reviews and evaluates the related research, and considers new research findings and practical applications. I always include some comparison of the theories on a number of dimensions. Over time, I found that students would repeatedly ask questions about how certain concepts differ across the theories, such as how Super's self-concept implementation differs from Holland's congruence or Dawis and Lofquist's correspondence. Table 1, reprinted from the original article, summarizes many of the areas in the four major career development theories that have some overlap. In considering how I might reply to student questions, I gradually realized that the concepts were basically the same, differing in subtleties involving measurement, explanatory concepts, and timing. These are important differences, yet surely the similarities are important as well.

Gradually, with no commitment to a particular conclusion, I began to write the convergence article. A careful reader of the paper will see that while I emphasized theoretical similarities, I also noted differences and indicated that each theory would work particularly well in a distinctive setting or with a particular clientele. This last observation, in which I indicated that the theoretical differences between the theories (though they may eventually disappear) are important, seems to have been lost in the emphasis given to the convergence aspect of the paper.

Finally, in my convergence article (Osipow, 1990b), I emphasized some aspects that I thought the important current theories needed to add or elaborate. Super's theory (Super, 1980; Super, Starishevsky, Matlin, & Jordaan, 1963) discusses the developmental press regarding decisions, as does the theory of work adjustment (Dawis & Lofquist, 1984); Holland (1985) has identified some of the barriers to effective career development, but little attention has been explicitly paid to those by other theorists; and, finally, none of the theories says enough about work adjustment, though that is one of the main emphases of the theory of work adjustment.

Of course, the theory convergence article (Osipow, 1990b) was based on the writings of the theorists of the 1980s. Some new ideas and integrations were presented at the conference. These should be briefly reviewed. For example, Bordin (this volume), as his recent work has suggested (Bordin, 1984), has now clearly moved toward a heavy emphasis on the important roles of play and spontaneity in work. He has further emphasized the importance of intrinsic motivations (and presumably, satisfactions) in work such as precision, nurturance, curiosity, power, aesthetic expression, and ethics.

Bordin's work may have begun before our recent economic recession, since choosing to emphasize such variables at a time when the economy is ailing and many people are unemployed (not by choice) or underemployed, seems inappro-

TABLE 1   Concepts, Classifications, Outcomes, and Predictions of Four Career Theories

Holland's Theory	Social Learning Theory	Developmental Theory	Work Adjustment Theory
Congruence	Reinforcement	Self-concept	Correspondence
Person types	Environment	Self-esteem	Reinforcers
Environment	Response skills	Vocational tasks	Work personality
Identity		Life stages	Skills
Consistency		Life roles	Satisfaction
Differentiation		Vocational maturity	Satisfactoriness
Classification			
People types Environ types	None	None	None
Outcomes			
Congruence	Skills	Self-concept implementation	Abilities

Occupational
    preferences
	Attitudes
	Traits
		Occupational
		  preferences
		Occupational fit
		Self-esteem
			Values/Needs
			Personality

Predicting?			

Satisfaction and
    persistence
    of choice
	Decision making	Satisfaction	Correspondence

Ease	Quality of process		Stability

From "Convergence in Theories of Career Choice and Development: Review and Prospect" by S. H. Osipow, 1990, *Journal of Vocational Behavior, 36*, p. 124. Copyright 1990 by *Journal of Vocational Behavior*. Reprinted by permission.

priate. Furthermore, as the Fitzgerald and Betz chapter in this volume points out, the labor force is increasingly diverse, and these diverse groups probably bring to their work new values, needs, and motivations that are likely to be far different from those that Bordin suggests. Bordin's notions seem to be targeted at an upper-level, affluent, highly educated worker who is probably male, while the labor force is moving toward greater diversity regarding income, gender, race, and ethnicity. Thus, Bordin's ideas would seem to have less applicability to any emerging integrated theory of careers.

Holland has reiterated his theoretical view in his volume. Among the strengths of Holland's work is its programmatic nature and Holland's ability to add to and modify his theory as new data emerge. Even more powerful has been his creativity in devising methods to measure, study, apply, and even merge his concepts with others' work. Two very notable examples of that last idea include the merger of Holland's theory with the *Strong Interest Inventory* many years ago (Campbell &

TABLE 2   The Distinctive Role of Each Major Career Theory

Theory	Function
Holland	What happens
Super	How it happens
Bordin	Why it happens
Theory of Work Adjustment	How it happens and its outcome
Social Learning Theory	How to make it happen and how to change what happens

Holland, 1972) and, more recently, the integration of his occupational classification system (Gottfredson & Holland, 1989) with that of the United States Department of Labor's (1991) *Dictionary of Occupational Titles*. There is a certain irony in Holland's insistence that efforts at theory convergence are inappropriate, even though some of his arguments against convergence are good, while at the same time he has extended his own work by merging it with other systems in order to make it more widely applicable.

In at least one important way, John Holland is absolutely correct: Developing a convergence in theory is not likely to be done effectively by a group, committee, or conference. Krumboltz makes that point effectively in suggesting that we should not take efforts toward convergence too literally. He implies that we are still at the divergence stage of career theory development, suggesting that many flowers should be permitted to bloom. He may very well be correct. Theory is best developed by one person, with perhaps two or three collaborators, who then need to integrate data and ideas, distill the good ideas and methods from the inadequate ones, formulate new ideas, and develop new theoretical integrations.

One's conclusion reflects individual perspectives on theory building. Each of the theorists whose work is represented here is and has been struggling to organize a body of knowledge in a distinctive and personal way. Most of the rest of us pick and choose from their products those features that are useful to us. That utility often varies reflecting our momentary needs. When I do research, I often use Holland's theory to guide me, or select aspects of social learning theory à la Krumboltz, or the theory of work adjustment. When I counsel, I rely on Holland's typology and measures, Super's stages, and psychodynamic processes. Others make their choices differently.

Table 2 summarizes, probably too succinctly, the most important distinctive emphasis of each career theory. This table shows my interpretation of the piece of career behavior best explained by each theory. Holland's (1985) person-environ ment typology is an excellent description of how people fit themselves into their most comfortable vocational niche. Super's emphasis on life stage development and self-concept implementation provides us with some explanation of the process. Bordin's (Bordin, Nachmann, & Segel, 1963) psychodynamic theory strives to permit us to understand the motivational forces that structure career decision making and development. Dawis and Lofquist's (1984) theory of work adjustment recapitulates in a distinctive manner how careers unfold using a developmental theme, but carries that theme over into the adult career by focusing on what happens to individuals under various workplace conditions. And, finally, Krumboltz's (1979) representation of the social learning theory approach to careers emphasizes how to enhance career decision making by understanding the personal and social forces that affect career choice initially and how it adjusts over time. Using Krumboltz's map analogy, it is possible to see how each theory looks at a different part of the terrain using a different scale of reference.

COMMENTS ON THE THEORIES

Some interesting points have been made by the authors of this book. Again, using a summary approach to the chapters, Spokane has focused on understanding how career decisions are made, Lent and Hackett and Blustein have focused on the cognitive-affective dimension in career decision making, Phillips has focused on understanding career development, and Fitzgerald and Betz and, to some extent, Spokane, have focused on understanding the person-environment dimension.

By implication, Spokane, Lent and Hackett, and Blustein raise the question of whether people decide at all, and what variables are important in their decision making. In some ways, their chapters remind me of my career choice and development concept (Osipow, 1990a) of "least resistance," that is, the notion that career "choices" may more significantly reflect ease of access than most career theories suggest.

Phillips' chapter, which raises questions about career maturity, reminds me of an issue that has troubled me for years: What evidence do we have that indicates that career maturity as it is measured in adolescence predicts the quality of eventual career choice, entry, and adjustment? Has career maturity been a useful construct? Do we have definitive data connecting career maturity in adolescence (or in any life stage, for that matter) with any meaningful career outcome, such as quality of decision, fit, satisfaction, effectiveness, productivity, stability, adjustment to changes, or congruence? I suspect that the predictive value is minimal, if only because so many social and economic variables intervene between early career maturity and later career behaviors. Those social and economic variables create noise in the system and reduce the predictive accuracy of career maturity. While Savickas (1993) believes such a criterion is too demanding, I think it is time to raise such questions about venerable constructs such as career maturity.

Spokane has raised questions about the nature of our interventions on behalf of good career decisions. How do we intervene, how do we evaluate the effectiveness of our interventions, and, considering the "least resistance principle," how do our career interventions fit into the system? One thing has become extremely clear in this volume: Career theories are not career counseling theories, and although career theories may have suggestions of value for career counseling practice, career counseling probably needs its own theory or theories.

Finally, Fitzgerald and Betz remind us of yet another of the great failings of our career theories, namely, that we really only consider some parts of the person-environment equation. That is, our theories represent "idealized" versions of career choice and development for some people and in certain environments, but leave out what is probably the majority of people. The work patterns, resources, and career aspirations of people of different backgrounds significantly affect their career paths in ways not fully considered theoretically.

Thus, in sum, the variety of corrective measures needed by the theories, and which a "converged" theory might resolve, include incorporating the least resistance principle, expanding the range of people and environments included, revising the concept of career maturity and empirically testing its potency, and recalibrating the impact our counseling interventions are likely to have on individuals in light of the concerns just mentioned.

WHERE DO WE GO FROM HERE?

I would proceed by building on Krumboltz's chapter (this volume). Krumboltz applies the analogy of maps of different scale to explain how the theories account for career behaviors in different ways. Some maps are very detailed, others are less so; some focus on topography, others focus on highways, and so on. It is a very good analogy and actually makes the point for theory convergence very effectively. Ideally, one should be able to move easily from the less detailed theoretical "map" to the more detailed one. Similarly, focusing on different content or populations would be facilitated by understanding how these concepts are related across the theories. If we were able to relate our current theories in that way, we would have moved significantly toward a "converged" theory. One of our problems in so doing is to develop the precise language that permits us to make those important translations.

Let me suggest the following as an example, one which is very far from a finished product. I consider Super's model to be one of those with relatively little detail, except in the developmental stages. Perhaps at a basic level we should focus on his plan to describe and explain life stage development. Holland's theory is a very detailed effort to explain the person aspect of career theory, and it might be connected to Super's developmental stages in the way Super has envisioned self-concept implementation. Dawis and Lofquist's theory has considerable detail describing adult adjustment issues and can be fit in to help us understand and predict work progress. Krumboltz contributes to our understanding of how individuals make decisions at different stages or in different settings. And Bordin's model may be helpful in providing an overall understanding of how work fits into life motivational issues.

My view is that, ultimately, new and more powerful theories emerge from the ashes and residue (or embers and sparks, to be more positive) of the failures of earlier theories. None of the theories perfectly (or even adequately) explains or predicts all the pertinent career phenomena. One might think of convergence theory in terms of building the "most wonderful theory" on the goals and methods of theory A, theory B, and theory N.

The "most wonderful theory" will select the most explanatory goals and methods available, that is, those that seem to best measure what we seek to assess and which explain the greatest number of phenomena, and develop links between them that make sense. The next step would be to test the links empirically, and revise them again, producing the "even more wonderful theory."

CONCLUSION

After reading all the chapters and making some further reflection, my conclusion remains that considerable convergence in career theory has already occurred. Granted, the theorists continue to emphasize the differences between the theories, but a fair reading should reveal many common points. In fact, I think theory convergence is part of a natural process. Indeed, if there is any reality to the idea of a career development process that is not a random event, it is only logical to expect the theories to resemble one another; otherwise, they would be at variance with reality. By their very nature, theories are doomed to extinction (and one [Roe, 1957] is virtually gone already). Itamar Gati (personal communication, 1992) reminded me recently that theories are revised by disconfirmation, not confirmation. It is easy to integrate new empirical findings supporting a theory, but difficult to understand how to fit new disconfirming findings into a frame of reference—yet this is what theory development is all about.

It is probably unreasonable to expect the theorists to be objective about their creations. Usually, an outsider is needed to see the flaws and suggest areas in need of change. One of my own professional roles has been as observer, and sometimes integrator, which grows out of my needs as a consumer of theory. Consequently, I strive to see how the theories relate to each other, while the theorists understandably are highly focused on their own work.

Should career theory be converged? The answer is an emphatic no. We need the creativity of the theorists, and part of the bargain is that we permit them the freedom to develop in their unique manner. However, the rest of us need to be aware of the links between the theories and strive to strengthen the links and reduce the distance between the theories where this is appropriate. In my view, that would be a sign of theoretical maturity.

Is career theory converging? I think it is, but the reader, and time, will be the final judge. Perhaps somewhere there is a reader who will create the next version of our career theory, which will reflect his or her independent view, yet build on the work of those who came before and bring us into the twenty-first century.

REFERENCES

Bordin, E. (1984). Psychodynamic model of career choice and satisfaction. In D. Brown & L. Brooks (Eds.), *Career choice and development* (pp. 94–136). San Francisco: Jossey-Bass.

Bordin, E., Nachmann, B., & Segel, S. (1963). An articulated framework for vocational development. *Journal of Counseling Psychology, 10,* 107–116.

Campbell, D., & Holland, J. (1972). A merger in vocational interest research: Applying Holland's theory to Strong's data. *Journal of Vocational Behavior, 2,* 353–376.

Dawis, R., & Lofquist, L. (1984). *A psychological theory of work adjustment.* Minneapolis: University of Minnesota Press.

Gottfredson, G., & Holland, J. (1989). *Dictionary of Holland occupational codes* (2d ed.). Odessa, FL: PAR.

Holland, J. L. (1985). *Making vocational choices* (2d ed.). Englewood Cliffs, NJ: Prentice-Hall.

Krumboltz, J. (1979). A social learning theory of career decision making. Revised and reprinted in A. Mitchell, G. Jones, & J. Krumboltz (Eds.), *Social learning and career decision making* (pp. 19–49). Cranston, RI: Carroll Press.

Osipow, S. (1990a). Careers: Research and personal. *The Counseling Psychologist, 18,* 337–346.

Osipow, S. (1990b). Convergence in theories of career choice and development: Review and prospect. *Journal of Vocational Behavior, 36,* 122–131.

Roe, A. (1957). Early determinants of vocational choice. *Journal of Counseling Psychology, 4,* 212–217.

Savickas, M. (1993). Predictive validity criteria for career development measures. *Journal of Career Assessment, 1,* 38–50.

Super, D. (1980). A life-span, life-space approach to career development. *Journal of Vocational Behavior, 16,* 282–298.

Super, D., Starishevsky, R., Matlin, N., & Jordaan, J. (1963). *Career development: A self-concept theory.* New York: College Entrance Examination Board.

United States Department of Labor. (1991). *The dictionary of occupational titles* (4th ed.). Washington, DC: U.S. Government Printing Office.

CHAPTER EIGHTEEN

Frustrations, Daydreams, and Realities of Theoretical Convergence

Lenore W. Harmon
University of Illinois

A SEARCH FOR CONVERGENCE among theories of career development and career choice is an ambitious undertaking. I believe that Donald Super, with his usual sweeping vision of our field, originally suggested that it was time for such an effort in 1989 or 1990. The charge given to me by the editors of this book—to reflect on all the presentations they had commissioned for the convergence project—was a daunting one. I accepted it only because of my frustrations with the current state of our knowledge and because of my hopes for change.

FRUSTRATIONS

As a professor, I find teaching theories of career development problematic. I tend to go from textbook to textbook, reorganizing my course outline and additional readings from year to year, never satisfied with the way the textbook authors or I have organized the available literature. There seems to be no satisfactory conceptual schema for organizing the things we know about career development, choice, and adjustment.

It is also difficult to explain the narrowness of our theories to students. The theories focus on a segment of the population that has become increasingly smaller—those who have the luxury of (a) relative certainty of employment, (b) choice about the type of employment they will seek, and (c) the power to effect changes in their workplace. The theories do not address the experience of people living in trying economic times when it is difficult for many people to find and retain jobs, let alone plan careers.

Another problem is that the concept of work that I want to espouse when I teach is not even fully realistic to me, yet I believe that it underlies many of our theories. The various authors represented in this volume have written about some aspects of work that I find appealing: Work can be seen as an extension of play in our lives; it can be seen as a way to develop skills and achieve mastery; it offers the possibility of experiencing satisfaction. But when I talk about these concepts with my students, they say that I am too idealistic and that I don't understand the real world. My wish and hope is that these concepts can be applied to greater proportions of our population.

My greatest concern is that the theories we have available do very little to tell us how to practice interventions that will change the experience of those for whom work is drudgery or not even worth pursuing. If we wish to limit our practice to the type of students who are able to attend college, then our theories apply, but they do not tell us what to do for the student who, like the fictional honor student at a Bronx high school in Tom Wolfe's (1987) novel *The Bonfire of the Vanities,* "attends class, isn't disruptive, tries to learn, and does all right at reading and arithmetic." If we wish to limit our practice to the most secure managers in our nation's businesses, our theories may be useful, but they do not tell us how to help the manager whose position has been terminated because of a merger and who has not been able to find a job.

In my own research, the lack of theoretical convergence doesn't bother me much at all. It is relatively easy to decide what variables I am interested in and to determine how I expect them to be related or influenced. But this is the case because I have chosen my research topics to inform counseling practice and social policy rather than to test or inform theory. The fact that our theories do not have the power to excite me to research theoretical questions may be more a result of my limited vision than of shortcomings in our theories. However, I have been in a position to monitor both published and unpublished research in this field for quite a few years, and it is my impression that comparing, testing, or integrating theories has not been the major focus of most programs of research. Clearly, the authors of the theories we have examined here have extensive research programs, as do those who have discussed integrating constructs, but their numbers are small compared to the numbers of researchers in the field. My impression is that most research is problem focused rather than theory focused. Thus, one of my frustrations is that our theories do not seem to be stimulating much exciting exploration. Alternatively, I am willing to recognize the possibility that researchers, myself included, lack the vision and creativity required to do theoretically-based research.

To summarize, theories of career choice and development do not form an elegant, intellectually satisfying, and cohesive body of knowledge; they do not inform practice with the most needy of our potential clients; and they do not excite researchers to do interesting, creative work.

DAYDREAMS

Given these observations, I had some expectations for the outcomes of the convergence project. I think that my hope was that we would together have some sort of collective "aha" experience in which we would find overarching organizing principles for looking at what we already know in new ways. In this, I was thinking along the lines suggested by René Dawis—of superimposing some larger picture on the linkages between theories. I also hoped that this might lead to more productive theory building and more effective practice. My fantasy of the outcome was not that theories would somehow be magically unified, but that we would have a more satisfactory way of explaining the relationships among theories of the present and the future. Looking at those expectations, I realized that I needed to make some compromises with my daydreams.

Compromises

I don't think that intellectual "aha" experiences are collective. They are probably very personal. I doubt that in the history of science there are very many new, innovative theoretical ideas that have been conceived by a group, although innovative ideas have sometimes been studied by research teams. Historically, it is the rather isolated individual who possesses the innovative insights. Often it has not been immediately obvious to those around him or her that the new ideas are worthwhile. In fact, it can be an uphill battle just to get new ideas accepted. The innovative thinker may be young and unburdened by the responsibilities that fame and fortune bring. The most tenaciously reactionary opponents may be those who have some vested interest in the status quo. In the field of career development, we are fortunate in this regard in that the most senior theorists, such as Donald Super, are among those who are pointing to a need for change and supporting younger theorists in their inquiries.

Recognizing that it was unrealistic to expect a group experience to emerge from the convergence project, I had to accept that I am the only theorist whose experience I know and control. As Kelly (1970) suggested, I am a very personal scientist, as is each person who attended the conference and who reads this book. Thus, my reactions to the ideas presented here must be completely my own and are certainly no better or more valid than those of anyone else. The most exciting reactions are more likely to come from respondents who are much less entrenched with the status quo than I am.

REALITIES

Limitations of Theories

We all recognize that theories are abstractions that will never completely encompass everything we need to consider as we try to conceptualize an individual client. Theories can only point us toward some general ways of conceptualizing the individual and the processes that the individual goes through. Several writers have acknowledged that theories are developed to be superseded. We certainly are not in search of some absolute understanding of truth, that, once elucidated, will prove satisfactory forever. It is our very awareness that theories can converge into new forms that motivates our participation in this project. The fact that those new forms may be very different from the material they emerged from and that they, too, are born to be superseded, is both a frightening and an exciting prospect.

Limitations of Our Ability to Conceptualize Reality

Originally, as I tried to think about the concept of convergence and the purpose of the project, I began to think in terms of dimensions along which theories might differ. My own concept of the task expanded when I heard Krumboltz's map metaphor—a very apt one for describing how our theories attempt to operate at different levels of explanation. Finally, I noted that most participants conceptualized the task in two- or, at most, three-dimensional terms. That led me to wonder if our theorizing is excessively two dimensional, if we are attempting to describe and explain phenomena that require a more N-dimensional outlook to arrive at the best description. It may be that our very dependence on a two-dimensional viewpoint points us toward explanations that can at best be partial.

The source of some of my frustrations may be that the phenomena I want to explain are not easily constructed from a two- or three-dimensional perspective. Most participants in this project have acknowledged the complexities of the phenomena we are trying to explain, yet few have spoken of examining more than two dimensions at a time. It is almost as though our tools have limited our thought processes. Perhaps our hopes for convergence have arisen at the precise time in history when the technology available to us may make it possible for us to get past the limitations of paper and the lines drawn on it. Perhaps we can utilize the full potential of holograms and computer imaging to explore more dimensions and interactions across dimensions than ever before. It remains to be seen whether the human mind is capable of grasping what these new technologies make available.

Another observation is that most participants tended to think in terms of linear relationships. I only heard two people speak in terms of nonlinear relationships at the conference. Blustein talked of the literature suggesting that some combination of attachment and individuation is more adaptive for young adults than an extreme level of either, and Brown spoke of an inverted U as the best description of the relationship between personal identity and a secure base. In general, we may be guilty of thinking in parametric terms, using ordinal or interval scales, when we really should be thinking in nonparametric terms and using categorical data.

What we hope to do may require us to adopt new ways of thinking and conceptualizing reality. Yet I find that I am no clearer about how to apply new approaches to reality than any of the other project participants. Even so, it seems important to remain open to the possibility that our way of construing what we want to explain may limit our explanations.

Promising Approaches

It is clear that we are able to find similarities in our theories. These similarities are at the level of theoretical concepts as well as at the level of processes and relationships. For example, Dawis asserted the compatibility of concepts between the theory of work adjustment and Holland's theory, and Krumboltz pointed out the compatibility of the developmental processes in his social learning theory of career decision making and Super's theory. We are also able to show that our career theories are related to theories in other areas of psychology. Super, for instance, claimed the relationship of his theory to differential, developmental, social, and phenomenological psychology, as well as to sociological and economic theories.

Holland's suggestions for restoring and renovating our current theories contain some useful ideas about looking for missing definitions and articulating new relationships that need not be limited to within-theory efforts. Krumboltz's idea of looking for anomalies is also useful. Although Krumboltz limited his observations to anomalies in the professional arena, I think that it may be at least as productive to look for theoretical anomalies—that is, predictions that differ for different theories—and to study the differential predictions and understand the basis for the results obtained.

The theorists and presenters on convergence concepts suggested a number of ideas that seem to be candidates for greater emphasis in our theoretical thinking. Bordin and Vondracek called attention to the individual's basic motivation to engage in activity that is worklike in childhood play, and Vondracek also noted similar activity in retirees. Bordin briefly noted the influence of family variables on the career development of individuals, and Blustein expanded on how family variables may facilitate identity development. Phillips reminded us of the nonrational nature of much of career decision making. Several reminded us of the agentic or constructionist nature of much of vocational behavior, with Lent and Hackett treating this topic extensively. This list of ideas that seemed important to me has the potential to expand the complexity of our theories tremendously as we attempt to integrate them more completely into our theory building.

Realities We Do Not Address

Perhaps one of the most profound questions to arise from the convergence project concerns the nature of change. If we accept the assumption that what is desirable is a satisfying person-environment fit, we must then also acknowledge that congruence between the person and the work environment is less than satisfying for a large proportion of our society. If we accept the assumption that what is desirable is a correspondence between the demands of the workplace and the accomplishments of the work force, we must then acknowledge that correspondence between the person and the environment is less than satisfactory in a large proportion of work environments.

The question of what needs to change to address these problems is an important one. Phillips posed the issue of how the decider can attain certainty of personal choice within the context of personal and social change. Spokane suggested that it is the individual's choice of environment, and not the individual, that must change. To be sure, Spokane understands the complex forces that shape the choice, but I believe that he has not gone far enough. There are work environments that make demands that no worker should have to fulfill. For example, who would choose to work unprotected in an environment contaminated by carcinogens? Only if Spokane's concept of individual choice rests on the assumption that there are no work environments that most people would find undesirable, does it fully address the locus of change.

What of those whose interests and abilities have not been allowed to develop because they live in poverty without enough to eat to support effective learning, or because they attend overcrowded schools where the most important lesson to be learned is how to survive physically? For what do they develop self-efficacy expectations? What of those who are discouraged by the barriers and constraints of society and who see no possibility that society will allow them to advance to work that is fulfilling or even life supporting? Gottfredson and Becker (1981) showed that congruence between aspiration level and job was achieved by changing aspiration level, not by changing position—even for middle class males. This suggests to me that when the level of change is individual, individuals must accommodate their views of what they can achieve to what society offers them. For many people, society offers very little. We, as vocational psychologists, are not skilled at looking at work from either the perspective of the socioeconomic system or from the perspective of the many individuals who are trapped in the nearly inescapable positions that such a system creates.

Fitzgerald and Betz's treatment of cultural and structural variables that affect vocational behavior raises important questions and points us to another locus for understanding change. It shows that the populations on which we concentrate are not those that predominate in our society. Those predominant populations do not have the type of freedom of choice that Spokane's analysis suggests. Thus, the workplace is also an important focus for change. Hackett and Lent, Chartrand and

Walsh, and Hesketh and Rounds all address the possibility of change in the environment and the individual's role in creating that change. To assume that the environment will provide nothing but desirable options for individuals flies in the face of such historical realities as child labor and unequal pay for equal work. Those problems were not even defined as problems until individuals formed groups that forced attention upon them.

Theorists like those represented in this book prefer to view work as an important source of fulfillment in people's lives. Society as a whole tends to see work as a solution to many social problems. For many years, candidates in national elections have offered promises of more jobs and better job training. Fulfilling these promises is expected to lead to solutions to other problems. Poverty, homelessness, crime, substance abuse and addiction, and domestic violence, as well as economic stagnation and the growth of the national debt, are, in many respects, tied to the lack of jobs and skilled workers in the minds of politicians and policymakers.

The people who are experiencing poverty, homelessness, crime, substance abuse and addiction, domestic violence, and economic insecurity do not see work as an intrinsic source of fulfillment. They see work as something the structure of our society denies them, as a means to get what other people have, and as a way to escape some of the conditions of their lives. They certainly do not see a long, hard workday at a minimum wage as an opportunity to express their playful motivations.

In viewing Super's "archway of career determinants," I was struck by the fact that "social policy" is depicted to rest on the economy, society, and the labor market, whereas I see the economy and the labor market as resting on social policy. Only in a completely laissez-faire system would social policy not impact the economy. Several of the participants in this project have suggested that our theories should influence social policy. The fact that they do not was seen as an anomaly by Krumboltz. Yet the analysis of Betz and Fitzgerald suggests that it would be very difficult for our theories to do so—they simply are not addressing the problems of most interest to either policymakers or the public. I would like to note that this is not a new observation. Linda Gottfredson (1982) suggested more than a decade ago that our research was not addressing the most pressing problems of work in our society.

Our theories are slow in accounting for recent changes in the world of work—even for those who have rewarding and fulfilling jobs. One of the comments reported from the work groups at the conference had to do with the changing economic arrangements in our society. It was suggested that while work provides much less permanence than it has in the past, it does provide more flexibility. Yet most of our theories assume rather stable opportunities in a given career over time.

In summary, we do not adequately address the realities of our social system or the people who are most negatively impacted by it. In addressing the problems faced by individuals in planning and choosing a career course, we tend to put too much faith in the power of individual solutions.

CAN THEORY INFLUENCE
PRACTICE AND POLICY?

One of the things the project organizers asked me to discuss was the research implications of the deliberations of the conference. I would like to point out that most people invited to be involved in projects like this tend to be observers. (See my own confession in the earlier section on Frustrations.) We sit back and watch the world and say, I wonder if *x* varies with *y*. If we find that *x* and *y* do covary, we tend to be fairly satisfied with our observation. We may go on to try to determine if *x* causes *y* or *y* causes *x*, but having answered our own questions, we are content to let someone else attempt to apply what we have learned. Yet one of the most poignant pleas I have heard in the last few years in counseling psychology is for researchers to do research that is relevant to the practitioner (Resnikoff, 1984; Seaquist, 1984). That plea surfaced again during this conference project.

One of the most interesting aspects of editing the *Journal of Counseling Psychology* for the last six years has been to see what authors do once they realize that in order to be accepted for publication under my editorship, research must have some relevance to counseling. Some authors, usually those who don't have to be prompted to think about the relevance of their research to the practice of counseling, spell out the importance of the question(s) they are asking as a part of the rationale for the study, and this rationale appears in the introduction to the research. Other authors, and they are in the majority, tack on the obligatory paragraph about what their research means for counseling at the end of the article, if they include it at all. Sometimes that paragraph is quite general and so loosely related to the actual topic of inquiry that it could be attached to almost any piece of research. This tells me that much research is undertaken without much regard for its practical applications. We need to decide how to invest our limited research resources in research that is likely to point the way to specific changes in policy and practice that will have an impact on the broadest range of people.

A related issue is that we have taken a nearly defeatist attitude about sampling problems in the study of vocational behavior, assuming that the psychology department subject pool is a sample of populations ranging from college students to business recruiters. Those who have done the difficult work of finding populations appropriate to important questions (e.g., unemployed workers or low-income individuals involved in subsidized training programs), and have engaged these people as participants in their research, have sometimes been criticized for small numbers and low return rates.

Clearly, there are trade-offs to be made in selecting research samples. I suggest that, at least initially, we make these trade-offs in favor of smaller samples that are demographically more similar to the groups to whom we wish to generalize than is the typical student research sample, even if it means that the research is more difficult to do as a result. Because the most sophisticated models and analyses often used to explore them require large samples, our need to be sophisticated and build complex models encourages our dependence on the psychology subject pool. What we need are long-range, multistudy plans that include a mix of large and small sample designs with an understanding of when each is appropriate.

At this point, it may sound as though I am suggesting that practice and policy are more important than theory in research, but this is not my intent. If we had no theory to organize what we know, we would become endless inductive researchers, never able to generalize beyond our last observation. Research that actually informs theory is intellectually exciting, elegant, and practical. It is just as rare as research that informs practice. As indicated earlier, the most common paradigm in our research is, Do x and y covary? I envision a research strategy that first says, Of all the xs and ys that might be studied, why is studying these particular xs and ys important? Some responses that I might find compelling would indicate that the answer to the research question is relevant to informing social policy, important to enhancing the lives of the most underserved of people, or suggestive of ways to provide career counseling services most efficiently or effectively.

Iterations of this first step should provide a list of research questions that have important practical implications. The next step in my proposed research strategy would be to examine all the potential theoretical settings in which x and y appear, not limiting examination to career counseling theories or concepts that have exactly the same names. Exploring the list of unresolved theoretical issues about x and y in relationship to the use I could make of what I learned in resolving them should help me see which of my questions have the greatest potential to enhance the contribution of my research to both theory and practice.

It is simple to outline such a research strategy because in an outline one need not take account of complex sets of variables that may be best represented by multidimensional models. Neither need one take account of honest differences of opinion about what is important, either practically or theoretically. It is worth noting here that one of the questions that arose during the convergence project was how theorists, researchers, and practitioners might come to discuss, if not agree on, what is important. My response to that question echoes one recommendation of a task force I chaired in the late 1970s (Harmon, 1982), namely, that we set aside time to talk to each other and debate these issues. The conference on which this book is based provided an opportunity to engage in such a dialogue.

Theory building is hard work, and it has fewer rewards than doing relatively isolated research projects with available samples. I would suggest that we are in an economic time when we do not have the luxury of each going our own way. An Israeli friend of mine once observed that Israeli society is less individualistic than that found in the United States, and that because Israeli resources are so limited, the situation forces cooperation. During the whole of my professional career, the priorities of various public and private funding agencies have influenced the type of research that is done because of limited resources. Today, more than ever before, we are asked to show that we spend both our research and practice efforts wisely. It seems to me that the best way to do that is to acknowledge and nurture solid connections between theory, practice, and research.

CONCLUSION

The convergence project solidified my conviction that we need to broaden the range of what we are trying to explain with our career theories. It raised more questions than it answered for me, yet I find questions about the scope of our theories and the linkages among them, our methods, and the constructs we use to be exciting. Although the project did not produce the theoretical convergence that I initially had unrealistically hoped for, it did arouse a renewed sense of how theory, practice, and research must converge in an attempt to help career counselors make maximum contributions to solving the major problems our society faces today.

REFERENCES

Gottfredson, L. (1982). Vocational research priorities. *The Counseling Psychologist, 10,* 69–84.

Gottfredson, L., & Becker, H. (1981). *Journal of Vocational Behavior,* 121–137.

Harmon, L. (1982). Scientific affairs—The next decade. *The Counseling Psychologist, 10,* 34–37.

Kelly, G. (1970). A brief introduction to personal construct theory. In D. Bannister (Ed.), *Perspectives in personal construct theory.* London: Academic Press.

Resnikoff, A. (1984). Untitled. In J. Whiteley, N. Kagan, L. Harmon, B. Fretz, & F. Tanney (Eds.), *The coming decade in counseling psychology* (p. 195). Schenectady, NY: Character Research Press.

Seaquist, D. (1984). Untitled. In J. Whiteley, N. Kagan, L. Harmon, B. Fretz, & F. Tanney (Eds.), *The coming decade in counseling psychology* (pp. 197–198). Schenectady, NY: Character Research Press.

Wolfe, T. (1987). *The bonfire of the vanities.* New York: Farrar, Strauss, and Giroux.

CHAPTER NINETEEN

Convergence Prompts Theory Renovation, Research Unification, and Practice Coherence

Mark L. Savickas
Northeastern Ohio Universities College of Medicine

T HE CONVERGENCE PROJECT sought to build connections among the major theories of career choice and development and to consider an agenda for future work on theory convergence. The general outcome of this effort was a communal consideration of the advantages and disadvantages of a convergence agenda for theories of career choice and development. This chapter examines this general outcome by identifying and evaluating the specific outcomes of the project from the perspectives of theory, research, and practice. Three conclusions will be explicated, namely, that convergence can aid theory renovation, advance the empirical process for knowledge making, and enrich practice. The first section deals with *theory renovation,* or what convergence offers career theorists as they elaborate their models of reality. The second section addresses *research unification,* or what convergence offers researchers who want to enhance their methods for knowledge making. The chapter concludes by considering *practice coherence,* or what convergence offers practitioners who use multiple theories to guide their work.

CONVERGENCE CAN CONTRIBUTE TO THEORY RENOVATION

The first inference I drew from the convergence project was that no one seemed interested in converging theories, or, if they were, then they were unwilling to admit it in public. Rather, most participants seemed willing to settle for theory renovation, to use a term offered by Holland. On reflection, I agree that it would be premature to pursue a theory convergence agenda for its own sake. Nevertheless, I concluded that the convergence project did generate several significant ideas for theory renovation. These ideas for refurbishing theories fall into two groups, namely, issues that we have neglected and principles that we have forgotten. First, let us consider the group of neglected issues that drew the convergence spotlight.

Theories Have Neglected Diversity, Salience, Context, and Ability

One of the most clearly articulated outcomes of the convergence project was not anticipated—that one of the strongest points of convergence among theories of career choice and development rests in the issues that our theories neglect. Fitzgerald and Betz as well as Subich and Taylor decried the fact that the theories converge in neglecting diverse groups. Bordin and Super argued that in their concentration on work, career theories neglect other major life roles. Walsh and Chartrand, along with Vondracek and Fouad, advised us that the theories neglect the reciprocal influence of context on vocational behavior. (See the respective chapters of these authors in this volume.) The following four subsections consider, in turn, our neglect of diversity, salience, context, and ability.

Diverse Populations.   Vocational psychologists have been so focused on career development that we have neglected the work behavior of people who do not have subjective careers. Careers can be thought of from two perspectives—from that of the actor and that of the observer (Hughes, 1958). From an observer's view, most people have a career, that is, they occupy a series of work positions during their lives. Thus, *objective career* denotes the work history of the individual, and in this sense most individuals have a career. In contrast, *subjective career* refers to individuals' own viewpoint on their vocational behavior. A subjective career consists of memories of the past, experiences of the present, and dreams of the future. These cognitions function to impose direction on vocational behavior.

Almost everyone has an objective career, but many people do not experience a subjective career. Individuals who lock themselves into the present, or are trapped in the nonce by their culture or by social oppression, do not enjoy the privilege of anticipating and planning for a better tomorrow. Instead of climbing a promotion ladder or moving along a career path, they must concentrate on getting a job—any job—and then keeping it. They have a job without a sense of career. Without a subjective career to envision, direct, and develop, these individuals have no occasion to seek career counseling. In turn, counselors have not been prompted to articulate career theory to address the concerns of people who do not have subjective careers.

Contemporary career theories concentrate on "mature" and "adaptive" behavior as these qualities are defined by the career culture of the American middle class, excluding the work experience of the diverse groups that populate our country and ignoring the frustrations of individuals with lower socioeconomic status (SES). For example, in talking about career maturity, we have emphasized constructs of independence, decisiveness, and future planning. These are value-laden constructs that not each socioeconomic level and every culture prizes. Holland (1969) once suggested that what Super calls career maturity may merely be the effects of SES, with high vocational maturity being a concomitant of high SES. Several cultural groups in the United States index maturity by past-oriented and interdependent behavior, rather than future-oriented and independent behavior. Renovating career theories must include adding new constructs and broadening the range of convenience of established constructs so that the critical variables in career theory embrace most workers.

Role Salience. Super (this volume) reminds us that work does not exist in a vacuum. Work is an important life role, yet it is not the only life role. Contemporary life in late modern and early postmodern times requires extensive revision of the "grand narrative" of the twentieth century, which instructed us that society uses its human productive capacities to advance toward the new or the better with a gradual yet steady forward march. We cannot continue to build career theory on this grand narrative or continue to inculcate the Puritan work ethic, which makes career salient and the work role the central life interest. In postindustrial society, the work role may not be the chief tie to reality or the bestower of social identity. No one philosophy of life will be shared by everyone in a multicultural society. Increasingly, career theory will attend to alternative common narratives, rather than a grand narrative, and concentrate on life design and the place of the work role in the constellation of life roles. At this point in our history, counselors must learn to enable clients to invent a workable personal framework for their lives. To assist counselors, career theory must broaden its focus beyond fixation on the work role and look to how different cultures and unique contexts provide different paths of development.

Relative to role salience, Bordin (this volume) urges us to renovate theory by reexamining the work role itself, not just contextualize it into a spectrum of life roles. He gently criticizes the restricted view of work as effort directed toward postponed or future rewards. He asserts that

> the key point of my work-play concept is that from that perspective one finds the press toward fusing work and play. This means that there can be intrinsic, therefore immediate, rewards in work that reside in the activities. To the extent that this is a valid assumption, it has major implications for work and personal adjustment. (Bordin, personal communication, May 20, 1992)

By mining Bordin's profound wisdom, career theory can be renovated to include play and leisure, not as additional roles but as part of the work role.

Context. The new interest in multiculturalism and multiple life roles underscores the importance of context as a neglected component in contemporary career theory. How participants in the convergence project defined context produced several ideas for theory renovation. Vondracek and Fouad (this volume) offer to theory renovation the framework of *developmental contextualism*. This framework promises to obviate the need for different theories for different groups because, at its core, contextualism incorporates socioeconomic and cultural influences on individual vocational behavior. Moreover, with embeddedness as a key concept, the developmental-contextualism framework comprehends the issue of role salience.

Spokane (this volume), along with Walsh and Chartrand (this volume), offer theory renovation the possible elaboration of the congruence construct using the variable of *affordance* (Gibson, 1979). They define affordances as functional utilities or action possibilities available in the environment. The construct of affordance can be used to more closely fit individual plans to environmental opportunities and to study the shaping conditioned by reciprocal transactions between individual goals and social opportunities.

The constructs of affordance and embeddedness may prove to be key concepts in theory renovation, especially if we take seriously Dawis' (this volume) affirmation of the individual differences tradition in psychology. This tradition views people as individuals, not group members, and assumes that an individual's present status results from opportunity or the absence of opportunity. In addition, affordance and embeddedness may serve to bridge the British (Watts, Super, & Kidd, 1981) view of career development as shaped by the social opportunity structure with North American career theory. Linking individual career development to the opportunities in the physical and social environment may eventually offer practitioners theory-based interventions to deal with real-world problems that are so often neglected by contemporary career theory.

Ability. The final construct that we may have neglected drew the convergence spotlight thanks to Dawis' (this volume) assertion that ability could be the convergence construct par excellence for career psychology, in part because ability is the integrative construct for much of the rest of psychology. Dawis' suggestion made me think of ability in broad terms, particularly ability as discussed by Phillips.

Phillips (this volume) commented that career choice theories converge on decision-making rationality. She offers the construct of intuition to theory renovation. Intuition, as a decision-making resource, is used by many counselors who urge clients to trust themselves and their own feelings. Practical intelligence offers an intriguing possibility for theory elaboration. The research on tacit knowledge in career development (Wagner & Sternberg, 1985), intuition as a global style of problem solving (Witkin, Oltman, Raskin, & Karp, 1971), and intuition in self-organizing systems (Tiedeman & Miller-Tiedeman, 1985) offers practical models to follow in renovating theories. Following these leads, we can look beyond the decisional objectivity of logical positivism to see the theoretical possibilities offered by the decisional subjectivity of constructivism.

We Have Forgotten How Practice Constitutes Theory

In addition to the prospects for theory renovation offered by attending to neglected issues, there are also possibilities offered by remembering fundamental principles that we may have forgotten. It seems to me that we have lost track of the intimate relationship between theory and practice, a relationship of mutual shaping. The following three subsections discuss career theory as a constituent of practice.

Theories Are Practice.   A pivotal question was raised at the conference: Can practice ever inform theory? The question presupposes a dualism of science versus practice, rather than recognizes that career theory is an applied science, a science of use. The question thus reflects the dichotomy of theory versus practice and the inherent tyranny of dualistic thinking. Maybe in reaction to this tyranny, the question of "practice informing theory" rang out with a hostile edge. A few individuals who advanced the question seemed frustrated by their experience with unidirectional communication from theory to practice. They concluded that practitioners were excluded from the theory-building enterprise. They contended that while career theories were designed and developed to inform practice, they do not address some real-world problems that practitioners encounter. In short, they argued that theory needs to be made more practical. From this view, theorists are adherents, whereas practitioners are pragmatists. As adherents, theorists and their disciples reify theory, thus further separating career theory from the practical problems of counseling practice.

The problem with this specious question is that theorizing itself is a form of practice, albeit practice at a distance. Theorists do their best to comprehend vocational behavior, and a few theorists like Holland even elaborate their theories to help practitioners serve clients and to allow clients to help themselves (e.g., the *Self-Directed Search*, which Holland designed as a counselor-free intervention). As Krumboltz (this volume) and others so clearly explained, the theories themselves map specific terrains. If a map was not designed to portray the concerns of a particular client, then the theory would not be useful to that client's counselor. This does not mean that the map is useless or that theory ignores practice. It only means that the theorist in question was not practicing, at a distance, on that problem (Nespor & Garrison, 1992).

The idea of practice at a distance transforms the dichotomy of theory versus practice into a continuum from close to distant. Such a continuum overcomes the tyranny of either-or. However, the continuum still separates theory and practice. Constructivist philosophy of science reconciles this separation. For example, Nespor and Garrison (1992) argued persuasively that "theories cannot be detached from practice—from their uses or 'consequences' [because] the meanings of theories and concepts are constituted through their uses" (p. 28).

What a powerful idea—the meaning of a theory is constructed through its use! Thus, situated activity, particularly the practice of career intervention, constructs the true meaning of career theories. Theories are conceptual tools or mapped routines that must be used in practice to be meaningful. Moreover, the meaning of a theory changes as it is used. Each time a concept is applied to a new situation, its meaning deepens. As Nespor and Garrison (1992) argue, the problem is not to make theory more practical but to rethink theory as practice at a distance.

Teaching Theory as Practice.   Why have so many of us forgotten that theories are practice? Well, maybe we did not forget; maybe we were taught to consider theory as distinct from practice by the structure of our graduate school curricula. Theories, when first introduced to students, can be presented as abstract, decontextualized principles and categorical definitions. After students pass a theory or "know what" course, students can take a practicum or "know how" course. The artificial breach between theory and practice courses needs to be repaired. "Know what" presented as part of "know how" discussions makes theories more useful and may enable students to encode and remember them better. Perhaps vocational psychologists could increase their use of case studies in teaching. Presenting theories from the vantage point of case studies may contribute to the success of textbooks that emphasize theory applications (Brown & Brooks, 1990; Sharf, 1992) and the "Getting Down to Cases" section in the *Career Development Quarterly*. These materials show how theorists use their theories as a form of practice.

Career Counseling Theories.   One of the outcomes of the convergence project was widespread agreement that we have theories of career development but not theories of career counseling. This could be true, yet I am not sure. Maybe this conclusion exemplifies the tyranny of the dichotomy between theory and practice. Before starting to design new career counseling theories, we need to improve our teaching and repair the gap between theory and practice by doing a better job convincing students that theory is practice and demonstrating how theorists and master practitioners use theory. Clearly, viewing career theories from a convergence perspective reveals numerous important ideas for renovation of the individual theories.

CONVERGENCE CAN SPUR RESEARCH UNIFICATION

This section addresses the issue of research unification, that is, convergence of career theories at the empirical level. I will first describe the concept of research unification, then discuss three potential focal points for research unification.

Research Unification

In vocational psychology, recognition is given to individuals who identify and measure a new construct. Thus, we find researchers expending great conceptual effort explicating a new construct, then operationally defining that construct with an inventory, and eventually using the inventory to elaborate a nomological network around the construct. When we think of colleagues, we often associate them with a construct or inventory that defines their specialization. Natural scientists gain recognition another way—by solving a problem. These scientists agree on which problems are most important, and then researchers race against each other to solve a problem. Recognition is given to the individual or research team that advances the attack on the problem. Maybe vocational psychology has matured as a discipline to the point where we, too, can coordinate our research efforts to investigate a set of widely agreed on problems. A first step toward research unification is to encourage vocational psychologists who hold different theoretical orientations to identify and prioritize research problems, then agree to pursue these problems using their own theory in tandem with one or more other theories.

Research unification was what we had in mind when we asked prominent researchers, whose chapters appear in part 2 of this book, to discuss how a particular problem or topic in vocational psychology could be elucidated by each of the five foundational theories represented in part 1. The problems that they discussed embody central topics in vocational psychology—the formation of a vocational *identity,* the influence of *self-cognitions* on career behavior, the process of *decision making,* the dynamics of *congruence,* and the *social context* that conditions vocational behavior.

Each theory attends to one or two of these problems in detail and addresses the remaining problems in a more cursory fashion. For example, Super concentrates on decision making, Holland emphasizes congruence, Krumboltz accentuates self-cognitions, Dawis highlights context, and Bordin underscores identity. Accordingly, we learned from the theorists' chapters in this book that their theories are not competing explanations of the same five problems. Instead, the theories are visions of reality that focus on circumscribed parts of the larger whole, that is, a problem or two. Career theories provide lenses through which selected segments of vocational behavior can be viewed. According to Krumboltz (this volume), "each theory is an attempt to depict some part of reality and does so by deliberately ignoring other complexities." The problem scrutinized with a particular lens reflects the interests of the theorist who fashioned the lens.

In their chapters, the theorists acknowledged some of their different interests regarding level of abstraction and audience. For example, according to Dawis (this volume), career theorists differ in the level of abstraction they prefer. Dawis explicates this assertion by contrasting his use of higher-order, disposition-type variables such as abilities to Krumboltz's use of lower-order, ongoing behavior variables such as task approach skills. Holland (this volume) noted that different theorists have disparate audiences and goals. Holland explained that his theory aims primarily to aid practitioners in providing effective career interventions.

To me, the differences in how the theorists view problems are even more fundamental than differences in abstractness and audience. Fundamentally, the theories comprehend vocational behavior by discerning cognitive *structures,* the *development* of these structures across time, and the *learning processes* that foster structural development. Holland and Dawis emphasize structure while downplaying development and learning; Krumboltz emphasizes learning while deemphasizing development and structure; Super emphasizes development while downplaying process and structure; and Bordin emphasizes structure, views development as change in structure, and deemphasizes process. In short, the theories concentrate on different problems and use the conceptual paradigm most pertinent to that problem.

On occasion, the theories directly address the same problems. When this occurs, the theories already converge. It is difficult to think of an instance when two or more career theories address the same problem with different predictions. Articulating this conclusion was a useful product of the convergence project. However, stating that the theories converge is not to say that they are the same. The theories are never the same, even when they address the same problem, because they use different paradigms, privilege distinct constructs, and employ unique operational definitions in making sense of that problem.

Let us consider one of the problems—person-environment (P-E) fit—from the viewpoint of the two theorists who seem to have the greatest similarity (both emphasize structure and concentrate on P-E fit), namely, Dawis and Holland. Although their two theories are compatible and both highlight P-E fit, the theories were constructed and elaborated to deal with different facets of P-E fit. Accordingly, even the words they use to denote P-E fit within their theories express, with precise connotation, their differing interests. Holland uses *congruence* to spotlight the accord or match between an occupational choice and a personality type, whereas Dawis uses *correspondence* to spotlight the co-responsiveness between the person and the work environment.

Dawis uses the construct of correspondence within a theory of work adjustment elaborated without specific concern for the practice of career counseling. Holland uses the construct of congruence within a theory of educational and vocational choice elaborated specifically to inform the practice of career intervention. Despite their shared interest in P-E fit, Holland writes little about correspondence and work adjustment, while Dawis writes little about facilitating congruent career choices. However, if we ask either theorist to consider the issue they do not emphasize, we get heuristic ideas. For example, when Dawis (this volume) wrote about career counseling, he speculated that there may be two types of career choice clients. In making a career choice, one group of clients may try to maximize satisfaction, whereas a second group of clients may try to maximize satisfactoriness. Hypotheses such as the one offered by Dawis suggest that exploring convergence at the level of research unification may produce innovative directions for inquiry. In fact, this is what we had in mind by research unification—researchers using the lenses of their preferred theories to look at the same problems and then generate testable hypotheses to advance our understanding of the problem.

Focal Points for Research Unification.   In short, one idea for advancing theory building and knowledge is to unify research by (a) identifying problems addressed by two or more theories, (b) investigating these problems through the core constructs and operational definitions of two or more theories, (c) interpreting the results of the investigations from the perspectives of multiple theories, and (d) advancing our understanding of the problem under investigation by drawing a comprehensive conclusion from the multiple interpretations.

I take as my model for this reasoning early attempts by Holland (1972) to implement a convergence agenda. In a dialogue with Super concerning vocational development theory, Holland (1972) stated that his concept of consistency among occupational preferences was operationally equivalent to Super's construct of vocational maturity:

> I have recently interpreted Don's vocational maturity concept in terms of my own theory and it boils down to something like this. Vocational maturity is having a personality pattern on the *Vocational Preference Inventory* that is consistent, that is, having peaks on two or three things which go together. The sort of thing that counselors have observed for many years. And that immaturity is having peaks on this particular inventory, which don't go together, which by any casual observation are nutty. For example, having artistic and conventional about the same height is a nutty profile. It is also rare, but it is also nutty. These people believe and aspire to have very divergent kinds of competencies.

Ensuing research did not support this convergence hypothesis. Nevertheless, it clarified both theories, suggested that consistency is a late developing trait, showed that the structure of vocational maturity varies across career stages, and contributed to the evolution of the construct of coherence.

I learned from this early attempt at convergence that it may be more productive to compare how two theories view the same problem than it is to translate the core constructs of one theory into the language of another theory. I would like to offer three examples of potential research unification studies that each approach a common problem from the perspectives of two different theories. I selected three important problems that counselors frequently encounter among their career clients: (a) educational and vocational indecision that precludes making an occupational choice, (b) career beliefs that debilitate vocational behavior, and (c) maladaptive attempts to implement an occupational choice and establish a career.

Educational and Vocational Indecision.   The theories of Holland and Super both address the problem of educational and vocational indecision. Taking the risk of oversimplifying the two theories, one might say that Holland views indecision from the standpoint of a trait-and-factor psychologist looking for individual differences in personality and adjustment, whereas Super views indecision from the standpoint of a life span psychologist looking for developmental changes. In making meaning of career indecision, Holland privileges constructs that emphasize differences between individuals, whereas Super privileges constructs that emphasize differences within an individual across time. Let us consider how their views shape the problem of career indecision.

Holland studies indecision from the standpoint of differences among RIASEC types and, more importantly, as differences in the degree of difficulty individuals encounter when they must adjust to an environmental demand to make a career choice. Holland, Gottfredson, and Nafziger (1973) operationally defined this view by constructing the *Vocational Decision-Making Difficulties Scale* (VDMD), while Osipow, Carney, Winer, Yanico, and Koschier (1976) operationally defined it with the *Career Decision Scale* (CDS). Both of these scales index indecision as the number of problems an individual claims to encounter in making educational and vocational choices. Thus, viewing career indecision as rooted in adjustment problems has produced inventories that identify decisional difficulties and interventions aimed at problem solving.

In contrast, Super studies indecision from the standpoint of differences in readiness to cope with an environmental demand to choose, not as differences in personality or adjustment. Until one has mastered the tasks of crystallizing a vocational self-concept and formulating a preference for occupational fields and ability levels, an individual is not ready to specify a career choice. While an adjustment view concentrates on decisional difficulties, a developmental view attends to decisional readiness. Super, Thompson, Lindeman, Jordaan, and Myers (1981) operationally defined the developmental view by constructing the *Career Development Inventory* (CDI), and Crites (1978) operationally defined it by constructing the *Career Maturity Inventory* (CMI). Viewing career indecision as rooted in developmental delay has produced inventories that identify immature attitudes and competencies, and interventions that foster developmental task mastery.

Clearly, differential and developmental theorists view indecision differently, not to mention dynamic theorists such as Bordin. The theorists have not been particularly open to examining the privileged constructs used in another theory. And at the extreme, some theorists have competed to enroll practitioners and researchers into their knowledge-constitutive networks (see Latour, 1987). For all practical purposes, we can conclude that most researchers stand in one camp. Contemporary ideas about philosophy of science, such as standpoint theory (Harding, 1991), suggest that where researchers stand determines what they see. The campsite or standpoint of career researchers determines whether they study indecision as a result of differential difficulties or an incomplete readiness to cope.

However, unification research that compares the views from the two campsites might significantly advance our understanding of indecision and its remediation. In a practical sense, a researcher or, better yet, a team of researchers, representing the camps of Holland and Super could administer the VDMD and the CDI to a common group of undecided college students to determine how decisional difficulties relate to choice attitudes and competencies. It would be a major advance to know if decisional difficulties and developmental resources are different sides of the same coin.

Holland has already merged his difficulties view with a developmental view, although not with a career development theory. Holland merged his work on difficulties in vocational decision making with Erikson's developmental model of psychosocial identity during adolescence and young adulthood. Early on, Holland and Nichols (1964) referred to indecision as "slow and complex rate of development" (p. 33). As noted herein, Holland eventually produced the VDMD (Holland et al., 1973). Holland's research on this scale caused him to notice that the VDMD consistently exhibited a strong inverse correlation to an Identity Scale that he had developed based on the work of colleagues at The Johns Hopkins University (Greenberger, Campbell, Sorensen, & O'Connor, 1971). Eventually, Holland, Daiger, and Power (1980) constructed the *Vocational Identity Scale* (VIS) by merging items from the 13-item VDMD and the 15-item Identity Scale because they produced a strong inverse correlation. In my view, this correlation suggests that difficulties and resources are flip sides of the same coin.

A research form of the VIS contained 23 questions, including one item from Crites' CMI Attitude Scale. The published version of the VIS has 18 items that to me represent the convergence of the individual differences and developmental traditions in studying indecision. I think the instrument works superbly because it melds the best of two traditions in vocational psychology, the differential and the developmental. Moreover, because of its converging traditions, the VIS can be used comfortably by researchers from both camps. Differentialists can view the VIS as an adjustment measure, while at the same time developmentalists can view the VIS as a readiness measure (although Holland may object to this view).

The VIS is an excellent example of theoretical convergence arising from research unification. Holland did not begin with the intent to converge theories; the linguistic explication and operational definition of the construct *vocational identity* arose rather as a by-product of Holland's creative, persistent, and multiperspective research on the problem of career indecision.

Career Beliefs. A second example of theory convergence arising from research unification involves social learning theory represented by Krumboltz and developmental theory represented by Crites. Krumboltz (1988) constructed the *Career Beliefs Inventory* (CBI) as a counseling tool to help individuals identify career beliefs that may block their vocational decision making, job search, or career advancement. Krumboltz (1991) described the CBI as a logical outgrowth of prior research (Lewis & Gilhousen, 1981; Thompson, 1976) and as an application of cognitive psychology and cognitive therapy (Beck, 1976).

In constructing the *Career Concepts Test,* the original name for the CMI Attitude Scale, Crites included a cluster of 11 items that dealt with conceptions of the choice process. Conception items measure the extent to which an individual accurately conceptualizes the process of making an occupational choice (Crites, 1965). The 11 items each state misconceptions about career decision making. Two sample items are "There is only one occupation for each person" and "By the time you are 15 you should have your mind pretty well made up about the occupation you intend to enter." Crites (1973) produced programmed instruction materials that counselors could use to correct these misconceptions. He also described a counseling process for teaching accurate conceptions that uses a three-step cycle of nondirective exploration, directive shaping, and active learning.

Interestingly, both Krumboltz and Crites converge on the social influence model of counseling as the preferred way to disabuse clients of career misconceptions or maladaptive beliefs. Moreover, they both emphasize the counseling use of their inventories over a psychodiagnostic use. Putting together the work of Krumboltz with that of Crites—one from the social learning perspective and one from the developmental perspective—may foster faster advancement of our knowledge.

Work Adjustment. A third area for convergence is adjustment. Dawis (this volume) states that the theory of work adjustment (TWA) focuses on a different level of abstraction than does Super's theory of career development. TWA is at the coarse-grain level, whereas Super's theory is at the fine-grained level. This statement implicitly invites us to consider theory convergence and, more importantly, research unification. Let us inspect the intersection of Super's adjustment stages with TWA's adjustment styles.

Super indicates that the work adjustment segment of the vocational development continuum starts with the establishment stage. The establishment stage initially confronts the worker with the developmental tasks of stabilizing in a position and, later, consolidating that position. Crites (1982) suggests that stabilizing requires that one adapt to the organizational culture and perform the tasks of one's position, whereas consolidating requires effective work habits and attitudes over the long haul and solid co-worker relationships. Reading Dawis' (this volume) description of adjustment styles suggests that individuals will vary in the flexibility, activeness, reactiveness, and perseverance with which they encounter the social demand to stabilize in a position through organizational fusion and position performance and to consolidate by working hard and getting along with co-workers.

This implies numerous hypotheses for a research unification agenda. What range of flexibility facilitates organizational fusion and produces optimal position stability? As a new employee is inducted into an organization's culture and socialized to perform work tasks in a normative manner, what are the roles of activeness and reactiveness? The hypotheses are almost endless when one examines the intersection of TWA with the vocational developmental tasks.

A simple yet important start for research unification on problems such as vocational indecision, career beliefs, and work adjustment might be to heed the wise counsel of Oliver and Spokane (1988, p. 459), who advise researchers on career intervention to agree upon a core set of standard inventories with which to assess outcomes. Such a move would prompt research unification and refocus attention on making new knowledge rather than naming a new construct and designing an inventory to measure it. Presumably, this new knowledge could improve practice.

CONVERGENCE CAN INCREASE
PRACTICE COHERENCE

One question continued to echo in my head long after the convergence project had concluded: What convergence have practitioners already wrought?

This question implies, and rightly so, that practitioners have somehow integrated the career theories and have drawn a practical map of how to use each theory. This thought reframed the issue of convergence for me. Maybe the most productive way to view convergence is from the perspective of practitioners, not the perspective of theorists. So, in an attempt to answer the question of what convergence have practitioners already wrought, I asked myself how counselors link the career theories in the typical practice of career intervention.

Given the issues discussed in the second section of this chapter, we know that each theory addresses distinct problems. Therefore, counselors must, at least implicitly, construct some framework for deciding when to use each of the five career theories (or some smaller set thereof) and with whom they will use them. Using Krumboltz's (this volume) map metaphor, this means that counselors know how to place the distinct maps within an atlas or on a globe.

In thinking about how to arrange the atlas, I gained direction from Dawis (this volume), who urged us to (a) look for convergence, not try to unify the theories and (b) seek convergence by superimposing a larger framework on the linkages among the career theories. In his table that depicts the distinctive role of each major career theory, Osipow (table 2, this volume) suggested a type of overarching framework that might converge the theories—namely, an assembly of motivational constructs. I sought to converge the theories from the perspective of practice by using the theorists' identification of which problems interest them, Dawis' recommendation to apply an overarching framework, and Osipow's example of using motivational concepts as the overarching framework. The first task was to select an overarching motivational framework.

I selected the overarching framework offered by Wagner's (1971) theory of structural analysis (SA) because it spans all three of the motivation paradigms used by the career theorists—structure, process, and development. A second reason for selecting SA is that Wagner assembled the framework from a practice base, not a theory base. This factor makes SA particularly attractive in addressing the question of what convergence have career practitioners wrought. Wagner constructed SA from his experience using projective techniques in the practice of personality assessment. SA functions to systematically organize or converge data from a variety of techniques or perspectives into a comprehensive and coherent structure.

The following section outlines SA, translates SA into the language of vocational behavior, and offers a framework for converging the career theories. I will then address the question of, What convergence have practitioners already wrought?, by using the convergence framework to offer one explanation of how practitioners have converged and assembled career theories to conceptualize discrete groups of clients and provide these groups of clients with distinct career interventions.

Précis of Structural Analysis

In presenting structural analysis, Wagner (1971) asserted that two structures mediate personality. The *facade self,* the first structure to develop, consists of attitudes and behavioral tendencies. The facade self maintains contact with reality and reacts to environmental stimuli. Later, following the acquisition of language, individuals become aware of their own behavior and formulate a self-concept and identity that lie at the core of the *introspective self.* The introspective self evaluates and corrects the facade self; it provides depth and complexity to the personality by adding an inner life. The facade self initially responds only to environmental programming, so an introspective self introduces two new possibilities: the self-programming of behavior and the interaction between the subjective self and the environment. The diagram in figure 1 shows a portion of Wagner's (1971) schemata for the functioning of a normal personality. Drives funnel through the introspective self and facade self for release; the facade self and the introspective self interact and modify each other through self-cognitions, and the facade self reacts to prompts from the environment.

I realize that Wagner designed and developed SA for the clinical practice of psychodiagnostics, yet I will take a moment to reflect on Wagner's (1971) succinct statement of SA from the perspective of a vocational psychologist:

> The growing child must develop an attitudinal and behavioral facade which organizes external reality so that the organism can react meaningfully to the welter of complex stimuli which are constantly impinging. Later, if all goes well, the individual takes cognizance of his [or her] own functioning, achieves a sense of identity and formulates a subjective set of ideals, goals, and self-appraisals. The [facade self] and the [introspective self] then interact to form a complex, unique personality. (p. 424)

This succinct statement shows that SA offers an overarching framework for converging career theory from the standpoint held by practitioners of career intervention. Wagner used SA to create an overarching framework for popular projective techniques, each of which had been created to assess distinct levels of personality functioning. The authors of the projective techniques were interested in different aspects of personality, much like our career theorists are interested in different aspects of vocational behavior. This coincidence makes it evident that by simply identifying similar constructs, we can translate SA from the language of personality theory and psychopathology into the language of career theory and vocational behavior.

Translating SA Into the Language of Vocational Behavior

The facade self, which coincides with Osipow's "what," denotes "an attitudinal and behavioral facade which organizes external reality so that the organism can react

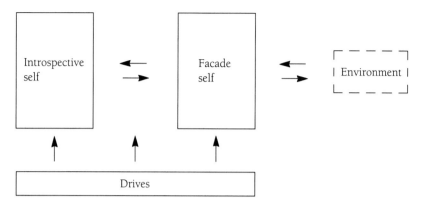

FIGURE 1   Schemata for Wagner's (1971) Theory of Structural Analysis

Adapted from "Structural Analysis: A Theory of Personality Based on Projective Techniques" by E. Wagner, 1971, *Journal of Personality Assessment, 35,* p. 426. Copyright 1971 by Lawrence Erlbaum Associates, Inc. Reprinted by permission.

meaningfully to the welter of complex stimuli which are constantly impinging." The facade self reminds me of Holland's typology. Each RIASEC type represents what Holland called an *adjustive orientation,* constituted by a constellation of attitudes, interests, and behavioral tendencies. Thus, Holland's description of adjustive orientation coincides quite well with Wagner's definition of the facade self. Moreover, like the facade self, RIASEC types emerge as adaptive repertoires early in life. Viewing traits as unitary adaptive mechanisms also places them in the facade self. Thus, stable person characteristics such as occupational interests populate the facade self.

The introspective self, which coincides with Osipow's "how," develops later than the facade self, when "the individual takes cognizance of his [or her] own functioning, achieves a sense of identity and formulates a subjective set of ideals, goals, and self-appraisals." The introspective self reminds me of Hughes' (1958) concept of *subjective career.* The introspective self includes developmental constructs such as Holland's vocational identity (i.e., a clear and stable picture of one's talent, goals, and interests) and the vocational self-concept articulated by Super. The introspective self evaluates and guides the facade self, and it offers the self-selected goals constituting vocational identity to direct the adaptive repertoire of the facade self.

In SA, drives press on the facade and introspective selves. The drives in SA coincide with Bordin's formulation of the psychodynamics of career, the view that emphasizes Osipow's "why." Like SA, vocational psychology has little to say about drives. Vocational psychologists, with the fortunate exception of the few like Bordin, have done little to develop the depth view of why people make the choices they do.

The process dimensions of SA are best understood from the perspective of Krumboltz's social learning theory. In the schemata of SA displayed in figure 1, arrows represent process. The arrows between the facade self and the environment represent the environment impinging on the individual (<—) and the individual's responses to the environment (—>), respectively. Krumboltz concentrates on this interaction. In addition, Krumboltz attends to the interaction arrows between the facade and introspective selves using constructs such as self-observation generalizations. Krumboltz's (1988) CBI can be conceptualized as assessing the arrows between the facade and the introspective selves. In addition to career beliefs, the arrows between the facade and introspective selves represent career maturity variables such as decision-making attitudes and competencies.

Lofquist and Dawis, in their concentration on the work adjustment process, emphasize core constructs attuned to the interaction between the facade self and the environment (skill, reinforcement value, person-environment correspondence), as well as the outcomes of this interaction (satisfaction and satisfactoriness). From the perspective of TWA, the arrows between the facade self and the environment represent the relation of personality structure (facade self) to behavior and the adjustment outcomes of that behavior. The interaction is conceptualized in terms of personality style and adjustment style variables, along with modes of adjustment behavior. The outcomes are conceptualized using the constructs of satisfaction and satisfactoriness. Because of the focus on the work adjustment process and its outcomes, TWA has been used extensively in work adjustment and vocational rehabilitation counseling but not in career choice counseling.

Having translated each element of SA into a corresponding career theory, we are now ready to integrate the translated elements into a new statement of an overarching framework for converging career theories.

A Framework for Converging Career Theories

Figure 2 displays a schemata applying Wagner's (1971) theory of structural analysis to the vocational realm. This facade self or, for our purposes, adaptive repertoire, could be termed a *vocational self*. (The term vocational was selected to coincide with Crites' [1969] use of "occupational" to denote environmental stimuli and "vocational" to denote behavioral responses.) As infants develop, they are inducted into the culture through social expectations that we call developmental tasks, proffered initially by the family and later by societal institutions such as the church, the arts, and the school. The vocational development tasks and their agents condition the individual to assume that the meaning of life is to cooperate with and contribute to the common good. In Western society, we provide three core role domains through which individuals can cooperate and contribute: work, friendship, and love. Commitment to these roles is the focus of Super's research concerning role salience. The arrows between the vocational self and the environment represent, to accept Crites' persuasive argument regarding precise terminology, *occupational stimuli* (<—) and *vocational responses* (—>).

With self-reflection made available by language, the individual eventually constructs and subsequently develops an introspective self or, for our purpose

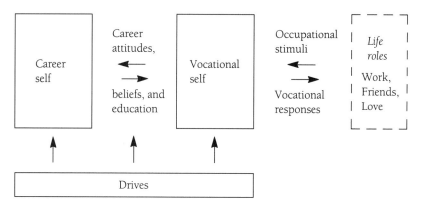

FIGURE 2   A Framework for Converging Career Theories

herein, *a career self*. (The term career was selected following theorists who [Hughes, 1958; Tiedeman & Miller-Tiedeman, 1985] explain the subjective sense of career as a self-reflective structure.) The career self adds self-awareness to the environmental awareness of the vocational self. Thought and its product, the career self, permit the individual to make meaning and to use this meaning to direct one's own behavior in a mature manner, not just in response to environmental stimuli. The enlarged worldview of the career self allows the person to develop life themes, abiding values, and long-range goals that are dealt with in vocational psychology using constructs such as subjective career (Hughes, 1958), vocational identity (Holland, Daiger, & Power, 1980), and self-concept (Super, 1963).

The career self is an organized subset of a person's cognitive universe, which enables the individual to identify and discriminate work roles as a focal experience. As such, this structure is an organized perspective for making coherent choices regarding behavioral alternatives. While the purpose of vocational behavior is to respond to vocational tasks and situations, the purpose of career mentation is to enhance the adaptivity of vocational behavior. Career mentation functions to (a) provide awareness of and orientation to vocational movement through time, (b) enhance self-control, (c) impose intention and direction on vocational behavior, and (d) evaluate outcomes relative to purpose.

When confronted by the environment with behavioral choices, people can use the career self to respond with thoughtful decision making. Behavior may occur at the provocation of the environment or be self-initiated. The arrows between the environment (work, friends, and love) and the vocational self denote occupational stimuli, developmental tasks, and vocational responses and connote reciprocal determinism (Bandura, 1978; Kohn & Schooler, 1973). The interactions denoted by these arrows are judged by their level of congruence or correspondence. The arrows between the vocational and career selves denote career beliefs, attitudes, and competencies pertinent to career choice and development and connote recursive thinking. The interactions denoted by these arrows are judged by their level of maturity or adaptivity. Both sets of arrows indicate the interactive molding that transpires between parts of the schema.

The normal functioning of the vocational and career selves can be thwarted by contextual oppression (Fitzgerald & Betz, this volume) or motivational distortion at the drive level (Bordin, this volume).

The Framework Offers a Convergent Model for Coherent Career Services

Now let us apply the framework to career intervention to see what convergence practitioners have wrought. Practitioners have wrought convergence by systematically applying distinct career services, grounded in discrete career theories, to client groups presenting particular needs. To comprehend the convergence wrought by practitioners, I have placed the distinct career services, along with the corresponding career theory that supports each service, in a separate section of the framework for converging career theories as portrayed in figure 3. The framework reveals the coherence among the services. The services are defined as occupational *placement,* vocational *guidance,* career *counseling* and *education,* personal *therapy,* and position *coaching.* Each of these services draws upon a different career theorist because each service addresses a distinct problem.

Placement.   The placement service corresponds to the environment (i.e., roles of work, friendship, and love) section of the model. Occupational placement assists individuals who have chosen an occupational field to secure a position in that occupation. It helps clients to negotiate the social opportunity structure by gathering information, writing resumes, networking, searching for jobs, and preparing for interviews. This service emphasizes social skills training. Counseling psychologists who provide placement services use social learning theory as articulated by Krumboltz and others to reduce job search anxiety, increase assertiveness, counter mistaken beliefs, coax exploratory behavior, increase social skills, and refine self-presentation behavior. Placement works best with clients who are ready to implement a choice, that is, those who have committed themselves to a field and seek a place in it for themselves. However, placement services do not work as well for clients who have no destination in mind. They need a guide to help them specify a choice.

Guidance.   The guidance service corresponds to the vocational self. Vocational guidance helps individuals who are undecided to articulate their behavioral repertoire and then translate it into vocational choices. It helps clients to perceive more options and make choices by applying Parson's (1909) venerable triad of clarifying interests and abilities, exploring congruent occupational fields and levels, and specifying suitable vocational choices. This service emphasizes guidance techniques.

Counseling psychologists who provide vocational guidance use the trait-and-factor theory as articulated by Parsons (1909), Williamson and Darley (1937),

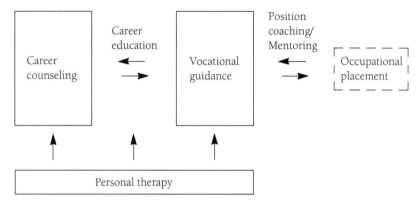

FIGURE 3   A Model for Career Services

Holland (1985), and others to interpret interest inventories and ability tests, provide educational and vocational information, encourage exploration, and suggest matching choices. Guidance, because it essentially translates self-concepts into occupational titles, works best with individuals who possess clear and stable vocational identities. Those people who cannot confidently and coherently answer the questions of, Who am I? and What do I want?, are not ready to make matching choices. They need a counselor to help them crystallize a vocational identity and envision a subjective career.

Counseling.   The counseling service corresponds to the career self. Career counseling facilitates self-reflection and cognitive restructuring in clients who need to mature and deepen their personalities. It helps clients to elaborate their self-concepts by introspection and discussion of their subjective careers (Hughes, 1958). Counseling psychologists who provide the counseling service use self-reflection models developed by ego psychologists, person-centered counselors, cognitive therapists, and others to conceptualize self and clarify choices through meaning-making activities like values clarification, identity articulation exercises, and life script analysis. Counseling works best with clients who want to learn more about their subjective views of life, develop their personal and vocational identities, or crystallize occupational field and ability level preferences. However, counseling does not work as well for clients who need to implement this self-knowledge. They need education.

Education.   The education service corresponds to the arrows between the vocational and career selves in figure 2. Career education assists individuals who encounter difficulties in enacting their subjective career intentions (career self) through their objective vocational behavior (vocational self). It helps these clients to develop self-management attitudes such as foresight and autonomy as well as competencies such as planning and decision making. It develops their readiness to cope with vocational development tasks. Counseling psychologists who provide career education services use deliberate psychological education (Mosher & Sprinthall, 1971; Tiedeman & Miller-Tiedeman, 1985) and developmental counseling (Blocher, 1974; Ivey, 1986) models to orient individuals to developmental tasks and foster coping attitudes and competencies that address these tasks. Career education works best with clients who want to learn to better manage their motivation and implement their self-concepts. However, education does not work as well for clients who experience motivational problems. They need therapy.

Therapy.   The therapy service corresponds to the drives section of the model in figure 2. Personal therapy assists individuals who have trouble developing a clear and stable vocational identity to examine what they need to feel secure (e.g., Phillips & Bruch, 1988). It focuses on the drama of recurring relationships to help clients examine personal motives, identify a central problem, and modify distorted motives. Counseling psychologists who provide brief therapy seek to integrate personal and career counseling models (Blustein, 1987; Subich, 1993) and use the working alliance (Bordin, 1979) to modify personality structure. Therapy works best with clients whose excessive indecisiveness, anxiety, and conflicts thwart their efforts to form a personally meaningful vocational identity. However, brief therapy does not work as well for clients who need extensive treatment to deal with fundamental psychopathology.

Coaching.   The coaching service corresponds to the arrows between the vocational self and environmental roles. Position coaching assists individuals who encounter problems adjusting to occupational positions to learn better adaptive mechanisms. It helps clients to cope with organizational culture, requirements of their positions, and co-workers by mentoring, rehearsing, and training. Counseling psychologists who provide career coaching use systems theory and organizational development theory as articulated by Dawis (this volume) and others to mentor individuals. Coaching works best with clients at the extremes of adjustment, such as individuals who need help entering the world of work through life skills training (e.g., Adkins, 1970) or progressing with managing their careers at a faster rate through mentoring (Carden, 1990). It also helps individuals resolve conflicts between work and family (Savickas, 1991). Needless to say, everyone can use a coach now and again.

This section presented a framework for converging career theories and showed the utility of this framework in examining the convergence in career services that practitioners have already wrought. The model assembles the singular perspectives of theorists into a framework to describe the multiple perspectives of practitioners. In so doing, it shows the potential of a convergence agenda for enriching the practice of career intervention by revealing a coherence among distinct career services. Systematic application of the coherent career services framework may advance contemporary efforts to devise better means for matching clients to interventions.

CONCLUSION

This chapter argued that a convergence agenda can aid theory renovation, advance the empirical process for knowledge making, and enrich the practice of career intervention. I have saved for last my favorite conclusion about the convergence project—we unified ourselves! The conference provided a period of self-examination and an opportunity for forging fresh bonds. We used this project to tell a story together. In telling the story, we each adopted multiple perspectives to empathically relate our own work to the work of our colleagues. We have already moved forward to a new position from which to shoulder the responsibility inherent in the challenge proffered by Hackett, Lent, and Greenhaus (1991)—to further unify our efforts to coherently expand the knowledge base of career intervention.

REFERENCES

Adkins, W. (1970). Life skills: Structured counseling for the disadvantaged. *Personnel and Guidance Journal, 49,* 108–116.

Bandura, A. (1978). The self-system in reciprocal determinism. *American Psychologist, 33,* 344–358.

Beck, A. (1976). *Cognitive therapy and the emotional disorders.* New York: International Universities Press.

Blocher, D. (1974). *Developmental counseling* (2d ed.). New York: Ronald Press.

Blustein, D. (1987). Integrating career counseling and psychotherapy: A comprehensive treatment strategy. *Psychotherapy, 24,* 794–799.

Bordin, E. (1979). The generalizability of the psychoanalytic concept of the working alliance. *Psychotherapy: Theory, Research, and Practice, 16,* 252–260.

Brown, D., & Brooks, L. (1990). *Career choice and development: Applying contemporary theories to practice* (2d ed.). San Francisco: Jossey-Bass.

Carden, A. (1990). Mentoring and adult career development. *The Counseling Psychologist, 18,* 275–299.

Crites, J. (1965). Measurement of vocational maturity in adolescence: I. Attitude Scale of the Vocational Development Inventory. *Psychological Monographs, 79* (2, Whole No. 595).

Crites, J. (1969). *Vocational psychology: The study of vocational behavior and development.* New York: McGraw-Hill.

Crites, J. (1973). *Rationales for Career Maturity Inventory Attitude Scale (Form A-1) items.* College Park, MD: University of Maryland.

Crites, J. (1978). *The Career Maturity Inventory.* Monterey, CA: CTB/McGraw-Hill.

Crites, J. (1982). Testing for career adjustment and development. *Training and Development Journal, 36,* 21–26.

Gibson, J. (1979). *The ecological approach to visual perception.* Boston: Houghton Mifflin.

Greenberger, E., Campbell, P., Sorensen, A., & O'Connor, J. (1971, July). *Toward the measurement of psychosocial maturity.* Center for Social Organization of Schools, Report No. 110. Johns Hopkins University, Baltimore.

Hackett, G., Lent, R., & Greenhaus, J. (1991). Advances in vocational theory and research: A 20-year retrospective. *Journal of Vocational Behavior, 38,* 3–38.

Harding, S. (1991). *Whose science? Whose knowledge?: Thinking from women's lives.* Ithaca, NY: Cornell University Press.

Holland, J. (1969). A critical analysis. *The Counseling Psychologist, 1,* 15–16.

Holland, J. (1972). *A dialogue on vocational development theory.* Washington, DC: American Personnel and Guidance Association.

Holland, J. (1985). *Making vocational choices: A theory of vocational personalities and work environments* (2d ed.). Odessa, FL: Psychological Assessment Resources.

Holland, J., Daiger, D., & Power, P. (1980). *My vocational situation.* Palo Alto, CA: Consulting Psychologists Press.

Holland, J., Gottfredson, G., & Nafziger, D. (1973, December). *A diagnostic scheme for specifying vocational assistance.* Center for Social Organization of Schools Report No. 164. Baltimore: Johns Hopkins University.

Holland, J., & Nichols, R. (1964). The development and validation of an indecision scale: The natural history of a problem in basic research. *Journal of Counseling Psychology, 11,* 27–34.

Hughes, E. (1958). *Men and their work.* Glencoe, IL: Free Press.

Ivey, A. (1986). *Developmental therapy: Theory into practice.* San Francisco: Jossey-Bass.

Kohn, M., & Schooler, C. (1973). Occupational experience and psychological functioning: An assessment of reciprocal effects. *American Sociological Review, 38,* 97–188.

Krumboltz, J. (1988). *The Career Beliefs Inventory.* Palo Alto, CA: Consulting Psychologists Press.

Krumboltz, J. (1991, August). The Career Beliefs Inventory. In W. Walsh (Chair), *Career assessment into practice.* Symposium conducted at the annual meeting of the American Psychological Association, San Francisco.

Latour, B. (1987). *Science in action.* Cambridge, MA: Harvard University Press.

Lewis, R., & Gilhousen, M. (1981). Myths of career development: A cognitive approach to vocational counseling. *Personnel and Guidance Journal, 59,* 296–299.

Mosher, R., & Sprinthall, N. (1971). Deliberate psychological education. *The Counseling Psychologist, 2,* 3–82.

Nespor, J., & Garrison, J. (1992). Constructing "relevance": A comment on Miller and Fredericks's "postpositivistic assumptions and educational research." *Educational Researcher, 21,* 27–28.

Oliver, L., & Spokane, A. (1988). Career-intervention outcome: What contributes to client gain? *Journal of Counseling Psychology, 35,* 447–462.

Osipow, S., Carney, C., Winer, J., Yanico, B., & Koschier, M. (1976). *Career Decision Scale* (3d revision). Odessa, FL: Psychological Assessment Resources.

Parsons, F. (1909). *Choosing a vocation.* Boston: Houghton Mifflin.

Phillips, S., & Bruch, M. (1988). Shyness and dysfunction in career development. *Journal of Counseling Psychology, 35,* 159–165.

Savickas, M. (1991). The meaning of work and love: Career issues and interventions. *Career Development Quarterly, 39,* 315–324.

Sharf, R. (1992). *Applying career development theory to counseling.* Pacific Grove, CA: Brooks/Cole.

Subich, L. (Ed.). (1993). How personal is career counseling? [Special issue]. *Career Development Quarterly, 42* (2).

Super, D. (1963). Toward making self-concept theory operational. In D. Super, R. Starishevsky, N. Matlin, & J. Jordaan, *Career development: Self-concept theory* (pp. 17–32). New York: College Entrance Examination Board.

Super, D., Thompson, A., Lindeman, R., Jordaan, J., & Myers, R. (1981). *Career Development Inventory.* Palo Alto, CA: Consulting Psychologists Press.

Thompson, A. (1976). Client misconceptions in vocational counseling. *Personnel and Guidance Journal, 55,* 30–33.

Tiedeman, D., & Miller-Tiedeman, A. (1985). Educating to advance the human career during the 1980s and beyond. *Vocational Guidance Quarterly, 34,* 15–30.

Wagner, E. (1971). Structural analysis: A theory of personality based on projective techniques. *Journal of Personality Assessment, 35,* 422–435.

Wagner, R., & Sternberg, R. (1985). Practical intelligence in real-world pursuits: The role of tacit knowledge. *Journal of Personality and Social Psychology, 49,* 436–458.

Watts, A., Super, D., & Kidd, J. (1981). *Career development in Great Britain.* Cambridge, UK: Hobsons Press.

Williamson, E., & Darley, J. (1937). *Student personnel work.* New York: McGraw-Hill.

Witkin, H., Oltman, P., Raskin, E., & Karp, S. (1971). *A manual for the Embedded Figures Test.* Palo Alto, CA: Consulting Psychologists Press.

CHAPTER TWENTY

Postscript

Is Convergence a Viable Agenda for Career Psychology?

Robert W. Lent
Michigan State University

Mark L. Savickas
Northeastern Ohio Universities College of Medicine

REFLECTING BACK ON the career convergence project from the present vantage point is both instructive and, in some ways, melancholic. Gone is the immediate excitement generated by the convergence conference, the high energy of creative and sometimes conflicting viewpoints being unveiled in the moment, the sense of history in the making, the optimistic expectations for the "event." Yet as the novelty recedes, time and distance afford a more sober opportunity to consider the project's achievements, limitations, and future prospects. In this postscript, we will measure the convergence project against its original goals and reassert the value of promoting rapprochement among the career theories, despite the many obstacles that such an agenda implies.

CONVERGENCE: A QUIXOTIC VENTURE?

In some ways, the aims of the convergence project seemed quite modest. As noted at the outset of this book, they entailed examining converging themes among the major career theories, considering the maintenance of important and useful distinctive features and applications of each theory, and nurturing an agenda for future research on theory integration. These aims did not include fashioning a unified career theory by committee fiat, forging a conceptual hegemony, promoting atheoretical eclecticism, or devaluing theoretical and empirical diversity in the search for knowledge about career behavior.

Despite its modest goals and explicit assumptions about the unique strengths of the diverse theoretical perspectives on career development, the convergence project proved quite controversial with many participants. Reactions among the five major career theorists, in particular, to the goal of seeking theoretical confluence seemed to range from somewhat optimistic (Super), to neutral (Bordin), to cautious (Dawis), to discouraging (Holland, Krumboltz). For instance, whereas Super argued that his work already embraces diverse conceptual positions, Krumboltz has asserted that a convergence of existing theories may be the last thing that is needed and that "theories are not designed by committees." Holland was somewhat more blunt, cautioning that the project's intent to promote theory integration was "ill-advised" and that one "cannot assemble theoretical constructs like Tinkertoy materials." Instead of pursuing a convergence agenda, Holland recommended that we renovate current theories, and Krumboltz counseled that we adopt different theories for different purposes.

While not precluding efforts at theoretical convergence, Dawis noted that "unified theory is the Holy Grail of science" and that such theories may prove to be a "will-o'-the-wisp." His four "iron laws" illustrated why all theoretical formulations, including integrative ones, are likely to enjoy an ephemeral existence, destined to be replaced or incorporated by next-generation models. Nevertheless, Dawis usefully made the distinction between unified theory and theory convergence, and suggested two general approaches to demonstrating or promoting convergence: (a) by showing how two or more systems overlap or are equivalent or (b) by building linkages among them.

Similarly, other project participants expressed caution or misgivings about the utility of convergence as a goal (e.g., Vondracek & Fouad, Subich & Taylor). Spokane noted that efforts at convergence are necessarily limited by the divergent assumptions that the theories make about particular facets of psychosocial functioning—for example, trait-and-factor and developmental approaches hold disparate views on the stability of behavior. He also emphasized the difference between a convergence of terms versus underlying philosophy, implying that the latter is considerably more difficult to achieve. Dollard and Miller's (1950) famous translation of psychodynamic concepts into learning theory terms is a good case in point: While a convergence in terminology is possible, it does not necessarily guarantee that the two positions will agree on fundamental issues, that the two sides mean the same things in their use of similar terms, or that more enlightening explanations (as opposed to new labels) for behavior will result.

Other authors were somewhat more sanguine about the goal of convergence, or were at least willing to consider vehicles for seeking convergence. Walsh and Chartrand, for example, suggested that the willingness to entertain theoretical convergence may be a "sign of a maturing field," though they asserted the need for care in the selection of potential unification constructs. Rounds and Hesketh recommended a general strategy for examining convergence, namely, study of the latent structure of our major predictor and criterion variables, together with the variables that moderate their relationships. Savickas advocated approaching convergence by comparing how different theories view the same phenomenon and by empirically examining the relationships among them. Lent and Hackett described one model intended to account for the relationships among a variety of person and environmental variables that emanate from different theories.

KEY BUILDING BLOCKS
FOR COMPREHENSIVE THEORY

Although the project produced no clear mandate for widescale convergence efforts, it did identify a variety of important and, in some cases, neglected elements that will need to be incorporated within truly comprehensive accounts of career behavior. On the person side of the ledger, Bordin argued for the inclusion of intrinsic motives and play as essential features of career development; Brown and Watkins, and Phillips each noted the need to attend to affective/emotional variables to a greater degree. Several sets of authors asserted the relevance of the Big Five personality dimensions to career choice, interest, and adjustment outcomes (e.g., Brown & Watkins; Walsh & Chartrand). Lent and Hackett discussed sociocognitive person mechanisms, such as self-efficacy and goals, that may enable the exercise of agency in career pursuits.

On the environment side, Fitzgerald and Betz offered a compelling plea, echoed by Harmon and others, for incorporating structural and cultural factors into career development theory and research to a much greater extent than is presently the case. These authors noted how environmental constraints limit the utility and relevance of current career theories for many segments of the population, and how a focus on structural and cultural variables may provide an "overlay to, or new perspective for, the consideration of career theories." This perspective seems to suggest that our major theories overrely on person constructs and assume that career paths may be freely chosen, without regard to contextual obstacles, if people bring their "rational" faculties to bear on their decision making (Phillips). One specific feature of the sociocultural environment, the family system, was cited by several authors as an important focal point for future study (Blustein; Bordin; Brown & Watkins); another was the concept of contextual affordance (Lent & Hackett; Spokane; Walsh & Chartrand).

Several sets of participants focused on the person-environment (P-E) interface as the basis for comprehensive theory. Rounds and Hesketh asserted, for example, that P-E transaction is a "unifying principle for career development theory," and Spokane identified the resolution of incongruence as a potential point of theory convergence. Blustein's embedded identity construct emphasizes the means by which people internalize environmental influences in seeking a stable, coherent sense of self. The life span perspective was offered as a general framework for studying career development in context (Vondracek & Fouad), and general social cognitive theory was used to explicate processes by which the person, behavior, and context may jointly shape career outcomes (Lent & Hackett).

ARCHITECTURAL PLANS
FOR COMPREHENSIVE THEORY

In addition to suggesting a number of important building blocks for a more comprehensive understanding of career behavior, the project highlighted some overarching plans for putting these basic elements together. In many cases, these plans hint at our larger paradigms (Borgen, 1992), questioning our business-as-usual approach to developing, testing, and applying career theories.

Perhaps the most frequently occurring argument that emerged throughout the convergence project involved the need to broaden the purview of career behavior and remove the conceptual shackles that constrain us. Descriptions of this ailment and its potential remedies took a variety of forms. Fitzgerald and Betz, in particular, noted how the literature has taken a myopic view of career development, focusing the majority of its inquiry on a relatively small segment of the larger population—namely, white college students. Along with Harmon, they urged that we extend the scope of career theory and research, including within our efforts those who do not enjoy the luxury of having a "subjective career" in Savickas' terms, for example, the underclass. Similarly, Vondracek and Fouad emphasized the need to attend to the cross-cultural utility of current career models.

Another variant of this paradigm-expanding argument involved the need to employ multiple perspectives to guide our efforts, along with diverse research tools to implement them. Vondracek and Fouad, for example, recommended that career inquiry become more multidisciplinary, drawing on advances in developmental psychology and other areas. Other writers pointed to personality, social, organizational, and cognitive psychology as wellsprings for career psychology. Recent constructivist positions, an outgrowth of the cognitive movement, were seen as offering potentially profound implications for the way in which career scientists and practitioners view their domains (Lent & Hackett). The nature of schemata allow for the expression of behavioral consistency and plasticity across time and context, thereby setting a place at the table for both developmentalists and trait-and-factor adherents.

Constructivism, and motoric conceptions of cognition, emphasize the active, feed-forward mechanisms by which people make meaning of their experiences and help regulate their own behavior. Such conceptions view cognitive, affective, and behavioral pathways as integral partners in guiding human functioning, thereby challenging earlier approaches that assume a simple "cerebral supremacy," or one-way causal influence of cognition on emotion and behavior. These approaches also call into question theories that offer decontextualized accounts of behavior.

In her chapter, Phillips illustrated the limitations of classical decision-making models that are founded on the ideal of the "rational person." She noted that decisions are often affected by factors such as affect, cultural norms, information processing constraints, and biases that are not well accounted for by rational-prescriptive decisional approaches. The latter tend to view affect as a problem to be solved, one that stems from irrational or maladaptive thinking. In contrast, constructivist formulations acknowledge the functional utility of personal beliefs. Importantly, in the realm of career counseling, constructivist and humanistic streams have recently found a confluence in novel methods that take a narrative, storytelling view of career development impasses (Savickas). Such an approach engenders efforts to "edit" unsatisfying stories, rather than impose an invariant sequence of rational problem-solving activities.

Finally, a number of authors suggested that an expanded base of inquiry on career development will require that we take a more ecumenical approach to selecting research methods. Although no one advocated abandoning traditional quantitative methods, several participants championed the use of qualitative methodologies to illuminate particular facets of career development, such as the embedded self, that may prove refractory to quantitative techniques alone (e.g., Brown & Watkins). Others considered ways to make traditional and emerging methods more responsive to our knowledge needs. For instance, Walsh and Chartrand admonished career psychologists to attend to basic measurement issues, ensuring that research scales adequately reflect the constructs they are intended to assess. Vondracek and Fouad advocated longitudinal designs to better capture the dynamic flow of P-E interaction. Harmon encouraged the harvesting of computer-technologic advances, exploration of nonlinear relationships, and use of nonparametric methods. Some noted, or implied, the utility of causal modeling procedures (Lent & Hackett; Rounds & Hesketh).

If all of these recommendations for theory and research expansion did not produce a definitive set of architectural blueprints for a comprehensive career theory, at the very least they suggested important qualities about the neighborhood of such an edifice, as well as its foundation, building materials and methods, and would-be inhabitants—a multicultural, multiclass, dual-gendered collective, to be sure.

HEALING THE THEORY-PRACTICE RIFT

Convergence project participants addressed at length in their chapters one significant controversy that was aired at the conference, namely, the gulf that many perceive to exist between career development theory and research on the one hand, and career counseling practice, including social policy, on the other. That such gulfs exist in other applied psychological specialties, such as psychotherapy, is well known, though it is not much cause for consolation. The fact is, this issue became a major subtext of the convergence project, quickly creating the momentum for a follow-up project exploring the convergence between career theory and practice (see the chapters by Savickas; Walsh & Chartrand).

In his chapter, Osipow noted that "career theories are not career counseling theories, and although career theories may have suggestions of value for career counseling practice, probably career counseling needs its own theory or theories." In the spirit of convergence and parsimony, theory-bridging efforts may prove valuable here. Indeed, there are inherent connections between career and personal development, and between career interventions and psychotherapy. Thus, rather than developing unique career counseling theories from scratch, it would be well to promote better efforts to link career practice with theories of change derived from personal counseling (cf. Rounds & Tinsley, 1984), as well as with more basic career, personality, learning, and development theories.

Such theory-bridging efforts will require the elaboration, modification, and the possible reforging of basic concepts and propositions within a more practice-friendly context. They will also require the cooperation of practitioners, scientists, and scientist-practitioners. The question raised throughout the project, Can practice ever inform theory?, sticks in academic psychology's collective craw. Of course it can and *should;* the problem may be that we too rarely ask it to.

Although practice-relevant theory and research might well form an integral part of the field's future mission, it is important that we not downplay the virtues of more basic research and theory. Kurt Lewin's observation that "there is nothing as practical as a good theory" has been invoked so often that perhaps it has lost its impact. The field's occasional tendency to dichotomize basic and applied science and to demand immediate relevance can be short sighted. For one thing, theorists live in the real world, too, and do not develop their ideas in a social void. For another, theorizing that may at first appear to be practice-distant tends to spin off practical applications. The contribution of theoretical physics to the development of nuclear technology is a case in point; there are many theory-into-practice examples to be found closer to home—for example, Holland's (1985) hexagonal interest model, Lofquist and Dawis' (1991) P-E correspondence counseling theory, and Super's career-development assessment and counseling model (Super, Osborne, Walsh, Brown, & Niles, 1992).

In sum, a reasonable argument might be made for supporting theorists to develop their models without the demand for instant consumption; some cakes simply take more time to bake than others. Such theories represent Savickas' notion of "practice at a distance." At the same time, a portion of the field's considerable energies can be devoted to elaborating practice and policy implications from existing theories, developing "bridging theories" that are specifically directed at practice issues, and launching research projects that test the applied implications of career theories. Part of the value of professional conferences, like the one included in this project, is that they provide the medium for a communal quest for future agendas. They may also, in their wake, facilitate the organization of programmatic research that addresses particular needs.

The point is that we need not try to eliminate the dialectic tension between theory and practice by forcing all theory to be immediately responsive to practical concerns or by abandoning basic theory; this tension can be healthy and heuristic. At the same time, however, we realize that our comments do not begin to address many practitioners' sense of alienation from the field's scientific base. Our field has clearly been slow to ponder innovative, structural methods that might unite scientists and practitioners in the common search for, and application of, knowledge. Clinical psychology has been struggling with this issue for some time; career psychology is just beginning to acknowledge it publicly. We can only hope that the career theory/practice project that follows this one will grapple openly and productively with the problems of scientist-practitioner dialogue and cooperation.

BACK TO TILTING AT WINDMILLS

The recent sensitivity to convergence and similarities among career theories (Borgen, 1991; Hackett, Lent, & Greenhaus, 1991; Krumboltz & Nichols, 1990; Osipow, 1990; Super, 1992) comes in the context of a broader dialogue about fragmentation versus unification in psychology's knowledge base. Arthur Staats (1991), one of the key figures in this dialogue, has argued that "psychology suffers from a crisis of disunity...[with] many unrelated methods, findings, problems, theoretical languages, schismatic issues, and philosophic positions" (p. 899). Let us briefly revisit Staats' thesis and its relevance to vocational psychology.

Essentially, Staats has argued that, in developing sciences like psychology, scientists tend to examine different phenomena, relying on diverse conceptual and methodological perspectives. The reward structure emphasizes identifying novel concepts and phenomena and generating competing theoretical accounts; it does not favor the search for commonality and interdependence. Staats contends that eventually this "chaos of disunity" is surmounted by movement toward a more unified state. This movement is marked by a change in goals "from preoccupation with the novel to inclusion of efforts to find interrelationships and to simplify and organize that which has already been found" (p. 900). As consensus emerges regarding underlying principles, language, and problems, competition in science begins to take on a different form. Rather than efforts to distinguish one's own work as unique, the prize involves being the first to solve complex problems.

Disunity in Career Psychology

Is career psychology a disunified science? If we apply Staats' criteria, perhaps it is. Are we as disunified as psychotherapy or certain other areas of psychology? Probably not. We currently have at least four dominant theories of career choice and development and a number of additional models that have proven heuristic to varying degrees (Hackett & Lent, 1992; Osipow, 1990). We also have a research literature that has grown exponentially in the past 20 years (Borgen, 1991), though, unfortunately, a good portion of it has not been explicitly ground in theory (Hackett et al., 1991).

One might argue that the unbridled proliferation of inquiry is healthy—an indication that our subject matter is fertile and our conceptual lenses acute. Alternatively, one might acknowledge that, while it has produced a rich and expansive literature, our tendency toward knowledge production without a corresponding focus on knowledge unification has yielded considerable conceptual disarray. In essence, we possess many unconnected fragments of knowledge, making it difficult to synthesize what we know into a coherent whole. Needless to say, if this burgeoning complexity is difficult to organize, efforts to apply what we know to practice will necessarily meet with considerable frustration. Thus, scientific diversity sans unification or convergence efforts likely contributes dramatically to the rift between theory and practice noted earlier.

Holland and a few other writers in this volume eschewed the search for convergence, noting the many pitfalls of such a quest. Indeed, it is hard not to be swayed by Holland's conclusion that "theoretical restoration or renovation looks like a productive strategy with relatively few barriers, but integration looks like a strategy with many barriers." We agree with Holland on the virtues of renovating existing theories, especially those that have proven their mettle in research and practice. However, at the risk of swimming against the tide, we also see value in nurturing more efforts at theoretical integration. Simply put, it does not need to be an either-or proposition.

If convergence is such a good idea, then why did it receive such a lukewarm, if not cool, reception from so many participants in this project? Part of the reason may lie in the multitude of meanings that were ascribed to the term *convergence*. Some seemed to view convergence or integration as implying a movement toward one grand career theory-to-end-all-theories, akin to physicists' quest for a unified theory of the universe (Hawking, 1988). From such a perspective, diversity would be stifled, current "partial" theoretical positions would be reassembled by committee into a larger "Tinkertoy" structure, and one monolithic theory would dominate all inquiry. Other participants, ourselves included, saw convergence in far more modest terms—essentially, as an effort to explore points of commonality, to account for the relationships among seemingly diverse constructs, to promote more comprehensive theories, and, where possible, to reduce redundancy and promote parsimony.

Unification Agendas

If one accepts the latter agenda for convergence, then how can it be pursued? It is perhaps ironic that a variety of strategies may be employed in the quest for convergence, recalling the Zen assurance that there are many roads to the same end.

Staats (1991) advocated several "theory tasks," or types of unification, ranging from relatively circumscribed theory-bridging efforts to grand, unified theory strategies at the more ambitious end of the continuum. We will highlight three of Staats' tasks that represent a relatively modest level of unification activity and which, we believe, might lend themselves particularly well to current career inquiry. These tasks do not require that one subscribe to the vision of a single grand theory of career development that would absorb, render obsolete, and transcend all separate career theories.

The first task involves devising what Staats (1991) called "unifying theory analyses" that attempt to bring common concepts and principles together within a shared framework to "produce parsimony, relatedness, and unity" (p. 905). P-E fit conceptions may offer a good example of how and where such analyses can benefit career psychology. Holland (this volume) and Dawis (this volume) have both noted the similarity between their respective concepts of congruence and correspondence. Though conceptually similar, each version of P-E fit involves somewhat different central matching constructs (e.g., interests in Holland's model versus values and abilities in TWA). Since it is reasonable to assume that P-E fit is multiply determined—for instance, there are many dimensions upon which people and their environments may be compatible or incompatible, with some potentially compensating for others (cf. Gati, 1989)—unifying theory analyses could be undertaken that attempt to identify, organize, and incorporate the major variables that are assumed to define fit. At the same time, unifying research could be conducted that examines whether different methods of defining fit are complementary, redundant, or differentially useful. Surprisingly, incidents of this sort of research are somewhat rare in the career literature (e.g., Rounds, 1990).

A second, related strategy involves the construction of "theory bridges" that relate seemingly separate phenomena (Staats, 1991). Arguing that isolated concepts need to be "woven into a general fabric for expanding knowledge," Staats has cited a number of variables that are quite familiar to career researchers, such as interests, attitudes, values, and preferences:

> We have separate studies of phenomena under these labels. Are there any relationships among these phenomena? Could theory bridges of common underlying principles be constructed?... We will never achieve a related, meaningful, coherent, compact, and parsimonious field of knowledge if we do not relate and organize the phenomena studied. (pp. 905–906)

Career psychologists appear to be increasingly sensitive to the need to explore such potential links. For instance, Brown (1990) asked, "what are the relationships among values, needs, aptitudes, and interests as they operate in concert to influence occupational choice making?" (p. 346). Betz (1992) called for more work examining individual difference variables' theoretical linkages, structure, and dimensionality. Rounds and Hesketh (this volume) advocated study of the latent structure of the field's predictor and criterion variables. And Lent and Hackett (this volume) described one bridging theory that attempts to account for the relations among a number of common career individual difference variables (e.g., interests, self-efficacy, ability, goals).

In constructing and researching theory bridges, it may be important to refrain from what Bandura (March 1, 1993, personal communication) described as "cafeteria theorizing," or what Holland (herein) has characterized as assembling theoretical constructs like "Tinkertoy materials." Bandura argued that "greater scientific progress is achieved by applying more aspects of a unified theory to career development than by stringing together constructs from divergent theories." The cafeteria approach may "spawn discordant eclecticism and needless redundancy," cautioned Bandura, rather than theoretical coherence and parsimony. Staats (1991) likewise counseled against "superficial eclectic combinations" that promote an "ephemeral peace" (p. 906) but do not fundamentally advance unification.

A third unification strategy described by Staats also seems quite relevant for current career psychology. This involves developing theories to reconcile general theoretical schisms or disparate philosophical positions, that is, broad disputes that transcend specific theories. For instance, in the career realm, developmentalists, trait-and-factor adherents, and social cognitivists hold differing views on the stability versus plasticity and globality versus situation-specificity of person attributes. Are these positions truly unbridgeable? Staats (1991) suggested that "theories are needed that show how the major findings of the schismatic positions can be related in a close, derivational way" and that such differences be viewed as *"problems* to be worked on toward a solution; they should not be accepted as foundations for mutual discreditation, for these sap the science's strength" (p. 906). Career psychology does not presently contain many examples of schism-melding unification efforts, though Vondracek, Lerner, and Schulenberg's (1986) attempt to bridge developmental and interactional positions is noteworthy.

We have tried to show in this book that there are many ways to approach theoretical convergence—and that the "big business" notion of a theory-conglomerate that would engulf and devour smaller theories actually offers a limited view of convergence. The common goal of the various unification strategies is not to restrain diversity or creativity, but rather to counterbalance "sheer production" with a

> strong investment in weaving the unrelated knowledge elements together into the fabric of organized science. Without that counterbalance...[of] unifying knowledge, the experimental productivity of the science simply makes it progressively more complex and disunified, less of a science, and less strong as a profession. (Staats, 1991, p. 910)

Activism Versus Letting Nature Take Its Course

In addition to the goals and methods of theoretical convergence, one area in which project participants disagreed was on whether convergence should be pursued actively and intentionally or whether a laissez-faire approach is best. Osipow (this volume) seemed to summarize the latter position well when he asked, "Should career theory be converged? The answer is an emphatic no." Osipow's stance places faith in the emergence of "new and more powerful theories" from the "ashes and residue…of the failures of earlier theories." He suggests that convergence represents a naturally occurring process of theory renewal and that to pursue convergence as an explicit agenda may constrain theorists' creativity.

Osipow's position is thoughtful and persuasive, yet the patient, noninterventionist approach to convergence is not without its downsides. Staats (1991) interpreted the history of science as suggesting that "letting nature take its course with respect to unification guarantees that a very long-term process results" (p. 910). He argued that increasing fragmentation of our knowledge base is the price we pay for shunning theoretical rapprochement. We agree with Osipow in the sense that it would be counterproductive for the field to expect all of its theorists to focus on convergence. Indeed, career psychology is well served by a diversity of theoretical positions. Yet it would seem that this diversity could be complemented by having some theorists and researchers build structures to unify our diverse fragments of knowledge. Thus, both diversity *and* convergence have their place. As Staats (1991) has observed, "psychology has enormous power in its building materials, but that potential will only be realized by adding the architectural direction of [intentional and systematic] unification efforts" (p. 910).

CONCLUSION

Unified theory, as Dawis (this volume) has observed, may well be likened to the quest for the Holy Grail—elusive, ephemeral, perhaps unattainable. But where would literature be if the knights found in medieval and Renaissance writings went on strike and refused the challenge of the quest, complaining that the Holy Grail probably doesn't exist or, if it does, it's too much trouble to find? The point may be that we need the quest, the challenge, and the striving involved in theory convergence. As the work motivation literature tells us, goals have orienting and motivating functions, sometimes enabling people to transcend the targets they work toward and to produce fortuitous outcomes. For instance, even though many viewed the goal of landing a person on the moon by the end of the 1960s as implausible, the goal nonetheless spurred important scientific and technological advances—and later proved to be achievable.

Unified science in the grand theory sense seems quixotic or Arthurian, in part, because it may appear to represent an end state, an advanced stage in which knowledge cannot be furthered. Yet we all know that science is a growth enterprise, and Dawis' four "iron laws" certainly mitigate against the framing of a finalized, universal theory that will explain all career-relevant phenomena. While unified science, the mythical end state, may ultimately be unattainable, unifying science—the process of seeking convergence among seemingly diverse theories and phenomena—somehow does not seem so farfetched. In this process, a multiplicity of convergence efforts is needed, not one single project or theory.

So what did this project achieve? Did it produce meaningful convergence, if only of opinion? Honestly, no. Its value may lie not in any immediate tangible product, but rather in its process—its ability to bring together a number of the field's foremost theorists and researchers who were willing to consider the merits of a convergence agenda. As Osipow (this volume) has observed, real theory developments, including theory convergence efforts, are generally pursued by individuals or small teams, far from the tumult of projects such as this one.

Nevertheless, the convergence project may have achieved a number of modest, though useful, intermediate objectives, such as (a) legitimizing the search for theoretical commonalities and relationships among our diverse phenomena of interest; (b) identifying several person, contextual, and P-E interaction mechanisms that could serve as a springboard for future inquiry on theory integration; (c) reaffirming the useful distinctions among the major career theories; (d) highlighting the theories' deficiencies and features needing renovation; and (e) recognizing a serious career theory-practice rift, leading to a new profession-wide project. Finally, we'd like to believe that the project helped set a valuable precedent in career psychology—that is, the coming together to identify and consider a communal response to pressing problems of scientific and practical import. This atmosphere of dialogue and debate may help nurture a sense of shared mission, a zeitgeist that promotes convergence as well as diversity.

REFERENCES

Betz, N. E. (1992). Career assessment: A review of critical issues. In S. D. Brown & R. W. Lent (Eds.), *Handbook of counseling psychology* (2d ed., pp. 453–484). New York: Wiley.

Borgen, F. H. (1991). Megatrends and milestones in vocational behavior: A 20-year counseling psychology retrospective. *Journal of Vocational Behavior, 39,* 263–290.

Borgen, F. H. (1992). Expanding scientific paradigms in counseling psychology. In S. D. Brown & R. W. Lent (Eds.), *Handbook of counseling psychology* (2d ed., pp. 111–139). New York: Wiley.

Brown, D. (1990). Summary, comparison, and critique of the major theories. In D. Brown, L. Brooks, & Associates, *Career Choice and development* (2d ed., pp. 338–363). San Francisco: Jossey-Bass.

Dollard, J., & Miller, N. E. (1950). *Personality and psychotherapy.* New York: McGraw-Hill.

Gati, I. (1989). Person-environment fit research: Problems and prospects. *Journal of Vocational Behavior, 35,* 181–193.

Hackett, G., & Lent, R. W. (1992). Theoretical advances and current inquiry in career psychology. In S. D. Brown & R. W. Lent (Eds.), *Handbook of counseling psychology* (2d ed., pp. 419–451). New York: Wiley.

Hackett, G., Lent, R. W., & Greenhaus, J. H. (1991). Advances in vocational theory and research: A 20-year retrospective. *Journal of Vocational Behavior, 38,* 3–38.

Hawking, S. W. (1988). *A brief history of time: From the big bang to black holes.* Toronto: Bantam.

Holland, J. L. (1985). *Making vocational choices: A theory of vocational personalities and work environments* (2d ed.). Englewood Cliffs, NJ: Prentice-Hall.

Krumboltz, J. D., & Nichols, C. W. (1990). Integrating the social learning theory of career decision making (pp. 159–192). In W. B. Walsh & S. H. Osipow (Eds.), *Career counseling: Contemporary topics in vocational psychology* (pp. 159–192). Hillsdale, NJ: Erlbaum.

Lofquist, L. H., & Dawis, R. V. (1991). *Essentials of person-environment correspondence counseling.* Minneapolis: University of Minnesota Press.

Osipow, S. H. (1990). Convergence in theories of career choice and development: Review and prospect. *Journal of Vocational Behavior, 36,* 122–131.

Rounds, J. B. (1990). The comparative and combined utility of work value and interest data in career counseling with adults. *Journal of Vocational Behavior, 37,* 32–45.

Rounds, J. B., & Tinsley, H. E. A. (1984). Diagnosis and treatment of vocational problems. In S. D. Brown & R. W. Lent (Eds.), *Handbook of counseling psychology* (pp. 137–177). New York: Wiley.

Staats, A. W. (1991). Unified positivism and unification psychology: Fad or new field? *American Psychologist, 46,* 899–912.

Super, D. E. (1992). Toward a comprehensive theory of career development. In D. Montross & C. Shinkman (Eds.), *Career development: Theory and practice* (pp. 35–64). Springfield, IL: Charles C. Thomas.

Super, D. E., Osborne, W. L., Walsh, D. J., Brown, S. D., & Niles, S. G. (1992). Developmental career assessment and counseling: The C-DAC Model. *Journal of Counseling and Development, 71,* 74–80.

Vondracek, F. W., Lerner, R. M., & Schulenberg, J. E. (1986). *Career development: A life-span developmental approach.* Hillsdale, NJ: Erlbaum.

Contributors

Convergence in Career Development Theories authors are pictured left to right as follows: (front row) J. Krumboltz, L. Harmon, E. Bordin, D. Super, R. Dawis; (second row) D. Blustein, S. Phillips, S. Osipow, J. Holland; (third row) A. Spokane, L. Fitzgerald, G. Hackett, J. Rounds; (fourth row) J. Chartrand, R. Lent, S. Brown, F. Vondracek; (fifth row) B. Walsh, L. Subich, K. Taylor, E. Watkins; and (back row) Rhonda Egidio, B. Hesketh, N. Fouad, M. Savickas. Rhonda Egidio served as the convergence conference registrar. Author Nancy Betz is not pictured.

Nancy E. Betz, Ph.D., is a professor of psychology at Ohio State University. Her research and teaching interests focus on the areas of psychological testing, barriers to women's and minorities' pursuit of many career fields, and the applications of self-efficacy theory to career choice and adjustment. She is a past recipient of the university's Distinguished Teaching Award. She has presented to national congressional groups on the underrepresentation of women and minorities in science and engineering and is a past recipient of the American Psychological Association's John Holland Award for Outstanding Achievement in Career and Personality Research. She has also served on the editorial boards of the *Journal of Counseling Psychology,* the *Journal of Vocational Behavior,* the *Journal of Career Assessment,* and *Psychology of Women Quarterly.*

David L. Blustein, Ph.D., is an associate professor in the Department of Counseling Psychology at the University at Albany, State University of New York. His current research focuses on understanding the factors that facilitate effective career development. His investigation addresses the role of the self and identity in career development and the career exploration and commitment to career choices processes. Dr. Blustein currently serves on the editorial boards of the *Journal of Counseling Psychology,* the *Journal of Vocational Behavior,* and the *Journal of Occupational* and *Organizational Psychology.* He has published extensively in the literature and is a frequent presenter at national conventions and conferences in career psychology.

Edward S. Bordin received his Ph.D. from Ohio State University in 1942. He joined the University of Michigan in 1948 and served as a professor of psychology and director of the Counseling Center until 1984, when he became professor emeritus. He served as editor of the *Journal of Counseling Psychology* and directed the influential Psychotherapy Research Project. He also served as President of the Counseling Psychology Division in the American Psychological Association and as President of the Society for Psychotherapy Research. After making an indelible mark on the discipline of counseling psychology, Dr. Bordin died on August 24, 1992, in LaJolla, California.

Steven D. Brown, Ph.D., is a professor of counseling and educational psychology and director of the graduate program in counseling psychology at Loyola University Chicago. He is a licensed clinical psychologist in the state of Illinois, where he maintains a small practice of vocational counseling. His research focuses on vocational psychology theory and on the roles of social cognitive and personality variables in the career choice and adjustment process. He coedited both editions of the *Handbook of Counseling Psychology.* Dr. Brown is currently developing a social cognitive model for vocational choice counseling that integrates social cognitive theory with basic personality research.

Judy M. Chartrand, Ph.D., is currently an assistant professor in the Department of Psychology at Virginia Commonwealth University in Richmond. Her research areas include the study of career decision making and person-environment fit theories. She has coauthored grant projects designed to enhance career planning for older adults and inner city adolescents and has conducted career planning workshops for Olympic athletes.

René V. Dawis received his Ph.D. from the University of Minnesota, where his mentor was Donald G. Paterson. After a year as assistant professor at the University of the Philippines, he returned to Minnesota to head up the fledgling Work Adjustment Project. Here he teamed up with Lloyd H. Lofquist and David J. Weiss to do research in vocational rehabilitation and produce, among other things, the theory of work adjustment. In 1963, he joined the faculty of the University of Minnesota's Industrial Relations Department and, in 1968, transferred to the Psychology Department, where he remains today. His research interests continue to be in vocational psychology.

Louise F. Fitzgerald, Ph.D., is an associate professor in the Departments of Psychology and Women's Studies at the University of Illinois at Urbana-Champaign and is coauthor of *The Career Psychology of Women.* Her research focuses on barriers to women in the workplace, particularly sexual harassment. In 1992, the Counseling Psychology Division of the American Psychological Association presented Dr. Fitzgerald with the John Holland Award for Outstanding Achievement in Career and Personality Research.

Nadya A. Fouad, Ph.D., is an associate professor in the Department of Educational Psychology and chair of the counseling area at the University of Wisconsin, Milwaukee. She has published numerous articles and chapters on cross-cultural vocational assessment, career development, interest measurement, and cross-cultural counseling, and in 1991 received the Ralph F. Berdie Research Award from the American Counseling Association. She serves on the editorial boards of the *Journal of Vocational Behavior,* the *Career Development Quarterly,* and *The Counseling Psychologist.*

Gail Hackett, Ph.D., is currently a member of the counseling psychology faculty at Arizona State University. She has written extensively in the areas of career counseling, career development, and gender issues in counseling. Her primary research emphasis has been the application of self-efficacy theory to career development. She has served on the editorial boards of several major publications and is currently the associate editor of the *Journal of Counseling Psychology.*

Lenore W. Harmon, Ph.D., is a professor of educational psychology at the University of Illinois at Urbana-Champaign. She served as editor of the *Journal of Vocational Behavior* from 1975 to 1984 and as editor of the *Journal of Counseling Psychology* from 1988 to 1993. She is the recipient of the 1993 Leona Tyler Award from the American Psychological Association's Division of Counseling Psychology. Her research interests include the career development of women and athletes and the development of interest inventories.

Beryl Hesketh, Ph.D., is chair of the Psychology Department at Macquarie University in Sydney, Australia. She was previously on the faculty of the School of Psychology at the University of New South Wales. Prior to moving to Australia in 1985, she served on the faculty of Massey University in New Zealand for 10 years. In addition to her research in vocational psychology, she has published and taught in the fields of selection, training, and performance appraisal. Currently, she is involved in two major research projects—one concerned with integrating training and career decision making and the other with testing the accuracy of fuzzy ratings as measures of distributional performance appraisal data.

John L. Holland, Ph.D., has been a researcher-practitioner and research supervisor and teacher for 40 years. He is best known for the *Self-Directed Search*, a leading interest inventory. His hobbies include art and music. Dr. Holland is considering a return from retirement so that he can influence change in the field of career practice and research.

John D. Krumboltz, Ph.D., is professor of education and psychology at Stanford University. He received a Guggenheim Fellowship and spent one year as a fellow at the Center for Advanced Studies in the Behavioral Sciences. On three occasions he received the Outstanding Research Award as well as the Distinguished Professional Services Award from the American Personnel and Guidance Association. He coauthored *Changing Children's Behavior* and coedited *Counseling Methods* and *Assessing Career Development*. He developed the social learning theory of career decision making in *Social Learning and Career Decision Making*, which he coedited. Dr. Krumholtz received the Leona Tyler Award from the American Psychological Association in 1990.

Robert W. Lent, Ph.D., is currently a professor and director in the Counseling Psychology Program at Michigan State University. His primary research interests include applications of social cognitive theory to career development, academic achievement, and psychological adjustment issues. Dr. Lent coedited both editions of the *Handbook of Counseling Psychology* and received the American Psychological Association's 1993 John Holland Award for Outstanding Achievement in Career and Personality Research. He currently serves on the editorial boards of the *Journal of Counseling Psychology* and the *Journal of Vocational Behavior*.

Samuel H. Osipow, Ph.D., is professor of psychology at Ohio State University in Columbus. He has been a faculty member there since 1967, serving as chair of the Psychology Department between 1973 and 1986. He is the author of *Theories of Career Development*, coeditor of the *Handbook of Vocational Behavior*, the founding editor of the *Journal of Vocational Behavior*, past editor of the *Journal of Counseling Psychology*, and current editor of *Applied and Preventive Psychology*. He is also the coauthor of the *Career Decision Scale* and *The Occupational Stress Inventory*. Dr. Osipow was recognized in 1989 with the American Psychological Association's Leona Tyler Award.

Susan D. Phillips, Ph.D., is on the faculty of the Department of Counseling Psychology at the University at Albany, State University of New York, where she is currently the Director of Doctoral Training and teaches graduate courses in career development and professional issues and practice. Dr. Phillips' research program has focused on decision making in career development. She was the 1991 recipient of the American Psychological Association's John Holland Award for Outstanding Achievement in Career and Personality Research, and currently serves on the editorial boards of the *Journal of Counseling Psychology* and the *Journal of Vocational Behavior.* She has published extensively in various professional journals.

James Rounds, Ph.D., is an associate professor and director of training in the Counseling Psychology Program at the University of Illinois at Urbana. He serves on the editorial boards of the *Journal of Counseling* and the *Journal of Career Assessment.* His research program concentrates on elaborating the theory of work adjustment and on investigating the structure of vocational interests.

Mark L. Savickas, Ph.D., is a professor and chair in the Behavioral Sciences Department at Northeastern Ohio Universities College of Medicine and is an adjunct professor of counseling in the Graduate School of Education at Kent State University. His research focuses on attitudes and behaviors that foster vocational development and interventions that promote career maturity. He edits the *Career Development Quarterly* for the National Career Development Association and serves on the editorial boards of the *Journal of Vocational Behavior* and the *Journal of Career Assessment.* Dr. Savickas also serves as the USA National Correspondent for the International Association for Educational and Vocational Guidance.

Arnold R. Spokane, Ph.D., is professor of education and psychology and coordinator of the Counseling Psychology Program at Lehigh University. A practicing career counselor for nearly 20 years, he is the author of *Career Intervention* and serves on the editorial boards of the *Journal of Career Development,* the *Career Devbelopment Quarterly* and the *Journal of Career Assessment.* He specializes in the study of the full range of career interventions, the overlap between career and mental health issues, including occupational-induced stress, and in the interactions of persons and environments at work. Dr. Spokane has authored or coauthored more than 50 journal articles, book chapters, and technical reports on career development.

Linda Mezydlo Subich, Ph.D., is currently an associate professor in the Department of Psychology at the University of Akron and teaches in the Counseling Psychology Doctoral Program. Her professional interests include vocational psychology theory and research, with special emphasis on issues relevant to women and minority group members. Her publications and presentations have encompassed the topics of career choice and development, self-efficacy theory, and counseling process. She is the associate editor of the *Career Development Quarterly* and serves on the editorial boards of the *Journal of Vocational Behavior* and the *Journal of Counseling Psychology*.

Donald E. Super, Ph.D., received honorary doctorates from Oxford University, the University of Lisbon in Portugal, and the Université de Sherbrooke in Canada. He is currently professor emeritus of psychology and education at Columbia University. He recently served as Distinguished Visiting Professor of Education at the University of North Carolina and as the international coordinator of The Work Importance Study at the University of Florida, as well as a consultant for the Department of Psychology at Armstrong State University. Among his published works are *Appraising Vocational Fitness, The Psychology of Careers,* and *Career Development in Britain*. He has authored numerous vocational assessment tools, including *The Work Values Inventory, The Career Development Inventory, The Adult Careers Concerns Inventory, The Salience Inventory, and The Values Scale*. His numerous awards include the American Psychological Association's Distinguished Scientific Award for the Applications of Psychology.

Karen M. Taylor, Ph.D., is currently the associate director of the Counseling and Consultation Service at Ohio State University. She is also director of the university's internship program in professional psychology. In addition, Dr. Taylor is an adjunct assistant professor at the university's Psychology Department. Her primary areas of professional interest include career psychology, the psychology of women, and training issues.

Fred W. Vondracek, Ph.D., is currently a professor of human development in Pennsylvania State University's College of Health and Human Development. Formerly the head of the university's Department of Individual and Family Studies, he has pursued an interdisciplinary approach to the study of career development, working toward an integration of life span human development and vocational psychology. He currently serves on the editorial boards of the *Career Development Quarterly* and the *Journal of Vocational Behavior*.

W. Bruce Walsh, Ph.D., is currently a professor in the Department of Psychology at Ohio State University, where he has served for 29 years. Dr. Walsh is the founder and first editor of the *Journal of Career Assessment*. He coauthored *Tests and Assessment* and coedited *Career Counseling for Women* and *Career Counseling*.

C. Edward Watkins, Jr., Ph.D., is currently an associate professor in the Department of Psychology at the University of North Texas. He coauthored *Theories of Psychotherapy* (5th edition). His primary professional and research interests focus on psychotherapy and psychotherapy supervision, career psychology, psychological assessment, and professional issues.

Credits

Acknowledgment is made to the following authors and publishers for their kind permission to reprint material from the copyrighted sources as follows:

Chapter 2 Krumboltz

Page 13 From "When Do Anomalies Begin?" by A. Lightman and O. Gingerich, 1992, *Science*, Vol. 255, pp. 690–695. Copyright 1993 by the AAAS. Reprinted by permission. **9–12 and 17–26** From "Integrating the Social Learning Theory of Career Decision Making" by J. Krumboltz and C. Nichols in *Career Counseling: Contemporary Topics in Vocational Psychology*, W. Walsh and S. Osipow, Eds. (1990), Hillsdale, NJ: Erlbaum. Copyright 1990 by Lawrence Erlbaum Associates, Inc. Reprinted by permission. **20** From *Appraising Vocational Fitness by Means of Psychological Tests* (p. 406) by D. Super, 1949, New York: Harper & Row. Copyright 1949 by Harper & Row. Reprinted by permission.

Chapter 7 Lent and Hackett

Page 80 From "Recent Developments in Cognitive Approaches to Counseling and Psychotherapy" by M. J. Mahoney and W. J. Lyddon, 1988, *The Counseling Psychologist,* Vol. 16, p. 200. Copyright 1988 by Sage Publications, Inc. Reprinted by permission.

Chapter 8 Fitzgerald and Betz

Page 104 From "Vocational Theories: Direction to Nowhere" by C. Warnath, 1975, *Personnel and Guidance Journal,* Vol. 53, p. 425. Copyright 1975 by the American Counseling Association. Reprinted by permission.

Chapter 9 Spokane

Page 121 From *Making Vocational Choices: A Theory of Vocational Personalities and Work Environments* (pp. 2–4, 53–54) by John Holland, 1992, Odessa, FL: Psychological Assess-

Chapter 19 Savickas

Index